The Politics of Slums in the Global South

Seeing urban politics from the perspective of those who reside in slums offers an important dimension to the study of urbanism in the global South. Many people living in substandard conditions do not have their rights as urban citizens recognised and realise that they cannot rely on formal democratic channels or governance structures.

Through in-depth case studies and comparative research, *The Politics of Slums in the Global South* integrates conceptual discussions on urban political dynamics with empirical material from research undertaken in Rio de Janeiro, Delhi, Chennai, Cape Town, Durban and Lima. The chapters engage with the relevant literature and present first-hand information on urban governance and cities in the South, housing policy for the urban poor, the politics of knowledge and social mobilisation. Recent theories on urban informality and subaltern urbanism are explored, and the issue of popular participation in public interventions is critically assessed.

The book is aimed at a scholarly readership of postgraduate students and researchers in development studies, urban geography, political science, urban sociology and political geography. It is also of great value to urban decision-makers and practitioners.

Véronique Dupont is Senior Research Fellow at the French Institute of Research for Development (IRD) in the Centre for Social Sciences Studies on Africa, America and Asia (CESSMA), Paris, France.

David Jordhus-Lier is Associate Professor in the Department for Sociology and Human Geography, University of Oslo, Norway.

Catherine Sutherland is Lecturer in the School of Built Environment and Development Studies, University of KwaZulu-Natal, Durban, South Africa.

Einar Braathen is Senior Researcher in the Department for International Studies at the Norwegian Institute for Urban and Regional Research (NIBR), Oslo, Norway.

Routledge Studies in Cities and Development

The Politics of Slums in the Global South
Urban Informality in Brazil, India, South Africa and Peru
Edited by Véronique Dupont, David Jordhus-Lier, Catherine Sutherland and Einar Braathen

The Politics of Slums in the Global South

Urban informality in Brazil, India, South Africa and Peru

Edited by
Véronique Dupont,
David Jordhus-Lier,
Catherine Sutherland and
Einar Braathen

Routledge
Taylor & Francis Group
LONDON AND NEW YORK

First published 2016
by Routledge
2 Park Square, Milton Park, Abingdon, Oxfordshire OX14 4RN

and by Routledge
711 Third Avenue, New York, NY 10017

First issued in paperback 2017

Routledge is an imprint of the Taylor & Francis Group, an informa business

British Library Cataloguing-in-Publication Data
A catalogue record for this book is available from the British Library

Library of Congress Cataloging-in-Publication Data
Dupont, Véronique.
The politics of slums in the global south: urban informality in Brazil, India, South Africa and Peru/Véronique Dupont, David Jordhus-Lier, Catherine Sutherland and Einar Braathen.
pages cm. – (Routledge studies in cities and development)
1. Urban policy – Developing countries. 2. City planning – Developing countries. 3. Low-income housing – Developing countries. 4. Urbanization – Developing countries. I. Title.
HT149.5.D87 2015
307.1′16091724–dc23
2015007595

ISBN 13: 978-1-138-05701-2 (pbk)
ISBN 13: 978-1-138-83981-6 (hbk)

Typeset in Goudy
by Florence Production Ltd, Stoodleigh, Devon, UK

Contents

Illustrations

Tables

Figures

Boxes

Settlement stories

Fact sheets

Contributors

Editors and contributors

Einar Braathen is Senior Researcher in International Studies at the Norwegian Institute for Urban and Regional Research (NIBR, Oslo), Norway. A political scientist, he has specialised in governance and policy analysis in the global South, particularly the linkages between multi-level governance (central-local relations, municipality-community relations) and policy delivery (poverty reduction, service delivery, climate change adaptation). For the last ten years he has mainly worked on two BRICS countries, South Africa and Brazil, and he has lived in Rio de Janeiro for longer periods. He was the project leader of *Cities against poverty: Brazilian experiences* (2010–13), funded by the Research Council of Norway, and the co-ordinator of the work package 'Politics and policies to address urban inequality' in the EU-financed project *Urban chances – City growth and the sustainability challenge* (Chance2Sustain, 2010–14). From 2015 to 2018 he heads the project *Insurgent citizenship in Brazil: The role of mega sports events*, funded by the Research Council of Norway. Braathen has authored and co-authored a series of articles and books including *Poverty and politics in middle income countries* (ZED Books, 2015). He is the editor of the website www.nibrinternational.no/Brazilian_Urban_Politics.

Véronique Dupont is Senior Research Fellow in Urban Demography at the Institute of Research for Development (IRD), France, in the CESSMA research unit – the Centre for Social Sciences Studies on Africa, America and Asia – in Paris. She is presently the joint director of CESSMA. She is also an associated member of the Centre for South Asian Studies in Paris, and a Senior Visiting Fellow at the Centre for Policy Research in Delhi, India. She was the Director of the Centre for Social Sciences and Humanities (CSH) of New Delhi from 2003 to 2007. Her research focuses on the socio-spatial transformations of Indian metropolises. She is particularly interested in the interrelations between urban policies and residential and coping strategies of the populations in informal settlements. Her recent publications include: *Cities in South Asia: Analysis and prospects* (co-edited with D.G. Heuzé, Paris: EHESS, 2007); *Circulation and territory in contemporary South Asia* (co-edited with F. Landy, Paris: EHESS,

2010); *Urban policies and the right to the city in India: Rights, responsibilities and citizenship* (co-edited with M.H. Zérah and St. Tawa Lama-Rewal, New Delhi: UNESCO & CSH, 2011).

David Jordhus-Lier is Associate Professor at the Department of Sociology and Human Geography at the University of Oslo, Norway. He is a political and economic geographer with a main focus on organised labour and social movements. His engagement with urban issues began with his PhD project, which focused on worker responses to local state restructuring in Cape Town, South Africa. He has since written on urban informal work and housing based on empirical research in this city in several book chapters and in journals such as *Transactions of British Geographers, Journal of Southern African Studies* and *Habitat International*. He was involved in Chance2Sustain through his position as a Senior Researcher at the Norwegian Institute for Urban and Regional Research from 2008 to 2012. He has recently led a three-year research project on hospitality workers. His recent publications include the anthology *A hospitable world? Organising work and workers in hotels and tourist resorts* (co-edited with Anders Underthun, Routledge, 2014).

Catherine Sutherland is Lecturer in the School of Built Environment and Development Studies, University of KwaZulu-Natal, South Africa. She is an urban geographer who focuses on urban sustainability and environmental governance. She was the Principal Investigator for the South African team for Chance2Sustain and this project has deepened her knowledge and understanding of Durban, particularly in relation to water governance and substandard housing. She has recently published research on sustainability in emerging economies, urban form and sustainability, water governance, social responses to large-scale projects and climate adaptation. She is currently leading a research project in partnership with the Norwegian Institute for Urban and Regional Research (Oslo) on the interface between water and climate governance in Cape Town and Durban. Her current publications include: C. Sutherland, M. Hordijk, B. Lewis, C. Meyer and B. Buthelezi (2014) 'Water and sanitation delivery in eThekwini Municipality: A spatially differentiated approach', *Environment & Urbanisation*; C. Sutherland, V. Sim and D. Scott (2014) 'Contested discourses of a mixed-use mega-project: Cornubia, Durban', *Habitat International*; and A. Taylor, A. Cartwright and C. Sutherland (2014) 'Institutional pathways for local climate adaptation: A comparison of three South African municipalities' (Focales, AFD, France).

Other contributors

Berit Aasen, sociologist, is Senior Researcher at the Norwegian Institute for Urban and Regional Research (NIBR, Oslo), specialising in governance, social and institutional change and development, and gender. She was formerly head of NIBR's Department for International Studies, and was a member of the Chance2Sustain research team. Her research interests are urban studies, gender, social mobilisation and justice. She is a member of the European Cooperation in

Science and Technology Research Network on Gender, Science, Technology and the Environment (GenderSTE).

R. Dhanalakshmi is a Social Science Researcher based in Chennai, India, with an academic background in social work. She worked in several Indo-Dutch social sciences research projects for the University of Amsterdam on issues of gender and labour market, urban waste management and urban governance. Her publications include 'Governance in urban environmental management: Comparing accountability and performance in multi-stakeholder arrangements in South India', co-authored with I.S.A Baud (*Cities*, special issue on Peri-Urban India, 2007), and *Solid waste management in Madras City*, co-authored with Shobha Iyer (Chennai: Pudhuvalvu Pathippagam, 1999).

Carlos Escalante Estrada has been an architect and urban planner for over thirty years. He has occupied various positions, including, from 2000 to 2008, co-ordinator of the Campaign for the Right to Adequate Housing for All in Peru. He is a member of the AGFE (Advisory Group on Forced Evictions) mission to the Dominican Republic and the Argentina Agency, and of the Regional Action Committee for the Global Campaigns led by UN-Habitat. In 2011, he became Chairman of the Board (COB) and Executive Director of the Metropolitan Planning Institute, and COB of Cadastral Institute of Lima. He has published on housing rights, the social production of habitat, and housing policies in Peru.

M.M. Shankare Gowda was a Post-Doctoral Fellow of the Indian Council of Social Science Research from 2009–12. He worked as Senior Researcher at the Centre for Policy Research (New Delhi) in 2014. Earlier, he was associated with the Centre for Social Sciences and Humanities (CSH) of New Delhi, India. His areas of interest include identity politics, government and politics, party system and local and urban governance in India. He has conducted extensive field research in several states in India.

Michaela Hordijk is a human geographer whose main interests are urban poverty, urban environmental management, (participatory) urban governance, participatory budgeting, youth in cities, and 'participatory action research'. These themes came together in her PhD research 'Of Dreams and Deeds: Community Based Environmental Management in Lima, Peru' (1995–2000), which resulted in the foundation of Aynimundo, supporting community participation initiatives in peripheral districts in Lima. She is Director of the Research Master's International Development Studies at the Graduate School of Social Sciences at the University of Amsterdam, and is Senior Researcher at the Governance for Inclusive Development Programme Group of the Amsterdam Institute for Social Science Research. She is Guest Lecturer at UNESCO-IHE in the water governance chair-group. Michaela Hordijk was Adjunct-Scientific Co-ordinator of the EU 7th Framework research project Chance2Sustain (2010–14).

Lisa Strauch is a graduate of the Research Master's International Development Studies at the University of Amsterdam, the Netherlands. Her thesis focused on informal housing development and the collective action strategies of the populations in urban poor settlements in Lima, Peru. She is currently working as an impact study researcher at the Partners for Resilience. Her main research interests include urban informality and strengthening climate resilience in Latin American cities.

Pamela Tsolekile de Wet works as a researcher at the African Centre for Citizenship and Development at the University of the Western Cape, Cape Town, South Africa. Her research interests focus on civil society organisation, development and democracy and she has written several reports and co-authored articles and book chapters on civil society organisations and participation in local communities on the Cape Flats. She has participated in developing score cards for residents to give feedback on local governance systems in Cape Town.

Acknowledgements

This book is one of the academic outcomes of the collective project 'Urban Chances – City Growth and the Sustainability Challenge' (acronym: Chance2Sustain), which was funded from 2010 to 2014 by the European Union under its 7th Framework Programme for research in Socio-economic Sciences and Humanities (FP7-SSH). The project was co-ordinated by the European Association of Development Research and Training Institutes (EADI), and involved the following research institutes: the Amsterdam Institute for Metropolitan and International Development Studies at the University of Amsterdam (AMIDSt – UvA), the Centre for South Asian Studies in Paris (CEIAS) under the French National Centre for Scientific Research (CNRS), the Norwegian Institute for Urban and Regional Research (NIBR), the School of Built Environment and Development Studies at the University of KwaZulu-Natal (UKZN), the School of Planning and Architecture (SPA) in Delhi, the Cities for Life Forum (FORO) in Peru, and the Centro Brasileiro de Análise e Planejamento (CEBRAP) in Brazil. In addition, the project benefitted from the support of the French Institute of Research for Development (IRD) and, in India, of the Centre for Social Sciences and Humanities (CSH) of New Delhi and the French Institute of Pondicherry (IFP).

The broad project explored how governments and citizens in fast-growing cities of the global South with a different economic base made use of participatory spatial knowledge to direct urban governance towards more sustainable development. The material for this book is drawn from one of the 'work packages' of this project, which focused on policies and politics to address the challenge of substandard settlements, with an emphasis given to related social mobilisation. This work package was led by Einar Braathen (NIBR). This book covers all four countries of the project, namely Brazil, India, South Africa and Peru, but only six of the ten cities were selected for further analysis: Rio de Janeiro, Delhi, Chennai, Durban, Cape Town and Lima.

Over the nearly five years of this project, our work has benefitted from the many fruitful exchanges and various meetings with the different researchers involved in this collective endeavour. At the outset, this project would not have materialised without the inspiration, perseverance and constant efforts of its initiator and scientific co-ordinator, Isa Baud (AMIDSt – UvA). We wish to express our most heartfelt gratitude to her. Michaela Hordjik (AMIDSt – UvA), as adjunct-scientific co-ordinator, also played a key role. Although it is not possible to list all the participants in this project, we are thankful to all of them for their stimulating discussions at some point or other during our research, and for enriching our knowledge on connected research issues. The Chance2Sustain network meetings organised in Amsterdam (June 2010), Sao Paulo (October 2010), York (September 2011), Lima (September 2012), Durban (October 2013) and Bonn (June 2014) were crucial moments for the development of our analytical framework and the building of our comparative approach. The participation of UN-Habitat officers, notably Jossy Materu, in some meetings provided us with especially relevant insights on substandard settlement issues at the global level. The staff of EADI, in particular Steffen Davids and Aurélien Lafon, as well as the staff and researchers of the local institutions involved in the organisation of these scientific meetings, need to be duly acknowledged. The country co-ordinators played a critical role in the organisation of these international meetings, as well as local workshops and seminars, and in facilitating field research and sharing their contacts. We would like to thank Sridharan Namperumal (SPA), Adrian Gurza Lavalle (CEBRAP), Liliana Miranda (FORO) and Catherine Sutherland (UKZN). Various dissemination symposia held in the four countries as part of the Chance2Sustain project also gave us the opportunity to submit our ideas and receive precious feedback from a number of observers or actors involved in the governance of cities we were studying, as well as from representatives of the civil society organisations involved in issues related to substandard settlements.

Two scientific events were particularly important for the research team involved in the preparation of this book. The first one was a panel entitled 'Reconfiguring the fast growing city: Exploring the interaction between urban governance, mega-projects and settlement dynamics in cases from India and South Africa', convened by Loraine Kennedy (CNRS, CEIAS), Glen Robbins (UKZN) and Einar Braathen (NIBR) at the EADI-DSA Conference on 'Rethinking Development in an age of scarcity and uncertainty' in York (19–22 September, 2011). Earlier versions of some of the settlement stories included in this volume were first presented during this panel, and benefitted from the comments of the convenors, the two discussants – Monique Bertrand (IRD) and Pushpa Arabindoo (University College, London) – and debates with the audience.

The second scientific event was a seminar on 'City governance, politics and the poor' organised by Einar Braathen along with Trond Vedeld, Berit Aasen and Peris Jones at NIBR in Oslo (24 April, 2013). This was followed by a two-day workshop focusing on the theme of our Chance2Sustain work package. This gave us the opportunity to present our first research findings, strengthen our comparative perspective and get invaluable feedback from the participants, whom we want to sincerely thank. Among these, we highly appreciated Colin MacFarlane's (University of Durham) precious comments. Other discussants included: Berit Aasen (NIBR), Rolee Aranya (Norwegian University of Science and Technology), Michaela Hordjik (AMIDSt – UvA), Yuri Kasahara (NIBR), Marianne Millstein (Nordic Africa Institute), Ingrid Samset (Chr. Michelsen Institute), Trond Vedeld (NIBR) and Henrik Wiig (NIBR).

We owe special and warm thanks to our colleague and friend Berit Aasen: she participated in our Chance2Sustain work package through all the stages of the project, contributed to our theoretical discussions, read and commented on our various reports; she also reviewed the entire draft of this book, and provided insightful comments. A special mention should also be made of Dianne Scott (UKZN), who offered valuable inputs to our analytical framework, and comments on parts of our manuscript. She also made a significant contribution to the empirical research for our work package in Durban and provided inputs for Cape Town. The book's internal coherence and overall vision has greatly benefitted from their contributions.

Many other colleagues from the Chance2Sustain project or researchers from other institutions have also offered their suggestions and engaged in discussions on preliminary findings from the field studies. We wish to thank them all. These include, for the research conducted in Brazil: Julia Cossermelli de Andrade, Denise Vitale, Eduardo Marques and Adrian Gurza Lavalle from CEBRAP, in addition to Helena Galiza (UFRJ) and Gilmar Mascarenhas (UFRJ); in South Africa: Mark Byerley and Faizal Seedat (eThekwini Municipality); for India: Sridharan Namperumal (SPA), Partha Mukhopadyay (Centre for Policy Research – CPR), Subhadra Banda and Yashas Vaidya (formerly with CPR), Pushpa Arabindoo (University College, London), Karen Coehlo (Madras Institute of Development Studies), Bhuwanesvari Raman (formerly with IFP), Nithya Raman (Institute for Financial Management and Research), Loraine Kennedy (CNRS-CEIAS), Eric Denis (CNRS), Aurélia Varrel (CNRS), Bérénice Bon (CEIAS); and for Peru: Liliana Miranda (FORO) and Michaela Hordjik (AMIDSt – UvA).

The research material presented in this book is based on in-depth fieldwork and we are deeply indebted to our associates and research assistants who helped us in our investigations. They include: Timo Bartholl, Ana Carolina Christovão, Valéria Pinheiro and Celina Myrann Sørbøe for Rio de Janeiro, M.M. Shankare Gowda and Tara Saharan for Delhi, R. Dhanalakshmi for Chennai, Dianne Scott, Sibongile Buthelezi, Njoya Ngetar and Bonang Lewis for Durban, Pamela Tsolekile de Wet, Athini Melane, Floortje Jacobs, Mandisa Ngcukanc, Adi Kumar, Tanja Winkler and Gerry Adlard for Cape Town.

Last but not least, we wish to express our profound gratitude to all the respondents to our interviews for their co-operation, their patience, and for the knowledge they shared with us. Among them, the residents of the settlements we were studying deserve a special mention. This book is dedicated to them.

During the preparation of our manuscript, a number of colleagues offered us their skills for specific tasks, and should be acknowledged. Karin Pfeffer (AMIDSt and GISlab, UvA) and Aurélia Varrel (CNRS) helped us with designing the map of Chennai, Vandana Solanki (CSH) for the map of Delhi, and Karin Pfeffer and Reza Shaker (GISlab, UvA) for the map of Lima. Michela du Sart (EduAction) designed the world map showing our case studies and the maps for Durban. Guillermo Takano (FORO) translated Carlos Escalante Estrada's contributions from Spanish to English. Timo Bartholl assisted in translating various documents from Portuguese to English. Vicky Sim (BEDS, UKZN) and Mayya Abou Faycal edited some sections of the manuscript.

We are also thankful to the eleven anonymous reviewers of our book proposal, who pointed out relevant issues, made constructive suggestions and helped us refine our publication project. We are further indebted to our colleagues who agreed to devote some of their precious time to carefully read earlier drafts of particular chapters and provide us with valuable comments. These include Richard Ballard (BEDS, UKZN), Agnès Deboulet (University Paris 8 Vincennes-Saint-Denis), Liliana Sara Miranda (FORO), Liza Weinstein (Northeastern University, Boston).

Finally we wish to thank our editors at Routledge, especially Khanam Virjee who encouraged us in this publication project, Bethany Wright for her patience and availability in replying to our numerous queries, and Margaret Farrelly for assisting us in the production process.

1 Introduction

Situating the politics of slums within the 'urban turn'

*Einar Braathen, Véronique Dupont,
David Jordhus-Lier and
Catherine Sutherland*

Urbanisation continues to transform both society and the environment in profound ways. Its impact on cities, their citizens and authorities therefore forms a major focus of research for both academics and practitioners. Contemporary urbanisation has become a phenomenon of the global South and it is happening at a rate and scale that is far greater than when the same process unfolded in the North (UN 2014). Urbanisation in the South occurs at a pace that renders formal urban planning processes and capacity insufficient. Hence, city growth is not matched by growth in housing and service opportunities, resulting in millions of people living in substandard conditions in cities across the world. These settlements are often identified as 'slums' in the global discourse (UN-Habitat 2003, Davis 2006). Most slum dwellers, or their parents, have migrated to cities in search of better income opportunities and livelihoods (IOM 2013). However, many of the urban poor find that their rights as urban citizens are not recognised and realise that they cannot rely on formal democratic channels or governance structures for their needs to be met. As a result many marginalised citizens mobilise politically in response to what they perceive as undignified living conditions, or to direct threats such as evictions. To complicate matters, this discontent often takes place in cities whose authorities have their eyes set elsewhere, on ambitious agendas for economic development and competitiveness motivated by visions of the 'world-class city'. This 'dressing up for the world' is often in conflict with the direct interests of the poor citizens of a city. It channels funds away from social spending or results in the spatial relocation of marginalised communities. In sum, cities in the South are arenas of intense tensions, that often result in the rise of urban social movements.

This book focuses on substandard settlements in the urbanising global South, and on the efforts of residents and authorities to secure housing and improve living conditions. How were substandard settlements addressed through urban policies? And how do civil society organisations mobilise and engage in both the formation and implementation of these policies? These two questions have guided the empirical research that is presented in this volume. While our main focus is on social mobilisation, we also explore mobilisation through two related research themes: policy-making on substandard settlements, and the politics of knowledge shaping interventions in these settlements. The book aims to connect these three main themes and to reflect on the relations between them. Social mobilisation can be understood as the encounter at the settlement level between public interventions from above, social responses from below, and struggles over knowledge construction and its legitimacy. The interactions between these dimensions are critical to participatory public interventions in pro-poor housing and determine when they succeed or fail.

Understanding the politics of slums from the perspective of those who reside in substandard settlements reveals much about the power struggles and tensions around urbanism in the South. Through in-depth case studies and a comparative approach, this book combines conceptual discussions with empirical material from a research project on six cities in Brazil, India, South Africa and Peru. The six cities – Rio de Janeiro, Delhi, Chennai, Durban, Cape Town and Lima – reveal similarities and differences in housing policies, knowledge production and social mobilisation emerging in the urbanising global South. The eleven case studies of substandard settlements are not viewed as isolated enclaves in their respective city. On the contrary, we analyse their dynamics in relation to transformation and development occurring elsewhere in the city, at other scales. Thus, the dynamics of slum formation, demolition, resettlement or upgrading are part of a broader urban restructuring process shaping metropolitan areas.

Consequently, the first section of this introductory chapter locates the politics of slums within the broader context of what we call the 'urban turn', in which city authorities are assigned new and sometimes conflicting roles. At an analytical level, this also requires that we focus on debates about urban governance, what is meant by governing cities and who takes part in doing so. The next two sections develop our conceptual and methodological research framework. We introduce our approach to urban informality and discuss the concepts of substandard settlements and slums. The comparative approach, which constitutes a main dimension of this research, is discussed, as well as the common methods of investigation that were applied to the case studies across the six cities. The last section presents the structure of the book, and outlines the three main themes with their related research questions.

Global context: the 'urban turn' and new strategic roles for the city

In this section we discuss how cities have come to inhabit a new and more central role in the world economy, and as a result in social sciences, and how this has encouraged new forms of urban governance and ascribed new roles for the urban authorities.

The 'urban turn': the growing importance of the city

Over the last decades, cities have acquired an increasingly important place in the social sciences, not only in human geography, but also in social anthropology and political science. This 'urban turn' reflects the increasing dominance of cities in all aspects of life, both globally and locally. This dominance is a result of a spatial reordering of the world, which many scholars see as linked to a wider process of neoliberal globalisation (Sassen 1991, Castells 1996, Jessop 2002). Arguably, the national state, and its spatial-political centre, the capital city, has yielded power and responsibilities to other nodes of power, including local governments and regional urban centres. Concomitantly, a group of so-called 'global cities' have emerged and claimed strategic positions in the new world economy (Sassen 1991), sometimes in ways that threaten to usurp the power of the nation-states that accommodate them.

Looking to the successes of other cities, urban authorities across the world are drawn into competing against other urban centres on a global stage. By developing urban growth strategies they aim for 'their' city to transform according to this model (see Robinson 2002). This point has also been made with special reference to some of the cities in this research (see Lemanski 2007, with special reference to Cape Town; Dupont 2011, for the case of Delhi; and Hannan and Sutherland 2015, for the case of Durban). Neoliberalism became a powerful dominant discourse and strategy to restructure, rescale, and reorder accumulation and regulation in capitalist societies, and numerous measures to sustain the neoliberal project at the urban scale were initiated by international organisations such as the World Bank (Jessop 2002). These efforts led to the transformation of the governance system of large cities. Technically oriented 'managerialism' was replaced by market economy-oriented 'entrepreneurialism' as the main principle of urban governance (Harvey 1989). It resulted in some cities such as Rio de Janeiro being managed almost like a private company (Vainer 2011). The main imperative of entrepreneurial cities is to create economic growth, often through attracting foreign (and domestic) investors by means of large-scale projects for infrastructure and business development (Kennedy *et al.* 2014). Decentralisation policies in many cases form part of this neoliberal agenda in practice, although these two phenomena are not necessarily linked. For instance, decentralisation drives in developing countries since the early 1990s often preserved privilege and prevented substantive democratisation, as sub-national governments and local municipalities were dominated by local oligarchies whose primary political agenda was to siphon off rents from entrepreneurial activities and build clientelistic networks, making their economic privilege and political control unassailable (Heller and Evans 2010).

In contrast to the neoliberal trajectory, the 'urban turn' has also manifested itself through a 'counter movement' of social movements and certain progressive city administrations, resulting in an alternative spatial reordering of the state. In some countries, or in federated states in some countries, decentralisation has encompassed other, more democratic possibilities. In India, the cornerstone of urban decentralisation reforms was the 74th constitutional amendment promulgated in 1992, which not only awarded greater autonomy to municipalities, but also promoted participatory democracy. This amendment guarantees the participation of women and the marginalised sections of society through the reservation of seats.[1] It further provides for the formation of ward committees to deal with local issues, including representatives from civil society. However, an assessment of participatory democracy as a result of the decentralisation reforms shows mixed results, revealing strong social barriers to inclusive urban governance (Tawa Lama-Rewal 2011). The states of Kerala and West Bengal in India are nevertheless good examples of this progressive 'urban turn' (Heller 2001). Brazil has also adopted more participatory forms of urban governance, as developed below (Heller 2001; see also Heller and Evans 2010). In South Africa, which has a transformative and economic growth agenda, the national and local state are sites of struggles to balance both pro-growth and pro-poor approaches to development.

Urbanisation in the global South: uneven and unequal

With urban dwellers outnumbering rural dwellers for the first time in history, and the global South being the main location of urban growth, the 'urban turn' is also starting to dominate the agenda in development studies. However, the level and pace of urbanisation across countries of the South is not equal, nor does it take place in a spatially even manner. For example, the level of urbanisation has remained much lower in India in comparison to Brazil. While the share of the urban population in the total population in India increased from 23 per cent in 1980 to 32 per cent in 2014, it increased from 66 per cent to 85 per cent in Brazil during the same period (UN 2014, see also Table 1.1). As a result of urban expansion, migration and natural population growth, cities in developing or emerging countries now occupy most of the places on the list of the thirty largest urban agglomerations in the world (UN 2014). Despite its relatively low level of urbanisation, India is, according to UN estimates, home to four 'mega-cities' in 2015, each with more than ten million people. With 25 million inhabitants, Delhi ranks as the second largest urban agglomeration in the world.

Cities of the global South have also grown in ways that create stark inequalities and produce acute shortages of decent housing. It is essential to indicate the magnitude of the urban population living in 'slums' in developing regions:[2] 820 million in 2010, corresponding to 33 per cent of the total urban population, as per UN-Habitat definition (see Box 1.1) and estimates (UN-Habitat 2012: 6). Table 1.1 shows the respective percentages for the four countries in this study, ranging from 23 per cent in South Africa to 36 per cent in Peru.

Such urban inequalities produce political responses. In Brazil especially, during the debates over the new constitution that began in 1986, urban social movements successfully made demands for more accountable forms of city governance, calling for decentralisation and citizen participation in the running of city affairs as a basic right of citizenship (Holston and Caldeira 2008). Brazilian municipalities are among the most autonomous and best resourced in the global South (Baiocchi

Table 1.1 Urbanisation and urban slums in Brazil, India, South Africa and Peru.

Country	Total population (in thousands)	Level of urbanisation: percentage of urban population in total population			'Mega-cities': urban agglomerations above 10 million inhabitants (or largest national urban agglomerations) – population in millions	Percentage of urban slum dwellers in total urban population at the country level
	2014 (mid-year)	1980	2000	2014	2015 (projection)	2009 (*2007)
Brazil	202 034	65.5	81.2	85.4	Sao Paulo: 21.1 Rio de Janeiro: 12.9	26.9
India	1 267 402	23.1	27.7	32.4	Delhi: 25.70 Mumbai: 21.04 Kolkata: 14.86 Bangalore: 10.09	29.4
South Africa	53 140	48.4	56.9	64.3	Johannesburg: 9.40	23.0
Peru	30 769	64.6	73.0	78.3	Lima: 9.90	36.1*

Sources and definitions:
i) United Nations (2014) *World Urbanization Prospects. 2014 Revision.* Department of Economic and Social Affairs, Population Division. Available from http://esa.un.org/unpd/wup/. Accessed on 15 January, 2015.
In this table, the concept of 'urban agglomeration' used by the UN Population Division refers to the population contained within the contours of a contiguous territory inhabited at urban level of residential density. In some cases, it includes not only a main city and its suburban fringes but also other cities situated in this same contiguous territory. Consequently, the administrative boundaries and population of the urban agglomeration do not necessarily correspond to the municipality of the main city.
ii) For slum population: UN-Habitat (2013) *Global Report on Human Settlements 2013*, Table B.3: 'Urbanization and urban slum dwellers'. See Box 1.1 for the definition of 'slum', which may differ from the national definitions (see Boxes 1.2 to 1.5).

Box 1.1 UN-Habitat operational definition of slum

The operational definition of a slum recommended by a United Nations Expert Group Meeting (Nairobi, 28–30 October, 2002) for international usage, defines a slum as an area that combines, to various extents, the following physical and legal characteristics:

- inadequate access to safe water;
- inadequate access to sanitation and other infrastructure;
- poor structural quality of housing;
- overcrowding;
- insecure residential status.

Source: UN-Habitat (2003) *The challenge of slums – Global report on human settlements*. Abingdon: Earthscan-Routledge.

2006). Social movements engage with the state and drive urban governance in the direction of democratisation to serve subaltern classes, while recognising that the national state remains fundamental to reduce inequality. The Brazilian cash transfer programme, the *Bolsa Família*, is one of the most successful redistributive programmes in the world, and it illustrates the role of both the local and national state. This programme is prepared through local governments, but it could not exist without the capacity and political will at the national level (Heller and Evans 2010).[3] Urban social movements in Brazil have long been striving for a deeper 'urban reform' (Rolnik 2011), and these efforts have escalated after the mass street demonstrations in June 2013 (see Box 7.2). Inspired by the visions of 'the right to the city' (Lefebvre 1968, Harvey 2012),[4] radical improvement and transformation of the urban transport system are now on the public agenda in the municipal, state and federal spheres of government, as a result of social action (Maricato 2013). As Sassen (1996) argues, neoliberal globalisation has nurtured resistance and alternate claims from urban social movements.

Urban governance: towards a critical understanding

Since the 1980s, governance has emerged as a dominant school of thought in political, sociological and administrative studies, particularly in the management of cities and other sub-national entities. It has provided a framework that has inspired reform strategies linked to the diverging constructions of the 'urban turn' in the socio-political domain, which were presented in the previous section. Urban governance can further be used as a dynamic framework for exploring the contested politics of land, housing and state-civil society relations in expanding cities, and hence it is adopted as an analytical framework for this book.

The governance school focuses on how the social is governed, and argues that hierarchical, political management – or 'government' – is increasingly being replaced by non-hierarchical modes of governing where non-state actors participate alongside state actors in the formulation and implementation of public policy – or what they term 'governance' (Jessop 2001, Mayntz 2003, Hajer and Wagenaar 2003). Given the constant change, uncertainty and risk evident in most city-regions, new forms of governance have placed a premium on adaptability, learning and reflexivity within local and regional economies (Pike 2004). Authorities attempt to combine vertical (hierarchical and state-centred) modes of governing with horizontal modes (networked and market-based) (Jessop 2001). The search for 'third way' solutions beyond the state and market, which emphasise horizontal networks, is part of this paradigm (Giddens 2002). The shift from 'government' to 'governance' emphasises the involvement of private and voluntary sectors in economic and social development, as well as quasi-autonomous non-governmental organisations (so-called 'quangos') (Jessop 2001). How local and national governments rely on non-state actors in the upgrading and formalisation of substandard settlements is discussed in Chapter 3. Local governments have become increasingly involved in network building with local business communities, and other important actors in the urban arena (Pierre 1999). Hence, the large-scale interventions that appear in many of the case studies of Chapters 4 and 6 represent complex interactions between different levels of government, private contractors and interests, as well as non-governmental organisations (NGOs) and community representatives.

The governance approach also stresses the importance of knowledge management in political processes, with many contributors arguing that the exchange of information is best managed by decentralised and polycentric processes, exemplified by markets. This thinking can be traced back to Friedrich Hayek, by many regarded as the father of neoliberal thought, who argued that the inability of central planners to comprehend or effectively manage social systems, often was caused by the failure to ensure the flow of information (Hayek 1988). Such an approach to information flows in governance tends to ignore power, however, in particular the distribution of governing resources between the nodes of a network. Therefore, different ideologies have underlined different strategies to reform urban governance. Some strategies emphasise more privatisation and marketisation of public functions (Pike 2004). Other strategies emphasise redistribution of power, democratisation and expansion of public services and spaces (Johnson 2001, Heller and Evans 2010). We will return to this discussion in Chapter 5, where we explore knowledge and power in the context of interventions in substandard settlements.

The city as strategic driver, mediator and responder

Attributing roles to 'the city' as a unified actor is problematic from an analytical point of view, but is increasingly being done by the marketing departments of city governments across the world. Slogans such as 'the city that reads' or 'the city that works for your business' are just a few examples of discourses that implicitly ascribe certain qualities to an urban region with the intent of communicating this quality to potential tourists, investors and attractive labour (Williamson, Imbroscio and Alperovitz 2003). Our case cities have engaged in similar branding exercises, not least linked to their bids for mega-events such as the FIFA World Cup and the Commonwealth Games. eThekwini Municipality, for instance, encompassing the city of Durban, states proudly on its website that it is 'ready to host you this festive season'.[5] At the same time, a drive around the poorer neighbourhoods of a city like Cape Town reveals another slogan on posters wherever construction is being undertaken – 'the city that works for you' – indicating that the city performs different roles, promoting itself to a wide range of audiences from local citizens to the international community. In fact, academic discourse has contributed to this personification of cities through concepts such as 'smart cities' (Caragliu, Del Bo and Nijkamp 2011). When we argue that neoliberal globalisation has resulted in three strategic, but sometimes contradictory, roles attributed to cities, we are specifically referring to roles taken on by their respective administrations. That being said, they perform these roles in concert with a host of other social actors, in line with the governance notion outlined above, leading to ongoing contestations over what the city is and who the city is for.

The first of these three roles is the role of 'the driver', based on an entrepreneurial notion, aiming to promote development and 'modernisation' of the city in a global market economy. Cities have been assigned the role of drivers of economic growth,[6] along with a distinct urban agenda that often includes attracting global investments and tourism through undertaking large-scale economic and infrastructure projects or hosting mega-events. More specifically, we note the creation of special agencies for mega-project implementation, the growing interest (and funding) from different spheres of government, the pervasiveness of public–private partnership arrangements, and the shifting boundaries of cities to encompass surrounding peripheries as a result of the expansion of infrastructure and economic-commercial ventures (Kennedy *et al.* 2014, Kennedy 2015). Governance arrangements are transformed by new instruments typically deployed in order to raise private capital for funding projects or to bypass normal planning practices in the interests of pro-growth agendas. Large-scale projects often affect substandard settlements directly or indirectly, negatively (causing evictions) or positively (offering social housing and upgrading), as presented in Chapter 3 on policies toward substandard settlements.

The second role, 'the mediator', can be seen as a transformation of the managerialism of the past (Harvey 1989), or as a 'reinvention of technocracy' (Braathen 2008). Here, city authorities mediate complex and sometimes conflicting global, national and local forces, including: multinational companies and investors; international development institutions and funding bodies; networks with other urban authorities; national and provincial/regional governments; national finance and business groups; and, finally, civil society organisations across all these political scales. Local forces also include private sector industrialists, businessmen, real estate developers and their associations and networks, and so-called non-state actors ranging from civil society organisations, NGOs, politicians and academics. With particular relevance for our study, they offer different discourses of slum, housing upgrading and resettlement. The 'city hall' must mediate between them. Mediation does not necessarily mean to bring these forces and discourses into harmony. Moreover, city authorities do not always have the autonomy and power to do so. Rather, 'mediation' means that the city authorities must decide which forces are more important than others in informing their own chosen policies, given the (limited) autonomy and power they enjoy. These processes are not value-neutral but reflect and sustain political values, albeit beyond partisan conflicts (Pierre 1999). Mediation may create certain disharmonies, and the purpose of the mediating efforts of the city authorities might be to cope with this disharmony, or even find ways to quell the 'noise' of dissenting discourses and social forces. Knowledge management, and the politics that surrounds it, is a key element in this mediation. According to Millstein (forthcoming), information is a critical means for exercising control in local political processes but also a source of contestation. The discussion of mediating knowledge is taken up in more detail in Chapter 5 of this book.

The third role, however, which we have labelled 'the responder', refers to how authorities react to the social demands of urban citizens, as they are articulated through formal processes (e.g., elections and stakeholder forums) and, more critically for this research, informal politics and social mobilisation. Several factors have led to the emergence of urban social movements that are created through the struggle for full urban citizenship. As underlined by Holston and Appadurai (1996: 189), 'place remains fundamental to the problems of membership in society, and (...) cities (...) are especially privileged sites for considering the current renegotiations of citizenship'. The notion of urban citizenship[7] refers to the struggle for the right *to* the city as well as for substantive rights *in* the city. Due to urban growth and the political mobilisation of urban populations, these pressures are manifested both within and beyond the formal democratic apparatus. There has been a democratisation process in the 1980s or 1990s in many of the cities we have studied with new, sub-local tiers of democratic decision-making emerging. Yet, many urban citizens, particularly residents in informal and substandard settlements, have to resort to different forms of social mobilisation to make their voices heard. This represents the main topic of the book, dealt with in all the chapters but more specifically analysed and theorised upon in Chapter 7 on social mobilisation. In the complex system of urban governance in any given city, these roles of driver, mediator and responder may coexist, but often in a conflict-ridden and dynamic way, and usually with the first two roles having far more weight in city politics than the third one.[8]

Conceptual clarifications on informality, slums and substandard settlements

In this section we first present our broad approach to urban informality, and, second, we explain what we mean by 'substandard settlements' and clarify our use of the related and much debated term of 'slum'. Other conceptual and theoretical discussions on urban policies, knowledge, and social movements and mobilisation will be developed in the corresponding chapters dedicated to each of these major themes.

Urban informality

Informality, by implication, can be considered to be the opposite of formality. In the context of urban housing, formality is often taken to encompass the urban planning system, the formal decision-making processes and the law. Urban informality is considered to operate outside of these practices. Formality reveals that which is recognised and mapped. Places with informal status are treated differently, often not being recognised as part of the urban fabric. What we know from experience to be thriving and close-knit communities can on formal maps of the city be shown as empty road reservoirs, wetlands or agricultural areas.

Roy's concept of urban informality has become authoritative through its nuanced definitions:

> As a concept, urban informality (. . .) is a heuristic device that uncovers the ever-shifting urban relationship between the legal and illegal, legitimate and illegitimate, authorized and unauthorized. This relationship is both arbitrary and fickle and yet is the site of considerable state power and violence.
>
> (Roy 2011: 233)

We adopt an approach that places the different substandard settlements in our research along a spectrum of informality: some settlements are characterised by the irregularity of their layout or they fail to conform to planning norms, in other cases informality refers to the illegality of tenure, or the substandard quality of housing and amenities. Our empirical cases might comply with any of these aspects or all of them.

Besides being defined by what it is *not*, informality is increasingly being associated with what it is *perceived to be*. In popular discourse, informality is often considered to be synonymous with criminal practices, filth and deprivation, in what Roy (2011: 224) has characterised as 'apocalyptic and dystopian narratives of the slum'. This narrative has arguably been supported by academic accounts such as – to some extent – Mike Davis' famous 'Planet of slums' (2006), which has since been challenged, in particular, by Ananya Roy.

In constructing an account of the politics of slums that contributes to a more nuanced and empowering account of urban informality, two recent theoretical discussions have inspired our approach: the notion of 'ordinary cities' as proposed by Robinson (2006), and the perspective of 'subaltern urbanism' articulated by Roy (2011).

An 'ordinary cities' approach acknowledges that 'ways of being urban and ways of making new kinds of urban futures are diverse and are the product of the inventiveness of people in cities everywhere' (Robinson 2006: 1). It challenges the ordering of cities, or typologies such as 'global cities'. In particular, it criticises the characterisation of non-modern cities as the Third World, under-developed cities or mega-cities and, relatedly, the perception of slums and substandard settlements as the embodiment of the non-modern city. Hence, such an approach can be articulated with Roy's concept of 'subaltern urbanism':

> Writing against apocalyptic and dystopian narratives of the slum, subaltern urbanism provides accounts of the slum as a terrain of habitation, livelihood, self-organization and politics. This is a vital and even radical challenge to dominant narratives on the megacity.
>
> (Roy 2011: 223)

Subaltern urbanism is a particularly relevant paradigm for our research as it 'seeks to confer recognition on spaces of poverty and forms of popular agency that often remain invisible and neglected in the archives and annals of urban theory' (ibid.: 224). Indeed, one way of challenging the hegemonic view of modern cities is to listen to the voices of the people living in these spaces and to map out the way they resist attempts to be excluded from the construction and production of their living environment. It can be argued that the modernist view does not recognise, for example, informal settlements as spaces of innovation and reason, but rather sees them as spaces of failure and survival, requiring development and outside intervention. In contrast, research on the innovation and multidimensional contributions of these spaces reveals slums, *favelas*, townships, invasions, auto-constructed peripheries as spaces of 'invention of the city' (Agier 1999) and 'invention of citizenship' (Holston and Caldeira 2008). It is important to understand and reflect on how the actors producing and living in these spaces define and respond to them.

In this book, we propose a critical exploration of the role of civil society organisations and individuals in responding to substandard settlements, and the politics and policy-making processes involved. This allows us to highlight what 'ordinary citizens' who live in these 'ordinary spaces' consider as important and necessary in their own path to development and greater sustainability. Our understanding of urban informality thus resonates with Bayat's (2007) examination of the politics of slums in the Middle East. Bayat suggests that 'key to the habitus of the dispossessed' is not a 'culture of poverty' but 'informal life, one that is characterized by flexibility, pragmatism, negotiation, as well as constant struggle for survival and self-development' (Bayat 2007: 579). Whereas some civil society formations in this study have either chosen self-help approaches (such as the case presented in Box 5.1), or self-help has been imposed onto them (as in the Peruvian case), there are other cases where residents and their organisations have been able to force the local state to act in its role as a 'responder' in innovative ways, through social mobilisation. In short, we are applying an approach where ordinary citizens do both ordinary and extra-ordinary things to claim their rights in the cities they inhabit.

Far too often, state authorities see the informality of the poor as a negative aspect of urban life, reflecting a lack of progress and development and hence as something that needs to be eradicated. Ordinary citizens might have different views about their informal status. On the one hand, they have to tackle the consequences of not being 'recognised' or 'supported', but on the other hand they might also view informality as a means of creating their own economic, political and social spaces within the city. Hence, some of the struggles we study can be seen as claims for recognition. However, this is not always the case. At other times, struggles for the right to the city entail seeking to defend a level of informality with its resultant flexibility. In many cases informal dwellers opt to return to their shacks or defend their informality against the interventions of states and developers. Nevertheless, their informal status makes them vulnerable to evictions and repression, as Chapter 3 reveals.

Interestingly, Roy suggests that mega-projects and other large-scale state interventions also might be characterised as informal insofar as they bypass regular planning practices, representing 'spaces of exception'. Thus, planning modalities produce urban informality 'as a state of exception from the formal order of urbanization' (Roy 2005: 147). As was evident in the case of Rio de Janeiro during the preparations for the FIFA World Cup 2014, legal and democratic norms were bypassed in these processes, and existing institutional frameworks and democratically elaborated master plans were circumvented or overruled (Mascarenhas 2012). The main legacy of such large-scale projects linked to mega-events is observed in the urban governance system in terms of a state of exception – or 'city of exception' (Braathen, Mascarenhas and Myrann Sørbøe 2015, Vainer 2011). Similar exceptional procedures were observed in Delhi in the context of the preparation for the 2010 Commonwealth Games (Baviskar 2011). In South Africa, the urban legacy of the 2010 FIFA World Cup was also extensively debated (Pillay, Tomlinson and Bass 2009), including reflections on both its impact on Cape Town (Swart and Bob 2009) and Durban (Bass 2009).

Substandard settlements or slums?

> Poor people used to live in slums. Now, the economically disadvantaged occupy substandard housing in the inner cities.[9]

In the quote above, the late comedian George Carlin makes fun out of the euphemisms he sees in modern societies, which he claims 'take the life out of life' and hide unpleasant truths from us. Acknowledging Carlin's point, social researchers are, however, required to use terminology that is precise in describing complex realities, even though that sometimes requires conceptualisations that supersede everyday language. The construction of a common vocabulary for our research on urban informality was a challenge given the different terminology that emerged as a result of engaging in fieldwork on six cities in four countries on three different continents. Human settlements, and their definitions, are outcomes of both particular processes of social-spatial differentiation and of normative-cognitive deliberations and political decisions. Each term triggers particular connotations in different regions of the world and is applied in particular local contexts, often associated with professional jargon and ideological stereotypes. To be able to compare analytically, we had to find a set of terms that reflected informal housing in meaningful ways.

For our research, we initially chose the term 'substandard settlements', rather than slums, as a heuristic device to designate the type of settlements we were focusing on. This term was broad enough to capture different normative perceptions or standards of housing across the different countries and cities. All the settlement case studies have in common a precariousness and deprivation that characterises the majority of their households, and sets them apart from much of the urban landscape that surrounds them. However, the type and magnitude of precariousness and deprivation may differ across spaces. Not only do these areas of the metropolitan region typically rank very low on socio-economic indicators (but not necessarily *the* lowest, see Baud *et al.* 2009), they also tend to be treated separately by urban authorities – through informal settlement departments and slum clearance boards – or are subject to less direct public control through targeted outsourcing (Lier 2008). Substandard settlements can thus be considered as indicators of urban inequality and socio-spatial segregation, rather than merely as markers of the lack of development.

Second, there are national legal standards expressed in law and urban policies, and technical standards applied by city planners, that categorise urban settlements in different countries. The term 'substandard' hence reflects that these are residential spaces failing to meet the standards accepted in formal urban planning and policy-making. Consequently, they are often a target for public policy that aims to transform them into 'standard' settlements, or to eradicate them from the city landscape. While people living in these settlements may claim the right to have these settlements recognised as ordinary and legitimate, they are by no means under the illusion that their standards are acceptable – and many community-based organisations are concerned with poor service delivery, poor housing materials and construction, or environmental hazards such as flooding. In other words, the term 'substandard' resonates with the claims and expectations of those who inhabit these settlements. That being said, residents might also place great value in their own self-sufficiency and the fact that homes and services are constructed and run by the community. To reiterate, classifications such as irregular–regular, unauthorised–authorised, illegitimate–legitimate, illegal–legal and substandard–standard are constantly being renegotiated and are at the core of many urban struggles. These settlements are therefore a reflection of both social and power relations within cities, regions and nations, and their politics.

We were not in favour of using the term 'slums' in our research, as this terminology is often associated with the stigmatisation of informal residents and hence is open to political manipulation. As Gilbert cautions:

> The very word 'slum' confuses the physical problem of poor quality housing with the characteristics of the people living there. And, with so many

unscrupulous governments in power around the world, the stereotype may be used to justify programmes of slum clearance.

(Gilbert 2007: 710)

It proved difficult to avoid using the word slum completely, however, particularly when referring to policy documents and official records that use this term. This was most evident in the Indian case. Furthermore, through our examination of the 'politics of slums' in Brazil, India, South Africa and Peru, we acknowledge the risk of stigmatisation, since the concept of 'politics' also includes the way in which the term 'slum' may be misused by policy-makers or other actors.

After careful consideration, we have allowed ourselves some flexibility in the terminology we employ, both in the conceptual chapters and the case-specific narratives, in order to adjust to different contexts. For instance, 'informal settlements' is a common term used in South Africa, while it is seldom used in Brazil. In Rio de Janeiro, it would be inappropriate not to use the term *favela*. In Lima, the local term *barriadas* is the most suitable when referring to substandard settlements, which have emerged from a process of land invasion by poor migrants. 'Squatter settlements' is most appropriate when we want to examine the law and the role of the judiciary in terms of the threat of eviction, particularly in the case of India. In Delhi, these 'squatter settlements' are also commonly designated by their local term, *jhuggi jhopri* clusters. In Chennai, the category of 'objectionable slums' is used to signify the impossibility of their regularisation.

We also needed to consider different official definitions of substandard settlements, in particular to inform the chapter dedicated to the analysis of policies towards these settlements (Chapter 3). We have therefore produced a series of boxes that review the various concepts of slums, *favelas*, informal settlements and *barriadas* in the four countries (see Boxes 1.2 to 1.5). We already presented above the definition of slums used by UN-Habitat (Box 1.1), as a means of standardising and providing a reference for some of the statistics provided in this chapter and elsewhere in the book.

Box 1.2   Official definition of *favela – aglomerado subnormal* – in Brazil

Einar Braathen

On the occasion of the 1991 national census, the Brazilian Institute for Geography and Statistics (IBGE) defined a *favela* as:

> A substandard settlement (*aglomerado subnormal*), of at least 51 housing units, with a haphazard layout, on illegally occupied private or public land, and lacking essential services.

The definition of *favela*, in the 2000 census, came to encompass those settlements on land that had been regularised. The emphasis shifted from the current (il)legal status of a settlement to whether it had originally been built on illegally occupied land, and to its ongoing haphazard layout and the lack of most essential services. In the 2010 census, the IBGE identified a substandard settlement as:

a) Illegal past (during the last 10 years) or current occupation and constructions on private and/or public land,

b) with at least one of the following characteristics: urban structures (house, streets, etc.) below current standards, and/or precariousness of essential public services.

Source: IBGE (2011) *Censo Demográfico 2010: Aglomerados subnormales.* Rio de Janeiro: Instituto Brasileiro de Geografia e Estatística. Available from www.ibge.gov.br/home/presidencia/noticias/imprensa/ppts/00000006960012 162011001721999177.pdf. Accessed on 13 December, 2014.

Box 1.3 Official definitions of slums and *jhuggi jhopri basti* in India

Véronique Dupont

The Slum Areas (Improvement and Clearance) Act, 1956

This benchmark Act (Chapter 2) deems as slums, old, dilapidated and overcrowded housing sectors where the buildings 'are in any respect unfit for human habitation' or that:

> are by reason of dilapidation, overcrowding, faulty arrangement and design of such buildings, narrowness or faulty arrangement of streets, lack of ventilation, light or sanitation facilities, or any combination of these factors, detrimental to safety, health or morals.
>
> (Sehgal 1998: 5)

This definition may apply to houses inhabited by tenants or proprietors with legal rights, as in the case of the old urban core of Delhi, which was notified as a slum area. This Act was first implemented in Delhi. Other states have later enacted their own Slum Areas Acts, with a definition of slums that may vary from state to state, but is usually based on similar notions.

There is no reference to the status of tenure (legal or illegal) in the Slum Areas Act. In contrast, the urban authorities and the judiciary designate as 'squatters settlements' informal settlements on lands occupied and built upon without the permission of the landowning agency. These are the 'illegal slums' locally called *jhuggi jhopri* clusters (or *basti*) in Delhi.

The Tamil Nadu Slum Areas (Improvement and Clearance) Act, 1971

The criteria to declare a 'slum area' under this Act (Chapter II-3) are the following:

>   (a)   any area [that] is or may be a source of danger to the health, safety or convenience of the public of that area or of its neighbourhood, by reason of the area being low-lying, unsanitary, squalid, over-crowded or otherwise; or
>   (b)   the buildings in any area, used or intended to be used for human habitation [that] are (i) in any respect, unfit for human habitation; or (ii) by reason of dilapidation, over-crowding, faulty arrangement and design of such buildings, narrowness or faulty arrangement of streets, lack of ventilation, light or sanitation facilities, or any combination of these factors, detrimental to safety, health or morals.
>
> (see TNSCB)

The Chennai Metropolitan Development Authority (CMDA 2008: 147) further introduced the category of 'objectionable slums':

> The slums situated on river margins, road margins, seashore and places required for public purposes are categorised as objectionable slums. The areas occupied by them have to be retrieved.

The Delhi Urban Shelter Improvement Board Act, 2010

This Act (Chapter 1) defines *jhuggi* and *jhuggi jhopri basti* as follows (see DUSIB):

> '*Jhuggi*' means a structure whether temporary or *pucca* [consolidated], of whatever material made, with the following characteristics, namely: (i) it is built for residential purpose; (ii) its location is not in conformity with the land use of the Delhi Master Plan; (iii) it is not duly authorised by the local authority having jurisdiction; and (iv) it is included in a *jhuggi jhopri basti* declared as such by the Board, by notification.
>   '*Jhuggi jhopri basti*' means any group of *jhuggis* which the Board may, by notification, declare as a *jhuggi jhopri basti* in accordance with the following factors, namely: (i) the group of *jhuggis* is unfit for human habitation; (ii) it, by reason of dilapidation, overcrowding, faulty arrange

ment and design of such *jhuggis*, narrowness or faulty arrangement of streets, lack of ventilation, light or sanitation facilities, or any combination of these factors, is detrimental to safety, health or hygiene; and (iii) it is inhabited at least by fifty households as existing on 31st March, 2002.

The board may notify any *jhuggi* or *jhuggis* scattered in the nearby areas as part of a nearby *jhuggi jhopri basti*.

Slums as per the Census of India

The Census of India (2011) defines slums in the following terms:

> (. . .) residential areas where dwellings are unfit for human habitation by reasons of dilapidation, overcrowding, faulty arrangements and design of such buildings, narrowness or faulty arrangement of street, lack of ventilation, light, or sanitation facilities or any combination of these factors which are detrimental to the safety and health (. . .) For the purpose of Census, slums have been categorised and defined as of the following three types:

- *Notified Slums*: All notified areas in a town or city notified as 'Slum' by State, Union Territory Administration or Local Government under any Act including a 'Slum Act';
- *Recognised Slums*: All areas recognised as 'Slum' by State, Union Territory Administration or Local Government, Housing and Slum Boards, which may have not been formally notified as slum under any Act;
- *Identified Slums*: A compact area of at least 300 population or about 60–70 households of poorly built congested tenements, in unhygienic environment usually with inadequate infrastructure and lacking in proper sanitary and drinking water facilities.

Sources

Census of India (2011) Available from www.censusindia.gov.in/. Accessed on 25 January, 2015.

CMDA (2008) *Second master plan for Chennai Metropolitan Area, 2026*. Vol. III, Chapter VI. 'Shelter'. Chennai: Chennai Metropolitan Development Authority.

Delhi Urban Shelter Improvement Board (DUSIB). Available from http://delhishelter board.in. Accessed on 25 January, 2015.

Sehgal, S.D. (1998) *An exhaustive guide to The Slum Areas (Improvement and Clearance) Act, 1956 – The Slum Areas (Improvement and Clearance) Rules, 1957*. New Delhi: Universal Law Publishing Co.

Tamil Nadu Slum Clearance Board (TNSCB) Available from www.tnscb.org.in/. Accessed on 25 January, 2015.

Box 1.4 Definition of informal settlements in South Africa

Catherine Sutherland

The term 'informal settlement' is used to define slums in South Africa. There is no 'official' or single definition of informal settlements in South Africa (HDA 2012, Tissington 2012). In most cases informal settlement definitions refer to the status of the land occupied (illegal or not officially documented), the nature of the dwelling in terms of its substandard materials and the lack of adequate municipal services (HDA 2012).

An informal settlement is defined as a settlement that consists of the following characteristics: lack of security of tenure, informality, poor and substandard building materials, a lack of access to services, although many informal settlements in South Africa are provided with basic services such as communal tap points and rudimentary sanitation. The National Housing Code, which contains the 'Upgrading of Informal Settlements Programme', identifies informal settlements using the following criteria: illegality and informality; inappropriate locations; restricted public and private sector investment; poverty and vulnerability; and social stress. The term 'shack' or 'informal dwelling' is used to define each house within a settlement. In each local context different terminology is used to define informal settlements. For example in KwaZulu-Natal the Zulu term, *mjondolo* is used.

The legal rights of informal settlers to *land* vary as they may be settled illegally on public or private land, they may pay rental to shack lords for their land (who in some cases are the owners of the land), and they may have obtained the right to remain on public land through agreements with the state and through the implementation of upgrading projects. Residents of informal settlements also have different levels of access to informal *houses*. Some are owners of their shacks, others rent them, and some are lodgers or tenants who have access to small rooms attached to the main shack and they pay rental to the owner or tenant of the main shack. Lodgers and tenants are the most vulnerable.

There is terminological confusion around the definition of an informal settlement that is problematic when estimating the number of informal settlers in South Africa. Unplanned informal settlements, informal structures that have been constructed on legal, formally planned serviced sites, and those built by the state as transit camps (temporary relocation areas) are all considered to be informal settlements (Huchzermeyer 2011, HDA 2012, Tissington 2012). However, their security of tenure and level of services vary considerably.

References

Housing Development Agency (HDA) (2012) South Africa: Informal settlements status. Available from www.thehda.co.za/images/uploads/HDA_Informal_settlements_status _South_Africa.pdf. Accessed on 12 January, 2015.

Huchzemeyer, M. (2011) *Cities with 'Slums': From informal settlement eradication to a right to the city in Africa*. Cape Town: Cape Town University Press.

Tissington, K. (2012) 'Informal settlement upgrading in South Africa: Linkages to livelihood creation, informal sector development and economic opportunity generation'. *Working Paper No. 2*. Johannesburg: Socio-Economic Rights Institute of South Africa.

Box 1.5 Official definition of *barriada* in Lima

Carlos Escalante Estrada

Although the essential definition of *barriada* has been maintained, new names such as *pueblos jóvenes* (young towns), *urbanizaciones populares* (popular urbanisations) or *asentamientos humanos* (human settlements) have been used. Back in 1961, the fourth article of Law 13517 – Organic Law of Marginal Settlements and Capital Increase of the National Housing Corporation – considered that:

- 'Marginal neighbourhoods' or *barriadas* are publicly owned (national or municipal government) or privately owned (communal) areas, located within the limits of capital towns or their suburban areas; any kind of housing groups built in these areas and which took place after land invasions, with no legal considerations on property (with or without a municipal permit), and no officially approved plot distribution plans. They lack one or more of the following services: potable water, sewerage, public lighting, roads and sidewalks, etc.

A few years later, in 1999, the second article of Legislative Decree No. 495 established that:

- 'Young towns', called also 'human settlements', are municipal, state or private land areas recognised by the competent body. They are able to follow physical and legal sanitation procedures that would lead to the granting of individual property titles if land tenure is proved, as well as the physical regularisation of plot plans, roads, and other public areas.
- 'Popular Urbanisations of Social Interest' (UPIS) and every informal settlement able to receive physical and legal sanitation from the national, provincial, and district authorities, or other competent body, are also considered as 'young towns'.
- Those settlements that have finished the physical and legal sanitation process keep their 'young town' condition, even if a judiciary or administrative resolution has nullified that condition.

> Finally, the fifth article from Law No. 28391 (16 November, 2004) defined as 'informal possessions' the so-called urban settlements, young towns, marginal neighbourhoods, *barriadas*, municipal housing programmes, populated areas, or any other form of informal tenure and occupation of urban plots whose characteristics comply with the Regulation for the Formalisation of Informal Property approved by Supreme Decree No. 013–99-MTC.

Within the spectrum of substandard settlements, this book focuses on those settlements that have resulted from a process of land invasion or illegal occupation. We include settlements that were initially classified as illegal settlements, but which later benefitted from land regularisation and upgrading programmes changing their status from illegal to legal. Our settlement cases include *favelas* in Rio de Janeiro, squatter settlements in Delhi and Chennai, informal settlements in Durban and Cape Town, and *barriadas* in Lima. All of them in their formation and initial development lacked security of tenure. In most cases these settlements have also been impacted by large-scale projects. Our settlement cases do not cover dilapidated and overcrowded tenements found particularly in old urban cores, such as: the *cortiços* in Brazilian cities, the *tugurios* in Peruvian cities, or the slum areas or overcrowded and dilapidated buildings in the historical cores of Indian and South Africa cities.[10] In our research we have therefore emphasised a dimension of vulnerability that is related to both the struggle of urban dwellers to secure their rights to land and to the impact of state interventions, including eviction, which often triggers social mobilisation.

Comparative strategy and research design

It is beyond the scope of this introductory chapter to review the wide range of methodological, epistemological and theoretical reflections on comparative urban research and its 'renaissance' (Ward 2008: 405) or 'resurgence' (McFarlane 2010: 725). However, one of the main learning experiences of this research has been how to conduct comparative urban research. It is therefore useful to reflect on the comparative approach we adopted[11] and to explain how we applied it at each stage of our research through the development of a common methodology.

The first question was how to compare four countries that at first glance, using various indicators of urbanisation and development, revealed large variations (Tables 1.1 and 1.2). India, in particular, lags far behind the other three countries in terms of its level of urbanisation, Gross Domestic Product per capita and Human Development Index. The country and city fact sheets in Chapter 2 present indicators of the four national contexts, and specificities of the local urban contexts.

Does this diversity of contexts constitute an obstacle to a *comparative* approach of urban informality in Rio de Janeiro, Delhi, Chennai, Cape Town, Durban and

Table 1.2 Gross Domestic Product per capita and Human Development Index of Brazil, India, South Africa and Peru in 2013.

	GDP per capita, PPP (current international $) in 2013		Human Development Index (HDI) in 2013	
	Rank (out of 185 countries)	US $	Rank (out of 187 countries)	Value 2013
Brazil	75	15,034	79	0.744
India	123	5,410	135	0.586
South Africa	81	12,504	118	0.658
Peru	87	11,775	82	0.737

Note: Brazil and Peru are classified in the group 'High Human Development' (HDI from 0.70 to 0.79); India and South Africa are classified in the group 'Medium Human Development' (HDI from 0.50 to 0.69).

Sources:
i) Gross Domestic Product (GDP) per capita based on purchasing power parity (PPP): World Bank. Available from http://data.worldbank.org/indicator/. Accessed on 9 August, 2014.
ii) HDI: UNDP (2014) *Human Development Report 2014*. Table 1: 'Human Development Index and its components'.

Lima? We argue that it does not and we assert the heuristic value of comparisons. We adopt the same approach as other scholars engaged in comparative urban research (such as Dureau *et al.* 2000, Gervais-Lambony 2005, Ward 2008, McFarlane 2010, Robinson 2011, Landy and Saglio-Yatzimirsky 2014) by rejecting the position of incommensurability:

> the often unarticulated assumption that no comparison is possible across cities that are regarded as substantially differentiated not only by their levels of development, but also by cultural or policy context, economic system or political environment.
>
> (Robinson 2011: 4–5)

Drawing on Robinson's (2011) argument, we contend that 'the comparative gesture' can be applied to all cities as long as a rigorous methodology is adopted in the comparison conducted. In a global context, where cities are connected through relational histories, economies, circulations of ideas and knowledge flows, comparative research is essential if we wish to gain a deeper understanding of 'the urban' and its relational processes. However, cities are also embedded in their local contexts, whose specificities need to be recognised, in developing a comparative understanding.

Our comparative methodology is based on a series of critical case studies of substandard settlements, which were carefully selected in the six cities to address our research questions (as detailed in the next section). It is important to stress that our purpose is not to compare cities as such, nor even specific urban settlements, but rather to compare *processes* and their relations, observed across different scales of the metropolitan landscape. More precisely, our comparative research targets policy discourses and the processes of policy-making and implementation for substandard settlements; the processes of social mobilisation that such policies are met with on the ground; and, finally, the way knowledge flows are produced, circulated or blocked with regard to interventions in these settlements. Our analytical comparison is inspired by how Robinson envisages case-by-case comparisons, by bringing case studies

> into careful conversation with one another in order to reflect critically on extant theory, to raise questions about one city [or about one urban settlement] through attending to related dynamics in other contexts, or to point to limitations or omissions in existing accounts.
>
> (Robinson 2011: 6)

We have pursued a flexible and inductive research approach, based on in-depth settlement case studies, nonetheless informed by theoretical discussions.

Research methodology

The main features of our research methodology include a multi-pronged strategy, an actor-centred approach, and qualitative methods, all of which are articulated within a comparative design. We combined a top-down perspective with an explicitly bottom-up and actor-centred approach, where the former approach involved analysing public policies around substandard settlements and interventions from above (as presented in Chapter 3) and the latter examining responses from social actors from within or connected to the settlement. In line with the perspective of subaltern urbanism, it aimed at highlighting the agency of substandard settlement dwellers in defending their visions and interests (as developed in Chapter 7).

Because these mobilisations may alter the initial intervention plans, their examination implied a bottom-up perspective, revealing their potential retroactive effects on policies. We thus paid special attention to the interactions between the state (as embodied by various institutions and actors) and the residents of affected settlements – forums, meetings and other structured dialogue, as well as demonstrations and open political confrontations. This relational approach was adopted as a general principle during our field investigations. An original contribution made by this research is the focus on the politics of knowledge, which plays out through the implementation of upgrading and resettlement projects on the ground (as shown in Chapter 5). In order to understand how residents in substandard settlements mobilise, we not only paid attention to their vertical connections and interactions, but also to their horizontal ones, for instance through networks between civil society organisations.

Data collection during fieldwork was based on an intensive qualitative research design.[12] This resulted in an interpretive orientation that, therefore, does not aim at producing statistical generalisations, but which rather tries to analytically generalise main processes across these case studies. We argue that questions related to the agency of the urban poor and the way they organise and mobilise can be best addressed through an in-depth qualitative approach.

The comparative approach introduced above was operationalised through a common methodology followed in each phase of our research, including: selecting the case studies, data collection through qualitative methods, and interpretation through a common analytical frame. Therefore, our comparative analysis is not the outcome of a mere a posteriori juxtaposition of case studies from six cities. Instead, it has been constructed through the multiple conversations between the researchers about their interpretations of the relations within and between the case studies, during each stage of the research process.

Selection of case studies

In each of the six cities, the settlement cases were selected through purposeful sampling. We initially identified two to five distinct settlements, or a string of connected settlements (as in Chennai and Lima), on the basis of our knowledge of the city and the application of two main criteria. First, some kind of mobilisation around critical issues should have taken place. Second, the settlement should have been impacted by a large-scale project, in order to relate the transformation of the settlement to broader changes at work in the city. Alternatively, the settlement should otherwise exemplify a particularly critical issue in relation to substandard settlement policies in the city.

For each short-listed settlement, a detailed profile was prepared. The information that was collected included: the historical background of the neighbourhood and the recent development of the settlement; the current characteristics of the settlement in terms of population, type of housing and layout, urban infrastructure and amenities; main issues at stake regarding its development and its future; and relevant actors in this regard. The main data sources used were direct field observations in each settlement and interviews with key informants, as well as secondary sources including: development plans and other official documents; reports from NGOs; project plans of developers if applicable; press cuttings; and web sources. This information was used to screen the pre-selected cases, and to determine which settlement(s) could be finally used for the in-depth case studies. For the settlements that were selected, this information provided a strong body of contextual data.

Data collection for in-depth settlement case studies

It was during this second phase of research that the full repertoire of qualitative methods was employed to create rich accounts of the organisational and political dynamics in these settlements, and how they relate to urban governance and planning processes. Three types of in-depth interviews were conducted: individual interviews with various categories of residents regarded as primary stakeholders through quota purposive sampling; focus group interviews with residents; and interviews with key stakeholders. Depending on the settlement cases, key stakeholders could include: local leaders in the settlements; representatives of civil society organisations working in the area; political representatives; government officials in planning and housing (or slum) departments; officials in other departments; corporate representatives; academics; and media representatives.

The various types of interviews were conducted using semi-structured, open-ended interview guides. Based on our main research questions, a set of interview questions had been developed that informed the interviews undertaken by the researchers in all the selected settlements. This generic interview guide aimed to facilitate the comparisons across different cities and countries. It identified a series of common questions, some appropriate for all interviewees, and some specifically directed towards particular stakeholders. The generic interview guide was subsequently adjusted to take into account the particular characteristics, issues, mobilisation, and governance context of the different settlements, opening up the type of comparative research being undertaken.

Participant observation (whenever possible), for example attending meetings, rallies and protests, functioned as an important complementary source of information and understanding. The consultation of official documents, plans and reports, minutes of meetings, as well as newspaper articles and other local media, also provided useful sources of information. Data collection for the selection of settlements and in-depth case studies was conducted over various periods of fieldwork, from 2011 to 2014. The findings presented in this book draw on eleven distinct in-depth settlement case studies.

Analysis and interpretation

The data collected during the different phases of the research were synthesised and examined according to a common framework. The framework was built collectively through the many theoretical and methodological conversations held between the researchers over the duration of the project. This framework, which was always under construction until the final stage of analysis in 2014, instructed the researchers on how to order and organise the findings in relation to the different overarching research questions. Structuring the data using the analytical framework enabled a relatively systematic comparison between the different contexts and research teams. The comparative strategy was strengthened through a constant dialogue between the small team of researchers working in the different cities and countries.

A guide to navigating the book

By drawing on eleven in-depth case studies of settlements, this collective endeavour responds to the pertinent call of Pushpa Arabindoo (2011: 636) for 'in-depth, empirical case studies' and the need for a new direction in collecting ethnographies of the urban poor in India [as well as – we can add – in Brazil, South Africa and Peru] as they negotiate the current political and policy drive for creating 'slum-free' cities.

Our findings are organised according to a few cross-cutting themes, and across different national and urban contexts. To strengthen our 'comparative gesture', we have avoided city-specific chapters, and instead we have developed thematic chapters drawing data and interpretations from all city and settlement cases. Chapter 2 provides contextual information on the four countries and six cities in the form of synthetic fact sheets. It briefly introduces the settlement cases and situates them on a city map. The case studies are presented in 'settlement stories' grouped in two distinct chapters. Chapter 4 comprises settlement stories that highlight issues of knowledge construction and the participation of residents in upgrading and resettlement projects. The settlement stories included in Chapter 6 illustrate the varied community responses to external interventions affecting their settlements. They can be read as settlement cases that stand on their own, or in relation to the subsequent thematic chapters they directly inform. Chapters 3, 5 and 7 are thematic and analytical, and need a more elaborated presentation.

In Chapter 3, we examine the main policies that have been adopted to address issues of substandard settlements in India, Brazil, South Africa and Peru, and their possible variations at the metropolitan level. In this regard, five types of approaches were identified: policies of self-help, policies of demolition and eviction, policies of in-situ upgrading, policies of relocation and resettlement, and policies of integrated human settlements. Some of the main research questions underpinning this comparative exploration are: Do we observe a convergence in policies towards substandard settlements, and how does this relate to globalised urban discourse? Do we observe gaps between policy discourses and their translation into tangible interventions? What does this reveal about urban governance?

Chapter 5 focuses on issues of knowledge and deals with the implementation of government programmes towards substandard settlements, making the connection between interventions from above (analysed in Chapter 3) and responses from below (analysed in Chapter 7). More precisely, this chapter discusses the politics of knowledge that play out when city authorities, business interests, expert communities and local representatives interact and become entangled in upgrading or resettlement projects. Both the inclusion of community-based knowledge and an open flow of knowledge have been highlighted as important pre-requisites for participatory public intervention in housing for the poor. However, this chapter focuses on the opportunities and barriers to a shared flow of knowledge, which we observe across many of the case studies. The main issues that are discussed include: retention of information as a strategy by various actors; the role of 'local knowledge brokers'; and community-based knowledge generation as a strategy by residents and community-based organisations.

Chapter 7 explores how residents in substandard settlements mobilise and organise in their struggle for decent housing and in resisting evictions and relocations. Several broad modalities of mobilisation, and several phases in the process of mobilisation, were identified, including: the everyday forms of resilience; protests or confrontational mobilisation; the judicialisation of struggle; engagement and partnership; division and demobilisation; and weak mobilisation. Through the case studies, we attempt to highlight the main actors and key factors of mobilisation campaigns, as well as aspects limiting or weakening collective action. The interpretation of the findings is articulated through the theoretical debates on social mobilisation, which are also presented in the chapter.

By way of conclusion, Chapter 8 revisits the original research questions and synthetises the main findings of our research. By drawing on the different conceptual and empirical chapters, we attempt to formulate a set of cross-cutting insights based on a theoretically informed analysis of our case studies.

Notes

1 One third for women, and for the scheduled castes – i.e. former untouchables – and tribes, in proportion to their demographic weight in the population of the corresponding constituency.
2 We refer here to the classification used by UN-Habitat in its publication (UN-Habitat 2012), without distinction between the less-developed countries and the emerging ones.
3 The same point can be made for the social housing programme in Brazil, *Minha Casa Minha Vida*. See presentation in Chapter 3.
4 As emphasized by David Harvey, the right to the city is "far more than a right of individual or group access to the resources the city embodies: it is the right to change and reinvent the city more after our hearts' desire" (Harvey 2012: 4).
5 See "Durban Festive Season Campaign Launched", 12 February 2014. Available from www.durban.gov.za/Resource_Centre/Press_Releases/Pages/Durban-Festive-Season-Campaign-Launched.aspx. Accessed on 28 January 2015.
6 Significantly, in India since the 1990s, the expression "engines of economic growth", or "engines of economic and social development" is coined in national urban policy documents while promoting the "tremendous potential" of cities. See for instance the website of the Ministry of Urban Development: http://moud.gov.in/urban_reforms. Accessed on 11 December 2014.
7 In the four countries under study, where people are free to move from one place to the other, the notion of *urban* citizenship has no legal content, unlike that of citizenship with reference to the nation: "urban citizenship is not so much about legality than about legitimacy" (Zérah *et al.* 2011: 4). For a discussion on the concept of urban citizenship and the right to the city with special reference to the Indian context, see Zérah *et al.* 2011.
8 Pierre (1999) argues that nation-state factors play an important role in shaping urban governance. Different sectors in urban politics display different models of governance and local political choice matters. Also, cities within the same national context differ significantly with regard to the degree of inclusion of organised interests in urban governance, which, in turn, is reflected in urban policy outcomes.
9 George Carlin (1990) "Euphemism". In *Don't do it again*. Available from www. dailymotion.com/video/xnipr1_george-carlin-euphemism-doin-it-again-1990_fun. Video viewed on 25 January 2014.
10 Cape Town presents an anomaly to urban blight in the inner city as the inner city of Cape Town, due to its location and the active role of local government in maintaining the urban core, has retained its high economic value and has not suffered from the 'white flight' experienced in other South African cities.

11 Diane Scott's presentation "A comparative approach in urban studies: Some tentative ideas" (Chance2Sustain Workshop, Durban, 10-13 September 2012) was a useful contribution to this exercise.
12 We acknowledge the contribution of Diane Scott in developing the methodological framework used in this research project.

References

Agier, M. (1999) *L'invention de la ville. Banlieues, townships, invasions et favelas*. Amsterdam: Editions des Archives Contemporaines.

Arabindoo, P. (2011) 'The rhetoric of the "slum"'. *City*, 15(6): 636–46.

Baiocchi, G. (2006) 'Inequality and innovation: Decentralization as an opportunity structure in Brazil'. In P. Bardan and D. Mookherjee (eds) *Decentralization and local governance in developing countries*. Cambridge (MA): MIT Press, pp. 53–80.

Bass, O. (2009) 'Aiming for Africa: Durban, 2010 and notion of African urban identity'. In U. Pillay, R. Tomlinson and O. Bass (eds) *Development and dreams. The urban legacy of the 2010 Soccer World Cup*. Pretoria: HSRC Press, pp. 246–64.

Baud, I., Pfeffer, K., Sridharan, N. and Nainan, N. (2009) 'Matching deprivation mapping to urban governance in three Indian mega-cities'. *Habitat International*, 33(4): 365–77.

Baviskar, A. (2011) 'Spectacular events, city spaces and citizenship: The Commonwealth Games in Delhi'. In J.S. Anjaria and C. McFarlane (eds) *Urban navigation. Politics, space and the city in South Asia*. New Delhi: Routledge, pp. 138–61.

Bayat, A. (2007) 'Radical religion and the habitus of the dispossessed: Does Islamic militancy have an urban ecology?' *International Journal of Urban and Regional Research*, 31(3): 579–90.

Braathen, E. (2008) *Decentralization and poverty reduction*. NORAD Report 22B. Oslo: Norwegian Agency for Development Cooperation.

Braathen, E., Mascarenhas, G. and Myrann Sørbøe, C. (2015) 'A "City of Exception"? Rio de Janeiro and the disputed social legacy of the 2014 and 2016 sport mega-events'. In G. Poynter and V. Viehoff (eds) *Mega-event cities: Urban legacies of global sports events*. Surrey and Burlington: Ashgate.

Caragliu, A., Del Bo, C. and Nijkamp, P. (2011) 'Smart cities in Europe'. *Journal of Urban Technology*, 18(2): 65–82.

Castells, M. (1996) *The rise of the network society. The information age: Economy, society and culture* (Vol. I). Cambridge (MA), Oxford (UK): Blackwell.

Davis, M. (2006) *Planet of slums*. London, New York: Verso.

Dupont, V. (2011) 'The dream of Delhi as a Global City'. *International Journal of Urban and Regional Research*, 35(3): 533–54.

Dureau, F., Dupont, V., Lelièvre, E., Lévy, J.-P. and Lulle, Th. (eds) (2000) *Métropoles en mouvement. Une comparaison internationale*. Paris: IRD-Anthropos [(2002) *Metrópolis en movimiento. Una comparación internacional*. Bogotá: IRD-CIDS-Alfaomega].

Gervais-Lambony, Ph. (2005) 'The challenge of comparative research in geography'. In Ph. Gervais-Lambony, F. Landy and S. Oldfield (eds) *Reconfiguring identities and building territories in India and South Africa*. Delhi: Manohar-CSH, pp. 31–42.

Giddens, A. (2002). *Where now for New Labour?* Cambridge: Polity Press.

Gilbert, A. (2007) 'The return of the slum: Does language matter?' *International Journal of Urban and Regional Research*, 3(4): 697–713.

Hajer, M.A. and Wagenaar, H. (2003) 'Introduction'. In M.A. Hajer and H. Wagenaar (eds) *Deliberative policy analysis. Understanding governance in the network society*. Cambridge: Cambridge University Press, pp. 1–30.

Hannan, S. and Sutherland, C. (2015) 'Megaprojects and sustainability in Durban, South Africa: Convergent or divergent agendas?' *Habitat International*, 45(3): 205–12.

Harvey D. (1989) 'From managerialism to entrepreneurialism: The transformation in urban governance in late capitalism'. *Geografiska Annaler. Series B. Human Geography, 71*(1): 3–17.

Harvey, D. (2012) *Rebel cities: From the right to the city to the urban revolution*. London, New York: Verso.

Hayek, F. (1988) *The fatal conceit: The errors of socialism*. London: Routledge.

Heller, P. (2001) 'Moving the state. The politics of democratic decentralization in Kerala, South Africa, and Porto Alegre'. *Politics and Society*, 29(1): 131–63.

Heller, P. and Evans, P. (2010) 'Taking Tilly South: Durable inequalities, democratic contestation, and citizenship in the southern metropolis'. *Theory and Society*, 39: 433–50.

Holston, J. and Appadurai, A. (1996) 'Cities and citizenship'. *Public Culture*, 8(2): 187–204.

Holston, J. and Caldeira, T. (2008) 'Urban peripheries and the invention of citizenship'. *Harvard Design Magazine*, 28: 19–23.

IOM (2013) *World Migration Report 2013*. Geneva: International Organisation for Migration.

Jessop, B. (2001) 'Institutional (re)turns and the strategic-relational approach'. *Environment and Planning A, 33*(7): 1213–35.

Jessop, B. (2002) 'Liberalism, neoliberalism, and urban governance: A state–theoretical perspective'. *Antipode, 34*(3): 452–72.

Johnson, C. (2001) 'Local democracy, democratic decentralisation and rural development: Theories, challenges and options for policy'. *Development Policy Review, 19*(4): 521–32.

Kennedy, L. (2015) 'The politics and changing paradigm of megaproject development in metropolitan cities'. *Habitat International*, 45(3): 163–8.

Kennedy, L., Robbins, G., Bon, B., Takano, G., Varrel, A. and Andrade, J. (2014) *Megaprojects and urban development in cities of the South*. Chance2Sustain, Thematic Report No. 5, Bonn: EADI. Available at: www.chance2sustain.eu/85.0.html (accessed on 27 January, 2015).

Landy, F. and Saglio-Yatzimirsky, M.-C. (2014) *Megacity slums. Social exclusion, urban space and policies in Brazil and India*. London: Imperial College Press.

Lefebvre, H. [1968] (2009) *Le droit à la ville* (third edn). Paris: Economica-Anthropos.

Lemanski, C. (2007) 'Global cities in the South: Deepening social and spatial polarisation in Cape Town'. *Cities*, 24(6): 448–61.

Lier, D.C. (2008) 'The practice of neoliberalism: Responses to public sector restructuring across the labour-community divide in Cape Town'. Unpublished PhD thesis. Manchester: School of Environment and Development, University of Manchester.

Maricato, E. (2013) 'É a questão urbana, estúpido!' In *Cidades Rebeldes: Passe Livre e as Manifestações que Tomaram as Ruas do Brasil*. São Paulo: Boitempo Editoral, pp. 32–46.

Mascarenhas, G. (2012) 'Produzindo a Cidade Olímpica: Neoliberalismo e governança no Rio de Janeiro'. In S.M.M. Pacheco and M. Sampaio Machado (eds) *Globalização, Políticas Públicas e Reestruturação Territorial*. Rio de Janeiro: Sete Letras.

Mayntz, R. (2003) 'From government to governance: Political steering in modern societies'. Paper presented at the International Summer Academy *From government to governance: The case of integrated product policy*. Würzburg, 7–11 September.

McFarlane, C. (2010) 'The comparative city. Knowledge, learning, urbanism'. *International Journal of Urban and Regional Research, 34*(4): 725–42.

Millstein, M. (forthcoming) 'Information and the mediation of power in Delft, Cape Town'. *Nordic Journal of African Studies*, accepted for publication: np.

Pierre, J. (1999) 'Models of urban governance: The institutional dimension of urban politics'. *Urban Affairs Review, 34*(3): 372–96.

Pike, A. (2004) 'Heterodoxy and the governance of economic development'. *Environment and Planning A, 36*(12): 2141–61.

Pillay, U., Tomlinson, R. and Bass, O. (eds) (2009) *Development and dreams. The urban legacy of the 2010 Soccer World Cup*. Pretoria: HSRC Press.

Robinson J. (2002) 'Global and world cities: A view from off the map'. *International Journal of Urban and Regional Research, 26*(3): 531–54.

Robinson, J. (2006) *Ordinary cities: Between modernity and development*. London, New York: Routledge.

Robinson, J. (2011) 'Cities in a world of cities: The comparative gesture'. *International Journal of Urban and Regional Research, 35*(1): 1–23.

Rolnik, R. (2011) 'Democracy on the edge: Limits and possibilities in the implementation of an urban reform agenda'. *International Journal of Urban and Regional Research, 35*(2): 239–55.

Roy, A. (2005) 'Urban informality. Towards an espistemology of planning'. *Journal of the Amercian Planning Association, 71*(2): 147–58.

Roy, A. (2011) 'Slumdog cities. Rethinking subaltern urbanism'. *International Journal of Urban and Regional Research, 35*(2): 223–38.

Sassen, S. (1991) *The global city: New York, London, Tokyo*. Princeton (NJ): Princeton University Press.

Sassen, S. (1996) 'Whose city is it? Globalization and the formation of new claims'. *Public Culture, 8*(2): 205–23.

Swart, K. and Bob, U. (2009) 'Venue selection and the 2010 World Cup: A case study of Cape Town'. In U. Pillay, R. Tomlinson and O. Bass (eds) *Development and dreams. The urban legacy of the 2010 Soccer World Cup*. Pretoria: HSRC Press, pp. 114–30.

Tawa Lama-Rewal, St. (2011) 'Urban governance: How democratic?' In M.-H. Zérah, V. Dupont and St. Tawa Lama-Rewal (eds) *Urban policies and the right to the city in India. Rights, responsibilities and citizenship*. New Delhi: UNESCO & Centre de Sciences Humaines, pp. 21–30.

UN (2014) *World urbanization prospects. 2014 revision. Highlights*. New York: United Nations, Department of Economic and Social Affairs, Population Division (ST/ESA/SER.A/352).

UNDP (2014) *Human development report 2014. Sustaining human progress: Reducing vulnerabilities and building resilience*. New York: United Nations Development Programme.

UN-Habitat (2003) *The challenge of slums – Global report on human settlements*. Abingdon: Earthscan-Routledge.

UN-Habitat (2012) *Streets as tools for urban transformation in slums. A street-led approach to citywide slum upgrading*. Nairobi: UN-Habitat.

UN-Habitat (2013) *Planning and design for sustainable urban mobility. Global report on human settlements 2013*. Abingdon: Earthscan-Routledge.

Vainer, C. (2011) 'Cidade de Exceção: Reflexões a partir do Rio de Janeiro'. *XIV Encontro Nacional da Anpur*. Rio de Janeiro: Anpur.

Ward, K. (2008) 'Editorial – Towards a comparative (re)turn in urban studies. Some reflections'. *Urban Geography, 29*(5): 405–10.

Williamson, T., Imbroscio, D. and Alperovitz, G. (2003) *Making a place for community: Local democracy in a global era*. Abingdon: Psychology Press-Routledge.

Zérah, M.-H., Tawa Lama-Rewal, St., Dupont, V. and Chaudhuri, B. (2011) 'Right to the city and urban citizenship in the Indian context'. In M.-H Zérah, V. Dupont and St. Tawa Lama-Rewal (eds) *Urban policies and the right to the city in India. Rights, responsibilities and citizenship*. New Delhi: UNESCO & Centre de Sciences Humaines, pp. 1–11.

2 National and urban contexts of the settlement cases

An overview

This book explores the politics of slums in a way that simultaneously attempts to be theoretically aware and empirically embedded, presenting original research in six cities across four countries of the global South (see Figure 2.1). In Chapters 4 and 6, the reader is taken through a series of settlement stories that forms the research base for the analysis of policy, social mobilisation and knowledge production. We believe that a systematic presentation of the metropolitan and national context in which these settlements are located will be useful as a reference guide when reading the remainder of the book. In Chapter 2, we therefore present relevant information about the national contexts of Brazil, India, South Africa and Peru, including information about urbanisation, economic growth and social indicators. This section is followed by six fact sheets on Rio de Janeiro, Delhi, Chennai, Cape Town, Durban and Lima. In addition to a photo from a settlement case and a map showing the case settlements for each city, these fact sheets contain information on the residential patterns of poor and marginalised communities and recent trends in social mobilisation.

The four countries and six cities studied

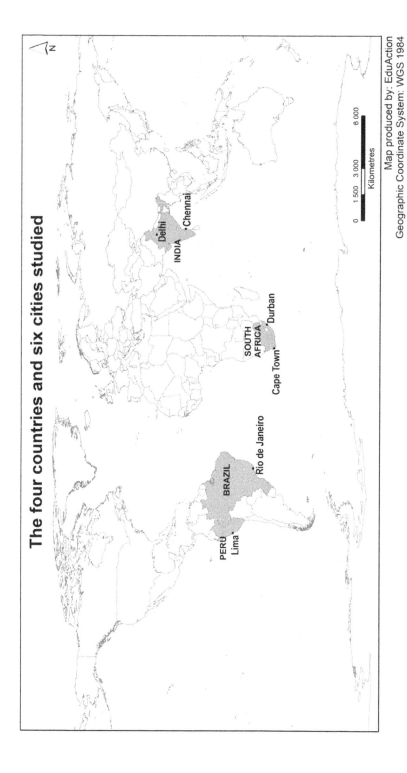

Map produced by: EduAction
Geographic Coordinate System: WGS 1984

Figure 2.1 The four countries and six cities studied.

Fact sheet 2.1 Brazil

EINAR BRAATHEN

The Federal Republic of Brazil is the world's fifth largest country, both by geographical area and by population. In 2013, its population passed 200 million. Brazil is highly urbanised, with 84.4 per cent living in urban areas. According to the latest national census (2010), 52.3 per cent of the population consider themselves being non-white: 43.13 per cent are Mixed (black and white, 'Pardo'), 7.61 per cent are Black, 1.09 per cent are Asian, and 0.43 per cent are Amerindian (indigenous) (IBGE 2011).

Its economy is the world's seventh largest, characterised by growth and relative stability since 1994, after two decades of economic downturn. Still, Brazil has experienced a recent 'roller-coaster decade', with the growth rate varying from 7.5 per cent in the peak year 2011 to a mere 0.9 per cent in 2012 (*The Economist* 2013). The GDP increased by 2.2 per cent in 2013 and 2.4 in 2014, according to the World Bank (O Globo 2015).

In terms of GDP per capita Brazil was in the 77th position globally. However, Brazil is one of the world's ten most unequal countries with a Gini coefficient of 0.54. It is ranked number 85 on UNDP's Human Development Index (UNDP 2014). Nevertheless, the proportion of population living in extreme poverty has been cut by half since a coalition headed by Luiz Inácio Lula da Silva took power in 2003. 16.2 million, or 8.5 per cent of the population, lived in extreme poverty in 2011 (with income below 40 USD per month). The reduction of extreme income poverty has been particularly linked to the Federal Government's expansion of cash transfer programmes (Singer 2012).

Sources

IBGE (2011) *Censo Demográfico 2010.*Instituto Brasileiro de Geografia e Estatística: Rio de Janeiro.

O Globo (2015) 'Banco Mundial vê expansão do Brasil abaixo da média global em 2013 e 2014'. 15 January, 2015. Available from http://oglobo.globo.com/economia/banco-mundial-ve-expansao-do-brasil-abaixo-da-media-global-em-2013-2014-11303961#ixzz3PwsKHZKG (accessed on 25 January, 2015).

Singer, A.V. (2012) *Os sentidos do Lulismo. Reforma Gradual e o Pacto Conservador.* São Paulo: Companhia Das Letras.

The Economist (2013) *Special Report: Brazil*, 28 September, 2013. Available from www.economist.com/news/special-report/21586667-having-come-tantalisingly-close-taking-brazil-has-stalled-helen-joyce-explains (accessed on 26 January, 2015).

UNDP (2014) *Human development report 2014. Sustaining human progress: Reducing vulnerabilities and building resilience.* UNDP.

Fact sheet 2.2 India

VÉRONIQUE DUPONT

The federal Republic of India is the world's second most populous country with 1.21 billion people in 2011 (last census). The urban population, around 377 million in the same year, represented 31 per cent of the total population.

Remarkably, the contribution of the urban sector to the gross domestic product (GDP) was estimated at 63 per cent in 2010 (GOI 2012). The liberalisation and opening of the Indian economy in the 1990s was associated with decentralisation reforms and ambitious national programmes in the urban sector, aimed at promoting cities as 'engines of growth' through large-scale investments and deregulation of land markets. The growing share of informal employment with respect to formal employment, and sharper income inequalities, evidence the contradictions of this growth model. The Gini index increased from 0.308 in 1994 to 0.339 in 2010 (UNESCAP 2014).

The national economy enjoyed high growth rates from 2003 to 2007 – around 9 per cent per year (as measured by the GDP at constant prices) – but the annual GDP growth slowed down to around 4 per cent in 2012 and 2013 (UNESCAP 2014). In 2013, India ranked 123rd globally in GDP per capita (PPP) (World Bank 2014), and was ranked 135th on the UNDP Human Development Index (UNDP 2014).

Poverty remains significant and widespread, despite its reduction. At the national level, the percentage of population below 1.25 dollars a day decreased from 49 per cent in 1994 to 33 per cent in 2010 (UNESCAP 2014). In urban areas, 26.4 per cent of the population was below the national poverty line in 2011–12 (GOI 2014). Urban poor are predominantly engaged in non-wage, informal employment. Depending on the definition of 'slums' (see Boxes 1.1 and 1.3), substandard and illegal settlements are home to between 22 per cent (Census of India 2011) and 29 per cent (UN-Habitat 2013) of the urban population.

Sources

Census of India (2011) *Census of India*. Available from http://censusindia.gov.in/ (accessed on 24 January, 2015).

GOI (2012) *Report of the steering committee on urbanisation. Twelfth five-year plan (2012–2017)*. New Delhi: Planning Commission, Government of India.

GOI (2014) *Report of the expert group to review the methodology for measurement of poverty*. New Delhi: Planning Commission, Government of India.

UNDP (2014) *Human development report 2014. Sustaining human progress: Reducing vulnerabilities and building resilience*. New York: United Nations Development Programme.

UNESCAP (2014) *Statistical year book for Asia and the Pacific 2014*. Bangkok: United Nations Economic and Social Commission for Asia and the Pacific.

UN-Habitat (2013) *Global report on human settlements 2013. Planning and design for sustainable human mobility*. Abingdon and New York: Routledge-Earthscan.

World Bank (2014) 'GDP per capita PPP (current international $)'. Available from http://data.worldbank.org/indicator/ (accessed on 24 September, 2014).

Fact sheet 2.3 South Africa

CATHERINE SUTHERLAND

Post-apartheid transformation continues to shape development in South Africa. South Africa has a population of 51.7 million (Stats SA 2011). Due to its particular history of racial segregation, the census still uses racial categories. In 2011, 79.6 per cent of South Africans classified themselves as Black African, 9.0 per cent as Coloured, 8.9 per cent as White and 2.5 per cent as Indian/Asian. The country has an urbanised population with 62.9 per cent of people living in cities (UNDP 2014). However, circulatory migration between rural and urban areas is common. South Africa is one of the most unequal countries in the world, with a Gini co-efficient of 0.69 and high levels of poverty and unemployment.

Cities play a critical role as growth engines in the South African economy. The nine largest cities in South Africa account for 60 per cent of the total output of the South African economy, revealing the dominance of urban areas in the national economy and the spatial concentration of economic activities in large urban centres (SACN 2011).

In terms of GDP per capita (PPP) South Africa ranked 84th globally in 2014 (World Bank 2014), and in terms of the Human Development Index (HDI) it was ranked 128th. Poverty remains significant with 23 per cent of the population living below the national poverty line (UNDP 2014). In South Africa, 13.5 per cent of the population live in informal structures and 10.4 per cent live in traditional structures (NPC 2010). South Africa experiences the tension of meeting both the pro-growth agenda, which focuses on the global competitiveness of the economy through a neoliberal approach, and the pro-poor agenda, which addresses poverty and inequality through redistribution. However, the pro-growth agenda continues to dominate the development agenda in the country (Scott *et al.* 2015). Development in the country is being impacted by the decline in the knowledge-based economy reflecting the poor standard of education, slow growth in internet access and poor funding for research and development (NPC 2010).

Sources

NPC (2010) *National development plan 2010: Development indicators*. Pretoria: National Planning Commission.
SACN (2011) *The state of the cities report*. South African Cities Network. Available from www.sacities.net (accessed on 24 September, 2014).
Scott, D., Sutherland, C., Sim, V. and Robbins, G. (2015) 'Pro-growth challenges to sustainability in South Africa'. In A. Hansen and Wethal, U. (eds) *Emerging economies and challenges to sustainability. Theories, strategies and local realities*. Abingdon: Routledge, pp. 204–17.
Stats SA (2011) *Census 2011*. Available from www.statssa.gov.za/census2011. Statistics South Africa (accessed on 24 September, 2014).
UNDP (2014) *Human development report 2014. Sustaining human progress: Reducing vulnerabilities and building resilience*. New York: United Nations Development Programme.
World Bank (2014) *World Development Indicators Database*. Updated on 1 July 2014. Available from http://data.worldbank.org/indicator (accessed on 2 September, 2014).

Fact sheet 2.4 Peru

Peru has a population of 30.9 million people (2014), making it the fourth largest country in South America. It is highly urbanised with 75 per cent of the population living in urban areas. In 2013, Peru ranked 87th in terms of GDP per capita (PPP) globally, and it was ranked 82nd in the world in the UNDP Human Development Index, with an HDI of 0.737 (UNDP 2014).

Politically Peru is defined as an independent, democratic and social republic. Its government is meant to be unitary, representative and decentralised. Peru has committed itself to building trust, and supporting dialogue and collaboration among multiple actors through 'infrastructures for peace', and this has reduced the amount of conflict over land and environmental resources in the country (UNDP 2014). In 1990, as a result of macro-economic adjustment, policies were developed to open up the economy and liberalise trade. This also led to the privatisation of major state enterprises, decentralisation of economic activities and the signing of free trade agreements (Gonzales de Olarte *et al.* 2011: 153). These reforms, together with rising mineral prices, generated an increase in the level of private investment, as well as an increase in the national GDP, which has almost tripled from 1990 to 2013. However, this macro-economic boom has not been reflected in significant social improvements. Despite this, the percentage of people living in poverty has decreased from 55.3 per cent in 1991 to 25.8 per cent in 2014, and extreme poverty decreased from 24.2 per cent to 6.3 per cent between 1991 and 2011. Social inequality remains high, and Peru's Gini coefficient was 0.48 in 2014 (UNDP 2014).

Land policy and housing for substandard settlements reflects a *laissez-faire* approach by the state as land invaders were able to occupy state land on the periphery of the cities and achieve recognition. After long periods of struggle and negotiation people living in *barriadas* were able to get access to water and sanitation services. In the early 2000s housing policy was reframed, providing limited subsidies to meet the demand for new housing.

Sources

Gonzales de Olarte, E., del Solar Rizo Patrón, V., del Pozo, J. M. (2011) 'Lima Metropolitana después de las reformas neoliberales: Transformaciones económicas y urbanas'. In C. de Mattos, W. Ludeña, L. Fuentes A. L. (eds), *Lima-Santiago Reestructuración y cambio metropolitano.* Santiago de Chili: Facultad de Arquitectura Diseño y Estudios Urbanos/ Lima: Centro de Investigación de la Arquitectura y la Ciudad, Pontificia Universidad Católica del Perú, pp. 135–176.
UNDP (2014) *Human development report 2014. Sustaining human progress: Reducing vulnerabilities and building resilience.* New York: United Nations Development Programme.

Fact sheet 2.5 Rio de Janeiro

EINAR BRAATHEN

Rio de Janeiro, is the second largest city in Brazil, with 6.4 million people living in the city municipality according to the national census 2010 (IBGE 2011), and twice that number living in a metropolitan region that covers 4,557 square kilometres. Rio is the epicentre of Brazil's fast-growing petroleum and tourist industries, the latter linked to the organisation of mega events such as the FIFA World Cup 2014 and Olympic Games 2016, causing numerous large infrastructure programmes.

Rio has followed the national trend and seen extreme income poverty cut by half from 1995 to 2010. Still, like in the other metropolitan regions in Brazil, housing precariousness has not been reduced substantially in the same period, and 22 per cent of Rio de Janeiro's population (1,393,314 inhabitants) lived in 'sub-normal settlements' or *favelas* in 2010. Rio is the city in Brazil with the highest number of people living in *favelas* (IBGE 2011). Historically, the *favelas* were built on steep hillsides (*morros*) next to affluent neighbourhoods, but for the last forty years the *favelas* have occupied the northern and western parts. The socio-spatial segregation of the city's residents has been scaled up (Gonçalves 2010).

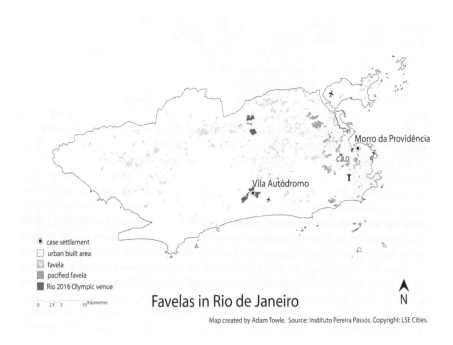

Map created by Adam Towle. Source: Instituto Pereira Passos. Copyright: LSE Cities.

Figure 2.2 Favelas in Rio de Janeiro.

Source: Adapted from Adam Towle, LSE Cities with his permission.

Vila Autódromo is a fishing village that developed into a working-class neighbourhood during the construction of an upper-middle-class boomtown, Barra de Tijuca, in the Western zone of Rio de Janeiro in the 1970s. The community has repeatedly been threatened by collective relocation, lately because of the construction of the Olympic Park.

Morro da Providência is Brazil's first *favela*, a self-built informal settlement dating back to 1893. It is located along the slopes close to the old port area, in the central part and historical downtown of the city. The community has been affected by a grand upgrading programme for the *favelas* of Rio de Janeiro, *Morar Carioca*.

Figure 2.3 Urban upgrading in Morro da Providência.
Photo: Anne Kjersti Bjørn, May 2012.

The city of Rio de Janeiro is, like most other cities in Brazil, governed in a centralised way with power concentrated in the hands of the mayor. Since 2008 the mayor, the governor (of the state of Rio de Janeiro) and the federal president have been aligned politically. This has increased the amount of public investments in the city, but the quality of governance in terms of transparency and democratic accountability has worsened. The lavish spending on public works for the mega-sports events, along with violent police actions against the first demonstrators, brought more than one million Rio citizens out on the streets in demonstrations in June 2013. Affected communities and civil society organisations have formed the network People's Committee of the World Cup and the Olympics. The urban social movement, that was strong in the 1980s, has been revived (Braathen *et al.* 2013).

Fact sheet 2.6 Delhi

VÉRONIQUE DUPONT

Delhi is the capital city of India, as well as a National Capital Territory of 1,483 square kilometres, mostly urbanised, a quasi-state with its government and legislative assembly. The central government retains the control on land, through the Delhi Development Authority (DDA). Within its administrative limits, the Delhi urban agglomeration had 16.3 million inhabitants in 2011 but the urban spread encompasses around 25 million people today. The agenda of transforming Delhi into a global city led to major socio-spatial restructuring. In the 2000s, urban renewal and infrastructure projects were boosted by the 2010 Commonwealth Games preparation, at the cost of large-scale slum evictions. As per the 2011 census, 11 per cent of Delhi urban population lived in 'slums'. As per the Delhi Urban Shelter Improvement Board, around 690 squatter settlements located on public land – the 'illegal slums' locally called *jhuggi jhopri* clusters – were home to approximately 1.5 million persons in 2012, or less than 10 per cent of the city population (27 per cent in 1998). Slum demolitions entailed the displacement of at least one million people from 1998 to 2010 and increased the homeless population.

Several NGOs, workers' unions and popular organisations have mobilised against slum demolitions and inadequate resettlement in Delhi. The types of actions include public meetings, rallies, sit-ins, resistance to the demolition squads, petitions, legal actions, awareness campaigns and capacity building

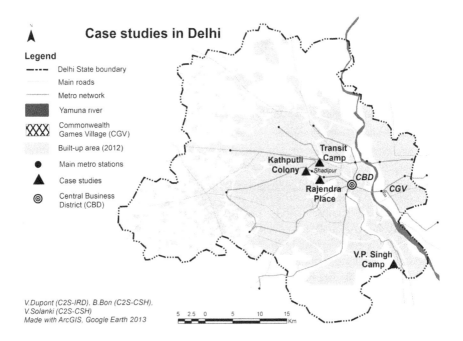

Figure 2.4 Case studies in Delhi.

Figure 2.5
A street scene in
Kathputli Colony.

Photo:
Véronique Dupont,
November 2011.

among affected people. In spite of some local successes denouncing large-scale slum demolitions and their brutality, these mobilisations have not altered the implementation of slum clearance. Attempts initiated by various civil society organisations in Delhi have been sporadic and fragmented. Coalitions and forums are not organised into a unified social movement. There is also a lack of efficient grassroots organisation among slum dwellers in Delhi, as local leadership remains split along political, regional, social and religious lines. Organisations representing the homeless are better co-ordinated, and managed to lead a successful campaign.

Kathputli Colony is a centrally located, forty-year-old squatter settlement where the DDA is undertaking its first project of in-situ slum redevelopment in partnership with the private sector. The residents have to be transferred to a transit camp before the construction of multi-storeyed buildings to re-house them in flats can start.

Rajendra Nagar, a demolished slum near Rajendra Place, was a small squatter settlement demolished in 2000 for the construction of a metro line. Its 125 families were rendered homeless. A municipal squad again evicted them from their temporary night shelter in December 2009 during the Commonwealth Games preparation. The subsequent death of two homeless people triggered a mobilisation campaign for the right to shelter.

V.P. Singh Camp, a squatter settlement in Delhi's southern periphery, provides an example of past successful mobilisation against an attempt of eviction in 1989–91. This contrasts with the absence of reaction when the DDA launched its Tehkhand redevelopment project in 2006 (later abandoned), and the present lack of collective action to improve the living conditions in the settlement.

Fact sheet 2.7 Chennai

VÉRONIQUE DUPONT

Chennai, the state capital of Tamil Nadu, is the fourth largest city in India with a population of 8.7 million in 2011. The Chennai Municipal Corporation (CMC) extended its limits in October 2011, covering now 426 square kilometres. As per the census data and definition of 'slums', 28.5 per cent of the population in the CMC area lived in slums in 2011. A survey conducted in 2003–04 for the Tamil Nadu Slum Clearance Board listed 444 'undeveloped slums' (not upgraded) within the metropolitan area; among those, 212 were categorised as 'objectionable slums', comprising a majority of squatter settlements located along waterways and threatened by eviction.

New clusters of poverty have been created in the 2000s by the construction in the southern periphery of large-scale resettlement colonies for displaced slum dwellers, Kannagi Nagar (16,000 dwelling units) and Semmenchery (6,800 dwelling units), with inadequate urban services and amenities.

Since the turn of the century, the construction of sector-specific corridors has impacted the urban and economic development of Chennai. Among those, the construction of an IT corridor in the southern zone was associated with land

Figure 2.6 Squatter settlements along the Buckingham Canal in Chennai.
Photo: Véronique Dupont, February 2012.

Arignar Anna Nagar is one of the squatter settlements of the Buckingham Canal Bank Road, in the IT corridor zone, categorised as 'objectionable slums'. In 2002, many families were evicted and relocated in Kannagi Nagar resettlement complex, in order to facilitate desilting and widening of the canal. The remaining residents are exposed to new threats of eviction.

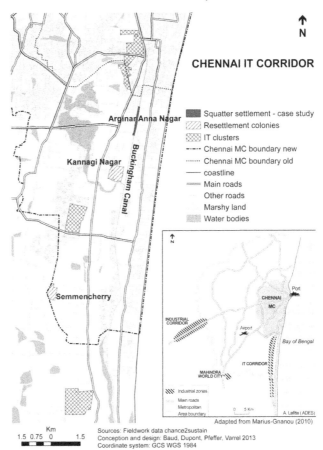

Figure 2.7 Chennai IT corridor.

speculation, the extension of the Mass Rapid Transport System, and 'beautification' operations, especially along the Buckingham Canal that flows parallel to the IT corridor – in short, transformations that usually entail slum evictions.

Collective action among slum dwellers is set in the context of political party control in slums, dominated by two main parties promoting both a regionalist and populist agenda (the *Dravida Munnetra Kazhagam* or DMK, and the *All India Anna Dravida Munnetra Kazhagam* or AIADMK). In the 1970s and 1980s, informal settlers resisted evictions and engaged in intense struggles aimed at securing their tenure on the occupied land and accessing basic amenities. Collective action resorted to massive street demonstrations as well as legal battles. However, in the 1990s, this type of slum-based collective struggle receded. Local residents' associations in slum areas have mostly abandoned confrontational strategies and are rather engaging in negotiations with the Slum Board.

Fact sheet 2.8 Cape Town

CATHERINE SUTHERLAND AND DAVID JORDHUS-LIER

Cape Town is the oldest and second-largest city in South Africa. The metropolitan area covers 2,461 square kilometres and has a population of 3.7 million. Since 2000, it has been administered by a unified municipality, the City of Cape Town. As the main economic centre of the Western Cape Province, it is home to 64 per cent of its population and generates 74 per cent of its GDP. Cape Town has grown rapidly as a result of rural-urban migration from the Eastern Cape Province. It has a diverse economy, focused on the service sector, and is the second wealthiest municipal area in South Africa after Johannesburg. It has high levels of inequality with a Gini coefficient of 0.67, which is lower than the national average but high in comparison to international standards. The metropolitan area reflects stark socio-spatial segregation: wealthy and affluent white-dominated areas are located adjacent to the Table Mountain National Park, whereas most of the coloured and black townships are located on more peripheral Cape Flats.

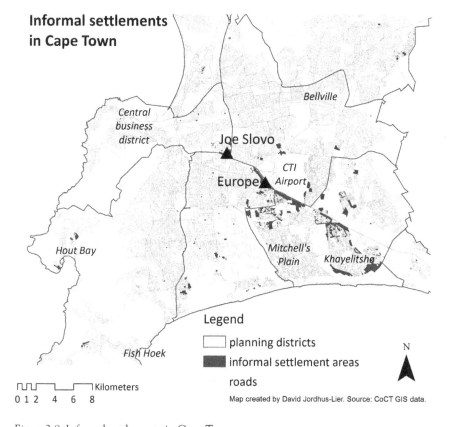

Figure 2.8 Informal settlements in Cape Town.

Joe Slovo informal settlement forms an outer band surrounding Langa township, the oldest black township in Cape Town, and is the informal settlement located closest to the city centre. Electricity, communal toilets and waterborne sewerage was installed in 2003. The N2 Gateway Housing Project, launched in 2004, has offered a number of residents a formal house, while many others have been resettled in another area.

Europe informal settlement in Gugulethu township forms part of a strip of shacks along the N2 highway. Established on top of a former landfill site more than 20 years ago, the unstable ground emits methane gases stemming from buried waste. Lack of proper drainage systems, yearly flooding and poor service-delivery systems add to the experience of poverty. Several NGO-led interventions have been initiated without leading to significant upgrading of Europe.

Figure 2.9
A community leader in Europe shows an unregulated waste site in the settlement.

Photo: David Jordhus-Lier, April 2011.

In 2011, 35.7 per cent of Cape Town households were living below the poverty line and 20 per cent of the population lived in informal settlements or backyard shacks. Since the late 1990s, many deprived communities in Cape Town have been in a state of permanent, high mobilisation. Initially, protests were revolving around eviction from formal housing, championed by the influential *Western Cape Anti-Eviction Campaign*. Over the course of the last decade, informal settlement dwellers, backyarders and other constituencies have also mobilised. Their protests focus on insufficient service delivery and upgrading across the metropolitan area. While some of these movements have chosen to align formally with political parties and politicians, the main mode of mobilisation has been relatively localised and fragmented expressions of resistance – often referred to as 'service delivery protests' in South Africa. Some notable exceptions include the *Social Justice Coalition*, the SDI-aligned *Informal Settlements Network*, a local branch of the Durban-based *Abahlali baseMjondolo*, and recently the ANC-aligned *Ses'Khona* movement.

44   *Various*

Fact sheet 2.9 Durban

CATHERINE SUTHERLAND

Durban, which is administered by the eThekwini Municipality, has a population of 3.6 million people and covers 2,297 square kilometres. The city has low economic diversity and high levels of poverty, where 41.8 per cent of the population are considered poor. Depending on definitions and data sources, between 12 and 31 per cent of the population lives in informal settlements in the municipality (Stats SA 2011). The fragmented, sprawling spatial structure of the city, its fast growth, which results in service and housing backlogs (411,783 households), and its socio-economic challenges are major obstacles to achieving sustainable, efficient and equitable development. The city has a relatively unique spatial geography as it has a dense urban core and a less dense under-developed rural periphery, which contains valuable environmental services, most of which is located on Ingonyama Trust Land. Large areas of the rural periphery are therefore governed by both the eThekwini Municipality and the Traditional Authority, which influences the nature of social mobilisation.

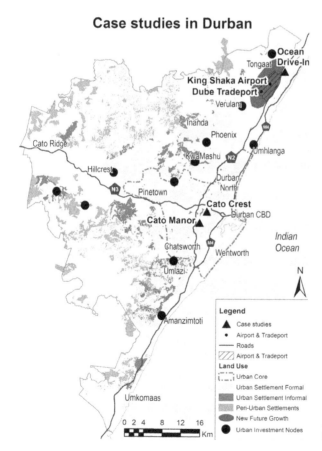

Figure 2.10
Case studies in Durban.

Ocean Drive-In is an informal settlement in the north of the municipality, located on private land in close proximity to the new Dube TradePort. In November 2012 the community were allocated houses in the state-subsidised formal housing project Hammonds Farm and hence were subject to a relocation process. Social mobilisation has taken on a variety of forms in the 30-year history of the settlement as residents have struggled for their 'right to the city'.

Cato Crest is a low-income settlement located in the inner core of the city that has been undergoing a enumeration and re-blocking process for upgrading. It consists of RDP housing and informal settlements and has a long history of social mobilisation and civic organisations as original community members resisted removal from the area under apartheid. It is a well-organised settlement with a history of strong social mobilisation and good leadership.

Durban reflects entrepreneurial urbanism with large-scale development projects, such as Dube TradePort, Cornubia and the World Cup 2010 stadium restructuring urban space within specific areas of the city. Since 1994, the eThekwini Municipality delivered a significant number of state-subsidised RDP houses. The municipality has always adopted a relatively tolerant approach to informal housing, recently committing to in-situ upgrading of informal settlements, as a result of its engagement with *Abahlali baseMjondolo* (AbM), a powerful national shack dwellers' movement that originated in Durban in 2005. Since 2010, the pace of state-provided formal housing delivery in the city has slowed down and programmes, such as the Interim Services Programme that provides basic services to informal settlements, have become more prominent.

Social mobilisation around housing is fragmented and localised with communities adopting different strategies including legal action, local protests, land invasions in association with protests, insurgent urbanism in the rural periphery and mundane adaptations that challenge the state. The most significant forms of social mobilisation in the municipality have occurred where there is strong leadership in settlements with robust civic organisations that have partnered with AbM.

Figure 2.11
Ocean Drive-In residents debating during a community mapping exercise.

Photo: Dianne Scott, April 2012.

Fact sheet 2.10 Lima

CARLOS ESCALANTE ESTRADA

Lima, the capital of Peru, is located in the central coastal part of the country, close to the Andes Mountains. The Metropolitan Area includes Callao seaport and covers 2,672 square kilometres. In 2007, its population was estimated at 8.5 million inhabitants, ranking as the fourth biggest agglomeration in South America. In 2009, 17.5 per cent of the population in the Lima province was in conditions of poverty. During the second half of the twentieth century, rural-urban migration led to invasions of vacant land located on the outskirts of the city. In the past two decades, the country experienced substantial economic growth. These dynamics boosted the real estate sector in Lima and entailed a noticeable increase in public and private real estate investments, as well as a steady increase in land values. It is estimated that 35 per cent of the population today live in self-help settlements (*barriadas*) and another 20–30 per cent in deteriorated inner-city tenements (*tugurios*).

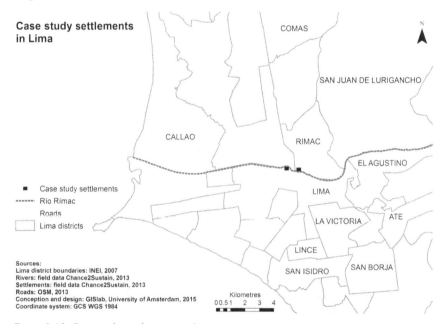

Figure 2.12 Case study settlements in Lima.

Margen Izquierda y Derecha del Río Rímac are two low-income settlements on the left and right banks of the river Rímac, located next to the city centre. They both have a long history of social mobilisation. They are now affected by an ongoing mega-project, the *Vía Parque Rímac* expressway, which combines road infrastructure with urban redevelopment. The threat of displacement triggered extensive community resistance.

Figure 2.13 Dwellings at risk of collapsing into the Rímac river.
Photo: Lisa Strauch, December 2012.

However, investments did not improve the conditions of low-income sectors and has rather increased inequalities within the city. The real estate market is structured around two modes of production and commercialisation of land: real estate companies that capture much of the land with good viability and access to basic services, which are aimed at middle and upper classes; and the informal urban developers named 'land traffickers', who provide land to lower-income families – these lands are located on the outskirts of the city, they lack access to basic services, are hard to access and are often situated in risky zones.

Social mobilisation for land and housing, borne by neighbourhood organisations, was particularly efficient in the 1970s. Its main claims for a place to live in the city included regularisation of informal land occupation and access to essential services. In the decade of the 2000s, the 'Citizen Campaign for the Right to Housing' managed to influence urban policies. Last, in the early 2010s, a new movement arose called the 'Roofless People Movement', which demands decent housing conditions for the urban poor.

References

Braathen, E. with Sørbøe, C.M., Bartholl, T., Christovão, A.C. and Pinheiro, V. (2013) 'Rio de Janeiro: Favela policies and recent social mobilizations'. *NIBR Working Paper 2013: 110*. Oslo: Norwegian Institute for Urban and Regional Research.

Census of India (2011) *Census of India*. Available from http://censusindia.gov.in/ (accessed on 24 January, 2015).

City of Cape Town (2014) *State of Cape Town 2014*. Available from www.capetown. gov.za/en/stats/CityReports/Documents/SOCT%2014%20report%20complete.pdf (accessed on 29 January, 2015).

Delhi Urban Shelter Improvement Board. Available from http://delhishelterboard.in (accessed on 24 January, 2015).

eThekwini Municipality (2012) *Spatial development framework report: 2012/2013*. Durban: eThekwini Municipality Economic Development Unit.

Gonçalves, R.S. (2010) *Les favelas de Rio de Janeiro – histoire et droit, XIXe et XXe siècles*. Paris: L'Harmattan.

HDA (2013) *Western Cape: Informal settlements status*. Available from www.thehda.co. za/uploads/images/HDA_Western_Cape_Report.pdf (accessed on 29 January, 2015). Johannesburg: The Housing Development Agency (HDA).

IBGE (2011) *Censo Demográfico 2010*. Rio de Janeiro: Instituto Brasileiro de Geografia e Estatística.

Marius-Gnanou, Kamala (2010) 'Nouvelles activités économiques et dynamiques métropolitaines: le cas de la périphérie Sud de Chennai'. *Annales de Géographie, 671–672*: 28–51.

Stats SA (2011) *Census 2011*. [Final set of data produced by Dori Posel based on census information]. Pretoria: Statistics South Africa. Available from http://beta2.statssa.gov.za/ ?page_id=3839 (accessed on 29 January, 2015).

Sutherland, C., Robbins, G., Scott, D. and Sim, V. (2013) 'Durban city report', *Chance2Sustain Working Paper*. Available from www.chance2sustain.eu.

Tamil Nadu Slum Clearance Board (TNSCB) & Tamil Nadu Urban Infrastructure Financial Services Limited (TNUIFS) (2005 and 2006) *Pre-feasibility study for identification of environmental infrastructure in slums in Chennai Metropolitan Area* [Indian Resources Information & Management Technologies, Ltd, Hyderabad in association with Community Consulting Indian Pvt Ltd (TGC India), Chennai]: *Final Report – Chennai Corporation Area*, September 2005 & *Final Report- Chennai Metropolitan Area (excluding CMC)*, April 2006.

UN-Habitat (2008) *State of the world's cities 2008/2009: Harmonious cities*. London: Earthscan.

3 Policies towards substandard settlements

Catherine Sutherland, Einar Braathen,
Véronique Dupont and David Jordhus-Lier

Introduction

The rapid and continuing growth of slum settlements in the developing world, in the face of the global call for 'slum-free cities', requires a paradigm shift in housing policy, urban planning and development (UN-Habitat 2013). The Millennium Development Goals (MDGs), under Goal 7, set as their target 'a significant improvement in the lives of at least 100 million slum dwellers by 2020' (www.un.org/millenniumgoals/environ.html, accessed on 7 August, 2014). Although these targets were met by 2010, the 'absolute numbers of slum dwellers have increased from 776.7 million in 2000 (when the MDGs were established) to 827.6 million in 2010' (UN-Habitat 2013: 14). Governments across the world continue to grapple with the challenge of providing adequate and affordable shelter for all. There has been a call from institutions such as UN-Habitat, NGOs, civil society, academics and progressive housing practitioners for a shift in housing policy for the urban poor away from the mere delivery of housing units to the development of integrated human settlements, including the upgrading of settlements. In the developing world, the economic, social, environmental and cultural dimensions of housing for slum dwellers are not adequately addressed and recognised (UN-Habitat 2013). Pro-poor housing in many countries in the South continues to be dominated by evictions and relocations, with resettlement projects being developed on urban peripheries or marginal land, and with limited consideration for the bundle of urban resources required to address urban poverty.

According to UN-Habitat (2013), political will and strong national housing policy are critical to the achievement of improved housing conditions for the urban poor. However, this 'strong' policy with clear frameworks may need to be implemented within emerging flexible and experimental governance regimes, which are considered as being appropriate for the development of more sustainable and resilient cities in the South (Pelling 2010, Roberts 2010, Swilling and Annecke 2012, Hordijk, Sara Miranda and Sutherland 2014, Taylor, Cartwright and Sutherland 2014).

Many post-2000 governments in the developing world have responded to the Cities Alliance's slogan of 'Cities without Slums'. This was incorporated as a long-term target in the Millennium Development Goal 7 (Target 11), creating a bold vision of 'slum-free cities' (Huchzermeyer 2011). This resulted in the emergence of a discourse on 'slum-free' urban areas, that was debated by multiple actors who held different positions about the role of slums in addressing the housing challenges of the South. It also led to multiple constructions of slum dwellers. These ranged from slum dwellers being considered as 'undesirable', to being seen as 'innovative makers and shapers of urban space'. The Cities Alliance supported participatory slum upgrading as best practice and it argued against slum evictions (Huchzermeyer 2011). However, the 'slum-free city' vision was not always interpreted in the socially progressive way in which it was intended. Many countries used this vision as a frame for eradicating slums through repressive programmes that undermine the rights of the poor to the city (Gilbert 2007, Dupont 2011b, Huchzermeyer 2011).

A long list of failures in public housing around the world reflects the complexity of the housing challenge. This reveals how difficult it is for the state to balance the multiple dimensions, including the participation of slum dwellers, that need to be addressed in producing integrated human settlements. However, public housing also represents enormous potential as housing projects can play a critical role in improving the economy, providing employment, alleviating poverty, addressing inequality and supporting human development. They also impact on the ecological and carbon footprints of cities and they shape mobility patterns and hence possibilities for public transport (Swilling 2006, UN-Habitat 2013). Housing policy must therefore be aligned with broader urban development programmes and be developed both for and with the poor.

International thinking on urban policy promotes the role of the local state in development, including the provision of housing and services, the development of economic growth and poverty alleviation strategies, the enhancement of participatory governance, and the promotion of sustainable development (Parnell, Pieterse and Watson 2009). Local government is at the closest interface to the urban poor and hence is best placed to engage with populations within each local context to find appropriate solutions to housing. However, the local state has to respond to these challenges within the frameworks set by regional and national government, and it is often constrained by the legislation, policy and funding mechanisms of higher tiers of government. It is also often influenced by international thinking and global agendas.

Many of the housing challenges found in local authorities today are a result of the intended and un-intended outcomes of state policies that focus on particular types of problems at particular times (Li 2007). It is useful to differentiate between policy formulations and state practices or interventions. Whereas the former provide general goals and guidelines and a repertoire of instruments for policy implementation, a state practice or intervention tends to be a specific policy instrument where the state takes direct and focused action in a specific place at a specific time. State interventions often emanate from the interpretation of policy formulations. In many cases, it is a specific state intervention or practice rather than a policy document that triggers mobilisation. The way in which policies translate into interventions and practices reflects the relationship between the state and its citizens. It also reveals the extent to which beneficiaries are able to participate in housing provision on their own terms.

In Brazil, India, Peru and South Africa, the state actors involved in housing governance include national, regional and local (city-level) governments. These actors produce various forms of legislation and policy which in turn lead to the practices that shape housing interventions. Housing policy is therefore constructed and enacted at the local, regional and national government level and should be understood as *multi-scalar*. These multi-scalar governance arrangements 'matter' in the countries under discussion.

In all four countries the Constitution or national legislation plays a significant role in shaping housing policy. For example, in South Africa a judicial challenge in 2000, known as the 'Grootboom ruling', led the Constitutional Court to argue that post-apartheid housing policy was not meeting the qualified right to housing as protected in the Bill of Rights. This ruling achieved international recognition. In the wake of the Grootboom case, the then Minister of Housing agreed to review the housing policy in light of its shortcomings (Huchzermeyer 2011). However, evictions continue to take place across the country, reflecting that shifts in policy do not always result in a change in state interventions (Huchzermeyer 2011). Legislation and policy may be supportive of the 'right to the city', however, the actions of state officials and other powerful development actors have at times served to undermine the formal policy framework (Pithouse 2009).

In Brazil, some local authorities, and more recently state/federal government, have championed pro-poor policy-making for housing. However, the regional state governments play an important role in the areas of environment, water and housing provision (Souza 2006). In India and South Africa the national state has driven such policy shifts, but along different trajectories. While India has adopted a market-orientated approach since the 1990s, South Africa employs strong central government control over housing provision through its state-subsidised housing programme (the capital housing subsidy model) (Gilbert 2004, Braathen 2011, Tissington 2011, Huchzermeyer 2014). In Brazil, Peru and South Africa, local government is mandated by law to improve the quality of life, housing, service provision and income-generating opportunities of their citizens. In India, the decentralisation policy adopted in 1992 devolved significant responsibilities to local authorities in urban areas. Nonetheless, regional state governments resisted this devolution of power and resources, and kept playing a major role in urban governance in India (Tawa Lama-Rewal 2011). However, budgetary constraints at the local scale impact on what can be achieved across all four countries (Gilbert 2004, Goebel 2007). In the Peruvian case, local government has a minimal influence on the budgets allocated to low-income housing, and hence is reduced to a similar role as local government in India. Actors protecting real-estate interests and the mass media and its partners have more recently been able to shape development outcomes in Peru, which serve to undermine the ability of the local state to address the housing challenge.

In both Peru and India, the national state government plays a direct role in urban development. Governance structures in India are particularly complex, with large cities being governed by a multiplicity of agencies. In India, two national programmes, the *Jawaharlal Nehru National Urban Renewal Mission* (JNNURM, launched in December 2005) and the *Rajiv Awas Yojana* (RAY or 'Slum-Free City Planning', initiated in 2009 under the Ministry of Housing and Urban Poverty Alleviation) are instrumental in shaping India's approach to housing for the poor. These policies reveal the shift in the role of the state in India since the late 1980s from being a provider of housing and services to being a facilitator that promotes public–private partnerships, relies on market mechanisms and uses land as a resource (Dupont 2011b, Mahadevia 2009). The RAY provides the main guidelines for housing provision for the urban poor. However, under the federal system of government, the regional states are assigned responsibility for land administration and land reforms, including the implementation of urban and slum policies. The National Capital Territory of Delhi is a notable exception as the central government retains control on land development.

In this chapter we present the main policies developed to address substandard housing in Brazil, India, Peru and South Africa. While we tend to move in this book from policy to practice, we recognise that practice does not always follow policy. As Holston (2008) and Bayat (2010) argue, the state has often had to catch up and craft policy as the insurgent practices and quiet encroachment of ordinary people 'make' the city. Cities are therefore not only made through specific (state) interventions, but through the actions of multiple actors that may require the state to respond through policy. Reality is not simply the linear outcome of design, but rather policy and practice are co-constitutive and entangled. As a result, the practices and actions of state authorities may be contradictory with one another and with the normative positions articulated in policies.[1] Policies are therefore relational as they contain the ideology, power and practices that exercise governance over citizens, and they constitute politics, when the implementation of policy triggers social action (Hajer and Wagenaar 2003). Policy approaches and their associated interventions are acted upon and often contested by multiple actors. The extent to which this action re-shapes policy is determined by whether policy-making and governance is authoritarian, technocratic or elite-based, or participatory, deliberative and democratic (Braathen 2011). The following section presents the different approaches to housing policy that are evident in the four countries we have studied.

Policies that address substandard settlements in Brazil, India, Peru and South Africa

Five approaches to housing policy have emerged in the six cities that have formed the focus of this research. These are: (i) policies of self-help; (ii) policies of demolition and eviction; (iii) policies of in-situ upgrading; (iv) policies of relocation and resettlement; and (v) policies of integrated human settlements. They reveal the shifts in housing policy that have taken place over time as a result of the political and socio-economic changes that have occurred in these countries.

Our five-part typology is not meant to be mutually exclusive, as concrete state interventions tend to draw on more than one policy approach. Moreover, shifts between policy approaches can take place over time, reflecting an evolution in international housing discourse and shifting political administration. In fact, even within a single intervention, efforts to legitimise the actions of the state can traverse from one policy approach to another. For example, the demolition of substandard housing continues in all four countries, but it tends to be justified under different legislation and policy in comparison to the eviction policies of the 1960s and 1970s.

Furthermore, we can analyse each of these five approaches in terms of their level of state intervention and community participation, as shown in Figure 3.1. This is a useful analytical frame as it enables us to understand these policies in relation to the politics of resistance and mobilisation discussed in this book.

The five policy approaches also result in different degrees of spatial disruption. This is an important point, given that beneath the technical implementation of housing policies and service provision lies the fundamental conflict over who has the right to urban space. Many poor people challenge exclusionary urban geographies by occupying land, individually or collectively, that is located closer to economic opportunity or to transport hubs. As Figure 3.2 illustrates, the degree

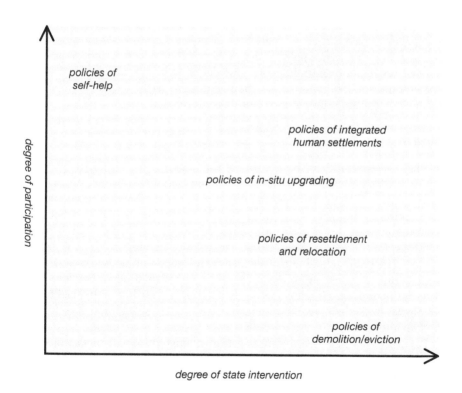

Figure 3.1 The degree of state intervention and participation in state housing policies.

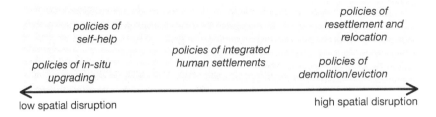

Figure 3.2 State housing policies and the level of spatial disruption.

of spatial disruption does not correspond directly with a policy's degree of state intervention or community participation.

Moreover, in practice the policies might be implemented in contradictory ways. Some of the settlement stories in this book show how in-situ interventions can begin to resemble the old eviction and resettlement policies. Patterns of policy intervention are mixed, complex and messy.

The remainder of this chapter presents the five approaches to housing policy for the urban poor in substandard settlements in Brazil, India, Peru and South Africa. It reflects on these broad policy approaches as they have been developed in each national context. Different programmes and practices that have emanated from policy in each case are presented. These policies inform state interventions, that then in turn generate political dynamics, which is reflected in the modalities of social mobilisation and politics of knowledge presented in subsequent chapters. These political contestations have the potential to feed back into the policy-making process and inform subsequent policy interventions.

Policies of self-help

Self-help approaches have been a part of the housing solution for the poor for centuries (Ward 1982, Harris 1998, Parnell and Hart 1999, Marais, Ntema and Venter n.d.). Self-help housing can take on a number of different forms ranging from collective house-building through co-operatives, to individuals building houses on invaded land. 'Co-operative house building' has been important in many countries, for instance in Brazil before the military dictatorship came to power in 1964. The Brazilian tradition of *mutirão*, or repeated voluntary and co-operative work, is linked, in *favelas*, to urban upgrading rather than house building. The Peruvian version of self-help housing, in contrast, is based on individual house building as its modus operandi, although this is often enabled through collective land invasions.

Policies of self-help housing are largely attributed to John Turner's thinking, which supports bottom-up, collective approaches where informal dwellers themselves are in control of the housing process. Turner argued that informal settlers should be given the 'freedom to build', since their knowledge about their housing context and potential housing solutions is as valid, and in many cases more valuable, than technocratic and professional knowledge (Turner and Fichter 1972). Turner based much of his work on his experiences in Peru between 1957 and 1965. In 1961, Peru was the first country to regularise 'self-help development' with the enactment of the Law for Marginal Settlements (the famous 'Barriadas Law') (Strauch, Takano and Hordijk 2015). Turner's ideas were later colonised by the World Bank, appearing as their neoliberal site-and-service 'aided self-help' policies (Pugh 1991). A detailed genealogy of urban policy development in Peruvian cities is given in Box 3.1.

Lima exemplifies the policy of self-help housing, as it was this approach that was adopted in the country from the 1950s until today, with some important changes post-2000. This resulted in Turner describing the city as socially progressive in terms of housing approaches for the urban poor (Strauch, Takano and Hordijk 2015). The national and local government allocated land on the urban periphery for 'invasion' by organised poor families so that they could self-urbanise and construct their own houses. Self-built housing on marginal land on the urban periphery along the banks of the Rímac river has been constructed through collective efforts 'from below' (Strauch, Takano and Hordijk 2015). Lima's pro-poor housing policies were participatory, supported by a national government that promoted incremental home-building. This was legitimised as an appropriate response to the large housing backlogs that had been generated by rapid urban growth and extensive urban poverty. Informal settlers were seldom evicted, and their collective organisation and incremental home-building was supported by the Peruvian government, who awarded legal status to informal settlements (Strauch, Takano and Hordijk 2015).

Over time, these peripheral settlements, which constituted vast areas with their own services, economy and dynamics, became part of the formal city as they sprawled outwards. Furthermore, collective organisation in the settlements was enhanced by the legal principle that the government would only discuss land issues with recognised neighbourhood associations, not with individuals (Hordijk 2000).

Pro-growth agendas that have swept the countries and cities of the South since the late 1980s have led to the demise of self-help approaches. In the 1990s, under the leadership of President Fujimori (1990–2000) and his structural adjustment reforms, Peruvian policies shifted away from a pro-poor to a pro-growth agenda with an increasing reliance on the market and privatisation to address development challenges. This was aligned with the policy approach of privatisation of the housing sector, which was advocated by the Washington institutions. However, the reforms introduced in the early 2000s remained more discursive than real. Their impact on low-income neighbourhoods was marginal. Policies supporting self-help housing continued through the Housing Materials Bank Programme, through which people could obtain building materials for house improvement. Self-help housing, land invasion and incremental home building in poor urban neighbourhoods in Lima continue to be the common practice.

However, this is countered by a new discourse that supports the aspirations to transform Lima into a globally competitive city. Some politicians now

Box 3.1 Self-help settlement and land policies in Peruvian cities

Carlos Escalante Estrada

Urban policies have made a significant contribution to the shaping of urban development in Lima. The modernisation of parts of the city due to private and public investment is evident from the beginning of the twenty-first century. In Lima, the first type of investment has been concentrated in global articulation nodes such as the port, the airport, shopping and financial centres, apartment blocks, etc; while the second aims to improve parks, roads, transport, etc. Urban entrepreneurship has become more dominant in the city, and this is evident in the development of small commercial and industrial agglomerations in former lower-income central areas and peripheral districts. The relationship between the city and human settlements is also changing (see Box 7.1).

Considering this changing scenario, policies from different governments towards human settlements in Peruvian cities have been based on a *laissez-faire* approach; permitting informal occupations in peripheral public land, providing limited self-help housing construction support to dwellers and slowly responding to their demands for basic services and collective facilities. This approach has meant that the government has withdrawn from its responsibility to implement housing policies for low-income sectors.

However, previous administrations with more authoritarian approaches were not that open to accepting land occupations and relied on the allocation of large areas of land, creating the space for large settlements such as 'Villa El Salvador' from 1971 and 'Huascar' from 1976. Both settlements defined Lima's neighbourhood expansion to the south and northeast. A similar effect occurred after the allocation of land for the development of 'Pachacutec' to the north of the city during the Fujimori administration. During this period, a new National Constitution eliminated the right to housing and restricted the possibilities for expropriating private land for the benefit of low-income populations.

State policy that aims to regularise informal land occupations was initiated in 1961 with the *'Ley de Barriadas'* No. 13517 and it is still in place today as administrations have constantly supported its validity. The land-titling policy had the greatest impact after the issuing of the Legislative Decree 803[2] that created the Commission for the Formalisation of Informal Property (COFOPRI) and the Urban Property Registry (RPU) in 1996. Nevertheless, massive land property deed provision did not stop more informal land occupations, but rather promoted them, obliging the government to appoint a multi-sectoral commission for formulating specific policies regarding legal and physical regularisation.[3]

An attempt to change this model occurred with the municipal housing programmes implemented in Lima by the *'Izquierda Unida'* municipal administration between 1984 and 1986. It incorporated a prevention focus to existing tenure regularisation programmes through the development of land access and progressive housing programmes that relied on territorial planning and the anticipation of further occupations.[4] This focus was replicated in other cities such as Ilo, Trujillo and more recently in Arequipa. It has taken thirty years since these experiences for the Municipality of Lima to approve a low-income housing programme.

The decision to turn a blind eye to informal occupations and the lack of urban control from local authorities has generated a vacuum in the management of urban land in peripheral areas that are occupied by informal real estate agents, known as 'land traffickers', who organise occupations and offer land plots to low-income families. While occupations tend to occur in more and more dangerous and inadequate areas, the best areas are taken by formal real estate developers in order to satisfy the demand from higher income markets due to better location and suitability for service provision. Policies from the Ministry of Housing and the Superintendence of National Assets tend to support this practice by auctioning desert land to real estate developers and undermining its transfer to the Metropolitan Municipality for the development of low-income housing programmes.

During the 1970s low-income populations, that represented more than one third of the population of Lima, constituted an important political constituency that was targeted by specific policies to gain their support. The reformist military government tried to co-opt the strong neighbourhood movement through political promotion organisations. During Fujimori's administration, populist pollcles greatly increased in extent with the creation of the Ministry of the Presidency (making it clear that the president was the only benefactor). These policies provided support for self-building and programmes for water, sewerage and electricity provision. The land-titling policy was also promoted and more than one million registered titles were issued in less than five years. This was inspired by a liberal approach that understands regularised and registered property as transferable capital for reaching credit and financial development, following De Soto's ideas (see De Soto 1989 and 2000). The APRA administration also tried to attract poor populations through the implementation of clientelist policies and the support of party-related neighbourhood committees as intermediaries of the 'Water for All' programme that, in fact, has been accused of the misappropriation of funds.

Post-2000, important transformations have occurred in relation to housing. In 2000 the Toledo administration assumed that the state should be a facilitator of private sector activities; deactivating the Bank of Materials BANMAT (that was financially unsustainable with a 90 per cent default rate) and replacing it with a new housing policy promoted by the Inter-American Development Bank in the whole region. The Household Bond policy aimed to cover the gap between the cost of a basic house produced by the market and the lack of spending capacities of low-income families. This subsidy was the basic component of the 'My Own Roof' programme (*'Techo Propio'*) related to greenfield and brownfield housing construction and upgrading.

Real estate operators mainly focused on greenfield housing while brown-field development and upgrading was left behind. The populist apparatus was dismantled and was replaced by a smaller but more sustainable scheme, given that the programme lacked funds. Its impact was even lower than BANMAT's.[5] Resources from the National Housing Fund FONAVI, which comprised of contributions from all workers and firms, were transferred to the MI VIVIENDA public fund in order to leverage the financial system that was used to address the housing demand from middle-income sectors.

Populations from old settlements that self-built their houses and acquired regularised land tenure only received support from the state in the form of basic service provision such as water, sewerage and access roads. Only after the 2000s, Mayor Castañeda included the construction of public stairways in the municipal agenda with a limited but theoretical approach. During the Villaran administration that followed, this programme developed a more integrated focus becoming the '*Barrio Mio*' programme ('My Neighbourhood'). This included building retaining walls to prevent rock falls, planting trees, paving local roads and building community facilities.

'*Barrio Mio*' is the most important programme of the Municipality of Lima but it is limited to those settlements that already have regularised land tenure, neglecting more recently occupied settlements. Since there is very little state control over new settlements, invasions on unoccupied neighbouring land held by land traffickers and the occupation of high-risk areas continue. In addition, people can access funds through 'participatory budgeting' for developing small public works in their neighbourhoods. These mechanisms, together with the '*Barrio Mio*' programme and water and sanitation programmes, are isolated actions that are not integrated with local planning, and have even promoted clientelism.

Planning and urban development approaches that consider the city as a whole will result in a large concentration of urban facilities (health, education, job opportunities) in the central area. Higher deficits remain in more peripheral districts formed by old informal settlements. The dominant policy for the last fifty years has regularised the existence of peripheral settlements with no kind of territorial planning approach, which reinforces inequalities and is particularly problematic considering the risky situation of populations living on steep slopes, sandy areas, wetlands and river cliffs.

References

De Soto, H. (1989) *The other path. The invisible revolution in the Third World*. New York: Harper and Row.
De Soto, H. (2000) *The mystery of capital. Why capitalism triumphs in the West and failed everywhere else*. New York: Basic Books.

argue that the city 'should grow through investment rather than by invasion' (Romero Sotelo 2006: 24, cited in Strauch, Takano and Hordijk 2015). This has meant a gradual shift away from developing the city 'from below' to development 'from above' (Strauch, Takano and Hordijk 2015).This has had significant implications for the policy of self-help housing. In the face of the development of large mega-projects in Lima, public land has been privatised in the heart of the city, especially in the old *tugurios*, where settlements and services have been relocated and land-use zoning has changed in the more profitable coastal areas.

Self-help policy, albeit socially progressive, also allows the state to withdraw from its responsibility of providing housing to the poor. One of the main responsibilities of the state in self-help housing is 'to create the conditions under which citizens (as right claimers) can fully develop their potential to build and gradually upgrade their own houses in a safe and dignified way' (Bredenoord and van Lindert 2014: 56). In South Africa the strong state interventionist approach has not been able to accommodate self-help as an approach, even though the BNG policy incorporates ideas of informal upgrading. This reveals that the role of the state in self-help housing should not be positioned as low or high state intervention, but rather somewhere in the middle (see Figure 3.1).

Policies of demolition and eviction

Policies that support the demolition and eviction of informal settlements were developed as a state response to the rapid urbanisation occurring in the developing world. However, these policies have been developed differently in Brazil, India and South Africa, reflecting both progressive and repressive approaches.

Slums increased dramatically in India, especially in Delhi, following the independence of the country in 1947, and the partition, which led to a massive migration of refugees. The Indian Parliament passed the Slum Areas Act of 1956 that included the improvement of old housing stock and the demolition of dangerous buildings. While it did not deal directly with illegal settlements, it was interpreted to justify evictions and demolitions (HLRN-HIC 2004). Moreover, the Slum Areas Act differentiated between 'notified' and 'non-notified slums'. This distinction legitimised an exclusionary provision of basic services. Under the Constitution of India, the right to shelter is indirectly recognised as a fundamental right, which draws from the right to residence under Article 19(1)(e) and the right to life under Article 21. Until the 1990s, the courts played an active role in protecting slum dwellers by passing orders that prevented the forced evictions of slum dwellers (Ahuja 1997). Several judgements also explicitly acknowledged an understanding of the living conditions of the poor, giving municipal authorities the responsibility to provide services to slums (Ghertner 2008). However, in an attempt to prevent the continued growth of squatter settlements, specific laws were enacted and court judgements passed to ensure that 'illegal encroachments' were considered an offence. With respect to demolition, it is important to mention the massive slum clearance that marked the notorious 1975–77 state of emergency in India, particularly in its capital city.

During this twenty-one-month break in the country's democratic regime, more than 150,000 families from Delhi's inner slums and squatter settlements were forcibly displaced to relocation sites on the outskirts of the city (Jain 1990).

Policies that supported the demolition of slums were prevalent in Brazil and South Africa during the 1960s and 1970s. This led to the large-scale destruction of informal settlements and increasing numbers of homeless people who often sought refuge in backyard shacks or in crowded houses that had escaped demolition. During the military dictatorship in Brazil, public removal policies resulted in the destruction of *favelas*. However, in the 1980s, Rio de Janeiro shifted its approach towards a political recognition and upgrading of *favelas*. This occurred as a result of the democratic election in 1982 that placed the left-oriented leader Lionel Brizola as the head of the regional state. Both politicians and social movements influenced the legal and institutional arrangements for housing policy, resulting in the notion of the 'right to the city' being included in the multi-level institutional framework – municipal, regional state and federal – developed for urban reform (Santos Junior 2009). 'Urban reform' – based on the notion of the 'right to the city' – was then a pendant to 'agrarian reform'. It emerged from the struggle of urban social movements and the recognition of all city residents as rights holders. The inclusion of the 'right to the city' in federal law (the City Statute of 2001) is an example of a breakthrough in recognising the rights of the urban poor (Fernandes 2007). National housing policies began to shift at the same time, but from 1985 to 2005 this shift did not materialise in significant, sustained social housing programmes in Brazil. Lack of federal investments was to blame, as well as the economic stagnation in the 1980s and the large-scale informalisation of the economy. Drug-trafficking gangs took control of the *favelas*. In the 1990s and 2000s, there was limited influence on housing policy from social movements, which by then had weakened.

Under apartheid, the national government of South Africa engaged in the demolition of informal settlements. Forced removals were a key instrument of the White minority regime's spatial engineering project under the Group Areas Act of 1950. Post-1994, a number of changes to legislation provided greater protection to informal settlers. Sections 26 (1) and (2) of the South African Constitution state that (1) everyone has the right of access to adequate housing; and (2) the state must take reasonable legislative and other measures, within its available resources, to achieve the progressive realisation of this right, which ensures a qualified right to housing and protection against arbitrary eviction. Poor households were protected against illegal and unfair eviction with the repeal of both the Prevention of Illegal Squatting Act No. 51 of 1951 with all its amendments, and the Slums Act No. 76 of 1979. The White Paper on Housing led to the promulgation of the Housing Act No. 107 of 1997, which refers to 'slum elimination' as a step towards the long-term goal of achieving adequate housing in South Africa. The 'squatting' and 'slums' Acts were replaced by the Prevention of Illegal Eviction from and Unlawful Occupation of Land Act No. 19 of 1998 (PIE Act), which reflects the principles of Section 26 of the Constitution. The so-called PIE Act makes the eviction of an unlawful occupier illegal, unless the eviction is authorised by an order of the court and complies with a number of procedural requirements. Legislation therefore afforded informal settlers a certain level of rights (Tissington 2011).

However, the African National Congress (ANC) government inherited cities with large, growing informal settlements. The eradication of 'slums' became, and still is, the dominant discourse of the ANC government, strongly influenced by the MDGs and the Cities Alliance's slogan *Cities without Slums*. According to Huchzermeyer (2011) informal settlement eradication was legitimised both as way of 'addressing' the legitimate goal of poverty eradication and reducing the housing backlog. This discourse was supported by the provincial Elimination and Prevention of Re-emergence of Slums Act, passed at provincial government level in KwaZulu-Natal in 2007 and taken up by national government later in that year, despite opposition from shack dwellers' movements and human rights organisations (Pithouse 2009). This Act enables court orders to be given that legitimise the demolition of shacks. According to Pithouse (2009), the discourse of 'slum elimination' makes shacks, which are nothing more than the self-built housing solution of the poor, appear as if they are a threat to society. The Land Invasion Unit in Durban, sometimes under court order and at other times illegally, removes new shacks that go up in the city, in an attempt to ensure that informal settlements do not grow in number.

Across our case study cities, demolition and eviction therefore remain part of state action, even as part of relatively progressive policies. More socially progressive policies developed in Brazil in the 1980s, India post-2009 and South Africa post-2010 did not prevent the state from intervening in informal areas in disruptive ways. Thus, in India, the agenda of transforming large metropolises into 'global cities', has led to a major restructuring of urban space, including slum clearance. This process, rooted in the liberalisation reforms of the 1990s, was most intense in the capital city, the country's showcase. Further, the hosting of the 2010 Commonwealth Games in Delhi supported this drive for global competiveness and its correlated image building where slum dwellers have no place (Dupont 2011a). Major infrastructure works, urban renewal projects and 'beautification' operations, all entailed slum demolitions and population displacement.

From 1990 until 2008 at least 221 squatter settlements (locally known as *jhuggi jhopri* clusters) were demolished in Delhi, and around 65,000 families, or about 325,000 people, were relocated in resettlement colonies on the outskirts of the city.[6] However, conservative estimates suggest that at least half of the total number of evicted families were not resettled (Bhan and Shivanand 2013). Ghertner (2010: 202) calculated that from 1997 to 2007 'close to a million slum dwellers have been displaced'. Although demolitions occurred in the entire urban area, the larger evictions affected the embankments of the Yamuna River and central and southern zones of the urban agglomeration. These are zones where the capital's reconstruction has been more conspicuous and/or are characterised by the presence of commercial and business districts and a concentration of residential colonies for higher-income groups.

Large-scale slum demolition without adequate resettlement programmes for the evicted families has also increased the number of homeless. To address the issue of homelessness in Delhi, the central government initiated a programme of night shelters in the mid-1980s, which is still in place. This consists of providing facilities for night stay in areas with high concentrations of homeless people. However, in the context described above, the programme proved to be grossly insufficient and did not meet the needs of the homeless (Dupont 2013).

The use of mega-projects as an urban growth strategy, which is evident in all six cities studied here, has been instrumental in driving demolitions and evictions. While not contained in a specific policy, demolition and evictions take place under the 'exceptionalism' of these projects, which opens up non-ordinary procedures. Demolitions occur where space is required to build mega-projects, but they also take place more indirectly as a result of mega-projects. In Durban, informal settlers of Ocean Drive-In were not provided with the alternative of having their settlement upgraded in-situ, as the settlement was located on private land in close proximity to the new Dube TradePort and King Shaka International Airport. The development of this mega-project led to an increase in the value of the land upon which Ocean Drive-In is located, placing pressure on the local state to relocate this informal settlement. The settlement also fell within the noise contour demarcated in the Environmental Impact Assessment of the new airport (Box 5.2) which served to legitimise removal.

Although there has been a shift away from more repressive urban housing policies in Brazil, India and South Africa, with the upgrading of informal settlements being recognised as part of the housing solution for the urban poor, evictions and demolitions continue to happen under the guise of upgrading and resettlement programmes, as the following sections reveal. In South Africa, informal settlements that for long have struggled against the threat of relocation continue to experience surveillance and control measures adopted by the state through their security-led approach to prevent the occupation of land by the urban poor (Huchzermeyer 2011, Tissington 2011).

Policies for in-situ upgrading

As states have recognised that upgraded informal settlements form part of the housing solution in rapidly growing cities, so they have shifted towards policies that favour in-situ upgrading. This shift has been driven largely by the recognition that governments are not able to keep up with growing housing demand through the provision of formal housing. The recognition that the location of housing for the urban poor impacts significantly on poverty and inequality has also led to a change in approach. This policy frame reflects, at least rhetorically, a recognition that the urban poor choose to live in particular locations because they offer access to a bundle of urban opportunities that are critical to the survival of the poor. Residents of informal settlements often develop strong social networks that form part of their coping strategies. The relocation of the urban poor away from their established locations, usually to areas on the urban periphery, increases their vulnerability and often deepens urban poverty.

This policy approach has emerged at different times in different places, depending on the particular political, economic and social context, and hence it has taken on different forms. In-situ upgrading can be implemented as minimal improvement, where only basic services are provided, but it can also lead to substantial upgrading where services, facilities and housing are significantly upgraded. In some cases, such as Brazil's processes of *urbanização* (upgrading), upgrades do not involve the large-scale demolition of existing structures, whereas in other cases, such as in India and South Africa, upgrading may result in demolitions where informal residents are moved to temporary or transit camps while the settlement is reconstructed. This can lead to evictions and homelessness as often the rebuilt settlement does not have enough housing to accommodate all those living in the original settlement. In many cases it is the tenants or lodgers that are displaced (Settlement Story 6.2). While Brazil has adopted a diverse approach to in-situ upgrading from the demolition of slums for the rebuilding of high-rise low-income blocks to community managed improvement programmes, South Africa has been slow to develop a range of alternatives, adopting a uniform approach to informal settlements (Huchzermeyer 2004).

In post-apartheid South Africa, the ANC government adopted a housing policy of large-scale delivery of state-subsidised formal housing. The housing subsidy system was accompanied by the widespread view among politicians, government officials and communities that informal settlements were temporary phenomena of South African cities soon to be replaced by formal housing. In 2004, this policy approach was replaced by the Breaking New Ground policy (Department of Housing, 2004) that adopted a more holistic approach to housing, including in-situ upgrading, flexible planning approaches and increased community participation. However, in-situ upgrading received very little support and was only promoted through rights-based action from within civil society (Huchzermeyer 2006). In 2010, in-situ upgrading received renewed impetus with the surprise announcement by President Zuma that 400,000 informal settlement units would be upgraded as a new housing target. However, it appeared that only settlements on land considered suitable for standardised low-cost township development would be considered in this programme.

In Durban, informal settlement upgrading is implemented in different ways depending on the suitability of the land. Informal settlements that are not eligible for in-situ upgrading, but face relocation, are provided with a minimum level of services that include communal tap points and pit latrines. For informal settlements that will not be relocated nor upgraded in the short-term, the municipality has developed the Interim Services Programme. This programme provides community ablution blocks that contain toilets and water points, all built in containers that are managed by caretakers. Substantial upgrading is undertaken on sites that are suitable for low-income housing and where the councillors support these upgrades. In this case informal housing is demolished, informal dwellers are relocated to transit camps and then moved back when the formal housing is complete. Conflict arises when some residents of the original settlement cannot be accommodated in the new housing project, as was seen in the violent housing protests in Cato Crest in Durban in January 2013 (Settlement Story 6.2).

In Brazil the victory of the left-oriented Ignácio Lula da Silva in the 2002 presidential elections led to significant urban reform. Institutions such as the Ministry of Cities and federal and regional state-level 'councils of cities' were established under the Lula administration (2003–10), which encouraged public participation in housing and sanitation projects. The federal government of Brazil implemented the *Programa de Aceleraçãodo Crescimento* (PAC, meaning 'Program to Accelerate Growth') and *Minha Casa Minha Vida* (meaning 'My House, My Life'). The PAC is an integrated development programme that has invested in a range of development projects including housing and sanitation. The PAC has allocated the majority of its funds to residents within communities, which means that it favours upgrading over resettlement of poor households. The *Minha Casa Minha Vida* programme includes the building of new houses on new sites, as well as the provision of new houses for in-situ upgrading.

In 2010, the Municipality of Rio de Janeiro, represented by the Municipal Board of Housing, announced a new housing and upgrading programme called *Morar Carioca*. The programme has the goal of upgrading and formalising all the *favelas* in the city by 2020. This was part of creating a lasting 'social legacy' of the 2014 FIFA World Cup and the 2016 Olympic Games.[7] *Morar Carioca* offered multi-sector territorial interventions such as urban upgrading, conservation of public space, control of the growth of *favelas* and urban legislation, as well as the resettlement of residents who were living in hazardous areas. During Phase I (2010–12), investments of more than USD 1 billion were made (Bittar 2011). The *Morar Carioca* programme included a number of innovations including a competitive public tender process that required architectural firms to develop participatory approaches to housing design. Projects were also required to include the provision of new houses for people who had to be relocated because of *favela* upgrading or because they resided in environmental 'risk areas' (Bittar 2011). In order to construct these housing units, the municipality drew on the federal housing programmes of *Minha Casa Minha Vida* and PAC.

Crucially, case studies from *favelas* such as Morro da Providência show that the preliminary upgrading projects implemented under the programme have repeated previous patterns of state interventions. This includes (i) lack of transparency of the formalisation projects and the low participation of local residents in their implementation; (ii) mismatch between the large number of removals and the low number of new houses built to be offered to the former residents of the *favelas*; (iii) new housing units being constructed in peripheral suburbs and not near the original *favelas* (Cardoso and Lago 2013). Thus, the interventions resemble the old eviction and resettlement practices, although the official policy since the 1980s has emphasised in-situ rehabilitation, in order to enhance social inclusion of the *favelas* into the city. A comprehensive academic assessment of the *Minha Casa Minha Vida* programme concluded that it had increased the socio-spatial segregation of Rio de Janeiro and the other larger cities by building most of the houses for low-income groups in the suburban peripheries

(Cardoso 2013). From a 'right to the city' perspective these programmes mainly benefited private entrepreneurs, denying people's rights to in-situ rehabilitation and consequently contributing to the development of a 'city of exception' (Vainer 2011).

In India, in-situ upgrading corresponds to an approach recommended in several current and historical policy documents, including the current RAY policy. They span different strategies, from minimal improvement to the full reconstruction of the settlement. The improvement of the living conditions in the existing slums through the provision of basic services post-independence in 1947 was a response of urban development authorities to sanitation and public health concerns, as in Kolkata and Delhi (Risbud 2009, Priya 1993). In 1972, the central government developed the Environmental Improvement of Urban Slums Scheme, which aimed to provide basic infrastructure in zones officially 'notified' as slums. Other schemes with similar or more comprehensive objectives followed, as part of poverty alleviation programmes. More recently, the JNNURM included the provision of basic services to the urban poor, with a focus on slums, as part of its agenda. This is a pragmatic approach that aims at addressing short-term needs of slum dwellers on site, similar to the Interim Services Programme that has been established in Durban and the Emergency Servicing of Informal Settlements (ESIS) project, which was launched in Cape Town (Box 3.2). Crucially, such interventions do not always guarantee slum dwellers rights of occupancy. In Delhi, slum dwellers remain vulnerable to evictions if the land-owning agency undertakes projects of 'better public utility' on the occupied sites (Dupont and Ramanathan 2008). In the state of Tamil Nadu, where the city of Chennai is located, in-situ development consisting of basic infrastructure provision and amenities, such as water supply, road and sanitation, has been among the strategies of the Tamil Nadu Slum Clearance Board (TNSCB) since its inception in 1971. In addition, while the central government housing policy began to emphasise the role of the state as a facilitator of housing rather than a builder, the regional ruling party in Tamil Nadu diverged significantly from the national trajectory, explicitly limiting evictions and focusing on the state provision and construction of housing. Under the progressive discourses of this regional state government, squatters could consolidate their hold on public land (Raman 2011: 75). Thus, multi-storied tenements for slum dwellers constructed on site by the TNSCB was the dominant approach in Chennai until the World Bank's intervention from 1975 progressively shifted policies towards resettlement solutions (see below).

Nevertheless, urban reforms introduced in the 1990s resulted in a new role for the private sector in Indian cities, as a developer and builder, including for low-income housing. Thus, in-situ rehabilitation schemes under public–private partnership were implemented, first in Mumbai and more recently in Delhi. This approach was promoted in the Master Plan for Delhi 2021 (notified in 2007) and supported by the national policy for *Slum-Free City Planning* (RAY, launched in 2009). Such slum redevelopment programmes require the demolition of existing slums before constructing multi-storeyed buildings to re-house families, who have to be transferred to a transit camp. A key element of these public–private partnerships is the strategic use of land as a resource according to the principle of cost recovery. In concrete terms, only part of the land occupied by the slum is used to accommodate its residents, the rest is cleared for high-end residential or commercial development for sale on the open market. The commercial component thus subsidises the social housing component. This new strategy provides a less land-intensive alternative to resettlement through 'site and services' schemes. The policy-makers' expectation is that 'vertical projects' will unlock the land stock occupied by slums. In 2008, the Delhi Development Authority identified twenty-one slum clusters for in-situ rehabilitation, projecting the construction of about 37,000 dwelling units to that end. Yet, by the end of 2014 none had been built (Dupont 2014). Kathputli Colony (Settlement Story 4.1) will be the first informal settlement in the Indian capital to be redeveloped under this strategy.

Policies of relocation and resettlement

Policies of relocation and resettlement have appeared in different forms in Brazil, India, Peru and South Africa. For example, ad hoc relocation and resettlement triggered by mega-project development can be observed across all six cities. Integrated policies of relocation and resettlement have also, at different points in time, become dominant in our different country contexts: in South Africa through large-scale formal state-subsidised housing under post-apartheid housing reform, in Brazil under the *Minha Casa Minha Vida* programme, as well as in Indian cities.

In Brazil, resources were made available in 2008 for the construction of 3.4 million new houses for the urban poor. These opportunities would be targeted at those families with an income of less than three minimum wages, and those displaced by mega-events. The overall aim of *Minha Casa Minha Vida* was to reinforce economic activity and support job creation during the financial crisis through rapid implementation. The programme relied on public–private partnerships where private sector contractors with public support, but also at times with civil society backing, presented projects to the federal government bank. This programme continues to operate under President Dilma Rousseff (2011–15). In Rio de Janeiro, new houses are built as part of in-situ upgrading programmes within more central areas and on greenfield sites on the periphery of the city. The municipalities have the responsibility for making land available (CEBRAP 2010).

A 'site and services' approach to housing was adopted by the apartheid national government in South Africa in the late 1980s. This approach was developed and implemented by the Urban Foundation and the Independent Development Trust (IDT), two connected business-funded think-tanks on urban and social policy. They supported development for the urban poor as a means of addressing both poverty and the economic downturn in the country (Huchzermeyer 2001 and 2004). The urban poor were provided with a plot of land, a platform upon which to 'self-build' a house, and basic services including a tap point, waterborne sanitation and electricity. The IDT programme obtained a grant of ZAR 2 billion from the national government and over a period of four years in the early 1990s 100,000 standardised serviced sites were delivered to those who qualified for subsidies. The Urban Foundation had a significant influence on the National Housing Forum, which was established to develop housing policy in the new democracy, and the state's capital housing subsidy model that was developed in South Africa post-1994 to deliver formal houses at scale. Many argue that the new post-apartheid policy was a continuation of the IDT 'site and services' approach, except that a top structure had now been added to the model (Nuttall 1997, Lalloo 1998, Huchzermeyer 2001).

The most striking example, therefore, of a state-driven resettlement programme is evident in South Africa. Post-democracy, South African housing policy was driven by the national Department of Housing (renamed the Department of Human Settlements in 2009). A state-subsidised system of large-scale formal housing delivery was adopted. These houses were colloquially known as 'RDP houses', after the Reconstruction and Development Programme that emerged post-1994 to guide transformation of the 'new' democratic country. The responsibility for housing delivery is vested with provincial governments that control the funding and facilitate and approve projects and schemes. Local governments are expected to identify housing demand and suitable sites for developments, and to motivate for the requisite funding for these projects.

Delivery was not the only goal of the South African state-driven housing programme. Five related objectives formed part of the programme: to demonstrate delivery to an expectant post-democracy constituency; to contribute to the economy;[8] to contribute to poverty alleviation; to establish housing markets; and to develop urban citizenship through the creation of a democratic and integrated society (Charlton 2009). The South African government claims to have built 3 million housing units since 1994 and the eThekwini Municipality, the administrative entity of Durban, has built over 160,000 units to date. Many informal dwellers and residents in precarious peri-urban and rural housing on the peripheries of South African cities, as well as people living in crowded housing in townships, have been relocated to formal housing projects. Although large numbers of houses have been transferred to the poor, these houses are often small and of substandard quality, and are located on greenfield sites on the periphery of cities, reinforcing the spatial legacy of apartheid. Due to their peripheral location these housing projects are isolated from social services and livelihood opportunities, they have not produced integrated and sustainable neighbourhoods, and they perpetuate urban sprawl (Charlton 2009, Pithouse 2009). These problems resonate with shortcomings observed in resettlement schemes in Indian cities, as described below. The formal housing process has not been able to adequately tackle the South African housing backlog (Tissington 2011). Hence, national and local state policy has turned towards informal settlement upgrading (as discussed above).

Chennai in India shows similarities to the resettlement policies developed in South African cities. Under the influence of the World Bank and its funding programmes, the Tamil Nadu Slum Clearance Board (TNSCB) began to shift towards relocation and resettlement under 'site and services' programmes from 1975 onwards. Later, resettlement and rehabilitation practices emerged, where dwelling units were provided in blocks of flats on alternative sites. In principle, these units would be connected to well-functioning infrastructure and services. As a result, 'by 2000 the TNSCB was almost exclusively involved in building large-scale tenement clusters on the outskirts of Chennai to house slum dwellers evicted and relocated from the central areas of the city' (Raman 2011: 74). The resettlement colonies of Kannagi Nagar (16,000 dwelling units until 2014) and Semmenchery (6,800 dwelling units), provide an illustration of this policy shift (see Chennai Fact Sheet 2.7 and Settlement Story 6.6). These large resettlement complexes were criticised for their lack of adequate facilities and limited access to urban resources (HLRN-HIC 2014), thus creating new 'ghetto[s] of poverty' (Coehlo, Venkat and Chandrika 2012: 53).

In Delhi, relocation to 'resettlement colonies' according to a 'site and services' approach was the favoured response to squatter settlements adopted by urban authorities from the late 1950s until 2009. Squatter settlements in Delhi mostly occupy public land, and their removal is in principle limited to untenable sites or land required for projects of public utility. Under this strategy, displaced families are allocated plots in relocation sites where they have to build their own dwelling. Like in Chennai, Delhi relocation sites are supposedly equipped with basic infrastructure, although this is often not the case (HLRN-HIC 2004, HLRN-HIC 2014, Menon-Sen and Bhan 2008). Leaseholds or licences with restriction provide security of tenure for the resettled families. However, beneficiaries are required to make a financial contribution, which means that the very poor are excluded from the resettlement programmes. Over time, due to land constraints, the size of the allotted plots was considerably reduced, from 80 square metres in the first scheme of 1960, to only 18 square metres (in the 1990s) and even 12.5 square metres (in the 2000s). Consequently, settlements became overcrowded and lacked adequate amenities.

Town planners and policy-makers in Delhi recognised some of the limitations of the 'site and services' programmes and consequently, in 2010, they shifted their approach towards the provision of flats instead of plots. As in Brazil and South Africa, resettlement often resulted in the dislocation of slum dwellers from urban opportunities and social networks that had sustained them. Most resettlement sites were on the urban periphery and this increased transport costs. Resettlement sites often had very poor facilities and services, creating 'housing areas' rather than integrated settlements. We will therefore now turn to the fifth policy approach, which explicitly attempts to address this flaw in previous policies.

Policy of developing integrated human settlements

The lack of co-ordination between actors, and the weak integration of policies that deal with the urban poor across different sectors, represents another critical disjuncture that impacts on housing for the urban poor. The development of integrated human settlements is increasingly being considered as critical to poverty alleviation and securing the 'right to the city' for the urban poor. In the past, as has been reflected in this chapter, the housing question has largely been addressed through a narrow focus on the formal construction of houses. However, in the face of increasing housing backlogs and homelessness, there is evidence that politicians, officials and consultants in some countries are responding more holistically to demands from civil society and research-based organisations. The message from these voices is that policies must be reoriented towards in-situ rehabilitation, which includes the development of economic, social and environmental infrastructure. The rationale behind the 'human settlements perspective' is to create integrated human settlements that provide the urban poor with access to a bundle of urban resources.

However, this more integrated approach to housing remains at the level of policy and there are limited examples of where this socially progressive approach to housing is being implemented on the ground. This approach has been developed in two pilot studies in Durban, where local government has worked with the private sector and an NGO to develop more integrated approaches to housing the poor. The shifts in Durban housing policy indicate that urban policy-making must be understood as a learning process, where policy-makers not only have to deal with new and growing challenges, but also the partial failures of their own interventions. This is elaborated in the case of Cape Town (Box 3.2), where a newly formed Human Settlements Directorate under the City of Cape Town is trying to adopt integrated policies towards upgrading of the city's informal settlements.

In India there is very little evidence of the implementation of more integrated human settlement policies, despite intentions stated in some policy documents such as RAY. Finally, in Peru the housing process is now dominated by pro-growth agendas that are undermining the opportunities self-built housing offers for more integrated housing development.

Conclusion

This chapter has used examples and cases from six cities in Brazil, India, Peru and South Africa to explore the shifts in housing policy that have taken place. The empirical research reveals that in several cities there has been a shift in official policy towards a more socially progressive discourse that supports the upgrading of informal settlements, recognising their 'place in the city'. In some countries this has led to more integrated approaches to housing, at least in their initial intentions.

However, the implementation of these new policies leaves a lot to be desired in all the countries and cities observed. Along with new policies that have been formulated, demolition and eviction remains a threat to informal dwellers. Their lack of security of tenure continues to undermine their right to the city. Moreover, living conditions of those who still live in slums remain tenuous and difficult.

Resettlement schemes provide informal settlers with basic services and in some cases formal houses, but the relocation of the urban poor away from sites that

Box 3.2 The development of informal settlement policies in post-apartheid Cape Town

David Jordhus-Lier and Berit Aasen

The way in which urban authorities address informal settlements reveals a great deal about the social sustainability of a city's development path. Importantly, the development of policies and strategies to deal with urban informality can be understood as a historically contested learning process, where managers and service departments learn from their own mistakes and 'experiments', amidst political and ideological shifts. The various post-apartheid upgrading and resettlement programmes of the City of Cape Town (CoCT) serve as an example of how these contradictions emerge over time.

Informal settlements in Cape Town

Like other South African cities, Cape Town has experienced rapid urbanisation as a result of migration and natural growth since the end of apartheid. From an official national figure of 300 informal settlements in 1994, there were 2,600 informal settlements in South Africa by the beginning of 2010 (Cities Alliance undated). While the exact number differs according to sources, CoCT managers claim that in 2014, 204 of these were located in Cape Town, housing more than 140,000 households. The proportion of households living in informal settlements has grown slightly since 2001, particularly those living in backyard shacks.

In Cape Town, the informal settlement landscape has some particular characteristics worth mentioning. First, and most importantly, the rapid growth in informal settlements in the post-apartheid era takes place in an urban geography still fundamentally segregated by apartheid. While migrants have erected shacks out on the Cape Flats where the so-called black townships were located – far away from jobs and economic activities – many bypassed this apartheid geography by occupying land closer to the city or transport hubs. This process has created a pattern of informal settlement clusters located along the N2 highway, which runs past Cape Town International Airport in to the city centre (see Cape Town Fact Sheet 2.8).

Second, according to municipal managers, informal settlements in Cape Town are more spatially concentrated and dense than elsewhere in the country. Many settlements, particularly those closest to the city centre, are now at the point where they are becoming 'dysfunctionally dense' (Interview, CoCT official, April 2011). Density is a crucial factor in upgrading processes because it entails that a higher share of residents will have to be temporarily relocated during in-situ upgrades. Combined with the high cost of social housing, this also means that a share of the informal settlement dwellers will have to be permanently relocated as the upgrading will not be able to accommodate all previous dwellers. However, the notion of informal settlements being too densely populated to be upgraded in-situ is disputed (Huchzermeyer 2011). Another consequence of density and strict land control is the mushrooming of backyard dwellings in the city (Lemanski 2009). Tensions between backyarders, formal housing residents and informal settlement dwellers are often constructed as corresponding to racial categories or binaries such as locals versus migrants (Eppel 2007). Such labels are in turn mobilised by different social groups to make claims of entitlement in housing allocation processes (COHRE 2009).

Shifting policy agendas

Following the democratic transition in the country, the main housing policy agenda was aligned with the Reconstruction and Development Programme (RDP). So-called RDP houses were rolled out on a mass scale, using a capital subsidy model. While the ANC government often point to the quantitative success of housing as a part of the RDP programme, critics argue that these houses were of substandard quality and on peripheral land. The 'RDP matchboxes' were seen as too uniform and supply-driven for meeting the needs of particular communities (Menguelé, Khan and Vawda 2006). Houses that were too far away from transport and jobs were simply left vacant, and there were widespread problems of vandalism and neglect. In an attempt to overcome the perceived lack of community participation, the National Department of Housing (NDoH) launched the *People's Housing Process* in 1998, intended to increase community involvement, but also criticised for reducing participation to 'sweat equity' and for being based on private sector principles (Millstein 2008).

While informal settlements are predominantly (but not exclusively) urban phenomena, housing policies are the responsibility of Provincial Government. In the Western Cape, a ZAR 1.4 billion 'special integrated presidential project' known as the *Integrated Services Land Project* (ISLP) became the key vehicle for housing policies in Cape Town from 1994 to 2004. A representative involved in the management of the ISLP claims it was innovative as it used community participation, available 'greenfields' land, as well as in-situ upgrading of informal settlements. However, the ISLP was unable to reduce the number of informal settlements. Informal settlement dwellers were offered formal housing, but other people were waiting to inhabit their shacks. The emergence of informal settlements might, in itself, be said to represent one of the shortcomings of the RDP approach: by prioritising the construction of formal housing, people's need to be close to employment opportunities and social networks are overlooked (Huchzermeyer 2006).

A fundamental problem in the policies of local government during this period lie in the diagnosis of the 'problem': one CoCT official claimed that in the initial post-apartheid era, informal settlements were treated as temporary phenomena that would disappear through the roll-out of formal housing. In 2004, a new National Housing Policy was presented by NDoH: *Breaking New*

Ground (BNG), which represented a move towards a more socially embedded, incrementalist approach through the Upgrading of Informal Settlements Programme (UISP).

In CoCT, the overall responsibility for implementation of informal settlement policies is placed within an expanded Human Settlement Directorate (previously the Housing Directorate), which has a Department for Informal Settlements in charge of planning and managing informal settlements. In addition, several other service departments and units are involved in servicing informal settlements, but finding ways to co-ordinate these efforts represents an ongoing challenge. The Human Settlements Directorate has an executive director for urbanisation, co-ordinating CoCT's policies on informal settlements, backyard dwellings and overcrowding. To strengthen the capacity of municipalities to implement upgrading of informal settlements, a national programme with World Bank/Cities Alliance support, the *National Upgrading Support Programme* (NUSP), has been set up to aid municipalities with technical assistance and best practice learning from pilot projects.

At a city level, Graham (2006) argues that the landmark Grootboom court case in 2000 (see section 3.1) and the shift to an ANC metropolitan government in 2002 served as drivers for articulating an informal settlement policy at a city level. In the same year as the national launch of the BNG policy, the CoCT launched their Framework for Upgrading Informal Settlements. The first phase in this framework was the *Emergency Servicing of Informal Settlements* (ESIS), launched in early 2004 (Graham 2006) which focused on providing basic water, sanitation and waste-removal services to all informal settlements at high speed. ESIS was pushed by the strong involvement of ANC Mayor Nomaindia Mfeketo, but Graham notes that while roll-out was achieved, capital investments were made at the expense of maintenance of existing structures.

An ongoing state of contested learning

CoCT's policy now acknowledges that informal settlements are 'here to stay', and therefore the city needs to both accept the challenge and provide the necessary policy and strategies. In practice, CoCT addresses the informal settlement challenge through a range of interventions, ranging from the mega-project approach of the N2 Gateway project (see Settlement Story 6.3) to an experimental, but essentially ad hoc, strategy of in-situ upgrading based on partnerships bringing together community and expert knowledge.

Two of the most significant initiatives exemplifying the latter approach are the Violence Prevention through Urban Upgrading (VPUU) programme, co-sponsored by German development institutions, and a partnership model with local organisations of the Slum Dwellers International (SDI) Alliance. Based on a CSO partnership between global and national NGOs and local networks of informal settlement dwellers, the SDI Alliance has, since May 2009, initiated a set of local government partnerships where managers and technical staff from CoCT meet with community representatives and NGOs to plan and implement upgrading in selected settlements. In 2011, there were fifteen to twenty partnership projects across the city, according to NGO representatives, focusing on re-blocking, new building materials, ablution blocks and other facilities.

Overall, the pilot projects chosen for testing new models in Cape Town do not seem to have been developed through a rigorous strategy, but rather by the availability of interested partners, competence and funding. Also, models seem to move in and out of political favour. While the re-blocking model promoted by the SDI was adopted as a draft policy by CoCT in 2013, we found that this model was being met with mixed responses by municipal officials a year later. The VPUU model, on the other hand, received a boost when it became a part of the showcase promoting Cape Town as the World Design Capital in 2014. Several senior CoCT managers interviewed for this research expressed a greater belief in a site-and-service model with substantial relocation to greenfield and brownfield sites, rather than in-situ upgrading as envisaged by the UISP policy. Interestingly, this latter policy direction shows strong continuities with the original ISLP approach of the 1990s.

By way of conclusion, as the number of informal settlements experiencing substantial in-situ upgrading is still very limited in Cape Town, current plans and policies have clearly not succeeded in providing upgraded housing at an aggregate level. Moreover, as a result of both emergencies and upgrading efforts, ongoing relocation of informal settlers continues and has placed a significant number of people in supposedly short-term temporary relocation areas (TRAs) and supposedly long-term incremental development areas (IDAs). Not only is this process intensely contested by communities, but it raises questions regarding the quality of emergency housing, the legality of forced relocation, the lack of a 'human settlement perspective' (e.g., access to employment and social services), and the risk of temporary measures becoming long-term (DAG 2007). In short, CoCT's policies and practices on informal settlements are illustrative of the contested, non-linear learning processes underpinning urban governance.

References

Cities Alliance (undated) *Upgrading South Africa's housing policy.* Cities Alliance in Action Project description. Available from www.citiesalliance.org/sites/citiesalliance.org/files/CA-in-Action-%20NUSP.pdf (accessed on 29 January, 2015).
COHRE (2009) *N2 Gateway Project: Housing rights violations as 'development' in South Africa.* Geneva, Switzerland: Centre on Housing Rights and Evictions.
DAG (2007) *Living on the edge: A study of the Delft Temporary Relocation Area.* Cape Town: Development Action Group.
Eppel, S. (2007) ' "They come here and take our houses!": Community conflicts in Langa in the context of the housing crisis in Cape Town: "Borners" against "migrants"'. *Thesis submitted for the degree of MPhil in Development Studies*, Department of Sociology. Cape Town: University of Cape Town.
Graham, N. (2006) 'Informal settlement upgrading in Cape Town: Challenges, constraints and contradictions within local government'. In M. Huchzermeyer and A. Karam (eds) *Informal settlements: A perpetual challenge*. Cape Town: UCT Press, pp. 231–49.

Huchzermeyer, M. (2006) 'The new instrument for upgrading informal settlements in South Africa: Contributions and constraints'. In M. Huchzermeyer and A. Karam (eds) *Informal settlements: A perpetual challenge*. Cape Town: UCT Press, pp. 41–61.

Huchzermeyer, M. (2011). *Cities with slums: From informal settlement eradication to a right to the city in Africa*. Claremont, SA: Juta Academic.

Lemanski, C. (2009) 'Augmented informality: South Africa's backyard dwellings as a by-product of formal housing policies'. *Habitat, 33*(4): 472–84.

Menguelé, F., Khan F. and Vawda A. (2006) 'The emergence and endurance of an evolving human settlements strategy'. In M. Huchzermeyer and A. Karam (eds) *Informal settlements: A perpetual challenge*. Cape Town: UCT Press, pp. 179–202.

Millstein, M. (2008) 'Challenges to substantive democracy in post-apartheid Cape Town: The politics of urban governance transformations and community organising in Delft'. *Thesis submitted for the degree of Ph.D*, Dept. of Sociology and Human Geography. Oslo: University of Oslo.

offer them urban opportunities presents other challenges. In-situ upgrading offers the opportunity of maximising the benefits of the sites chosen by informal residents. However, these programmes do not always result in much improved living conditions. They too can lead to displacement and exclusion as the housing developed on these sites is not always adequate for meeting the needs of all the original residents. And in-situ solutions have yet to deliver an improvement of informal settlements at a scale that is satisfactory given the huge expectations put on political authorities in all our case cities. However, in-situ solutions still represent the best option from a policy perspective of addressing the growing numbers of informal settlers in the six cities.

Unsurprisingly one of the main 'policy' lessons from our research is that practice does not necessarily follow policy. Often policy principles and practice are not aligned, with policy principles promoting a more progressive approach to housing, and practice and implementation resulting in a very different outcome on the ground, which is often repressive, impacting significantly on the lives of the urban poor. Cities are constructed through the complex interactions between top-down and bottom-up processes, some of which are driven by intended programmes, while others are a result of everyday practice.[9] Policy design and practice therefore form a dialectical relationship, revealing the tensions between goals and reality. This complexity and entanglement of policy and practice suggests that new approaches to housing policy need to be found. Huchzermeyer (2014: 346), in referring to the South Africa case, argues that there is a 'call for greater diversification, innovation and incrementalism' in housing policy and that participatory informal upgrading is critical. In the countries explored in this book, it appears that Brazil may be closest to this type of approach, although the practice on the ground is still strongly contested due to the policy-practice discrepancy. As the research has revealed, the impact of 'exceptionalist' large-scale projects on housing practice is significant in all four countries studied.

The following chapters in this book explore the encounters between those living in substandard settlements and policy-making authorities, revealing the ways in which policy shapes living conditions on the ground and how people living in these areas respond to state interventions, thereby (in some cases) re-shaping policy.

Notes

1 As contributed by Richard Ballard in his review of this chapter.
2 Law for the Promotion of Informal Property Formalisation.
3 Supreme decree Nº 100-2003-JUS.
4 A predecessor of this policy was the 'Popular Urbanisations of Social Interest' (UPIS) that were established by Law 13517 from 1961. Nonetheless, UPIS were created for reallocating populations living on valuable land that did not have enough resources for accessing to housing programmes.
5 BANMAT gave 184,297 loans in 1997 while only 17,500 bonds were given in 2012.
6 Source: Slum and *Jhuggi Jhopri* Department, Municipal Corporation of Delhi.
7 There are 900 *favelas* in Rio, and it is not realistic that the programme will reach all of them.
8 The Housing Code notes that housing practices should also 'reinforce the wider economic impact and benefits derived from effective and adequate housing provision in the domestic economy' (NDoH 2000: 11).
9 This invaluable contribution was made by Richard Ballard in his review of Chapter 3 of this book.

References

Ahuja, S. (1997) *People, law and justice. Casebook on public interest litigation*. New Delhi: Orient Longman.

Bayat, A. (2010) *Life as politics. How ordinary people changed the Middle East, ISIM Series on life in contemporary Muslim societies*. Amsterdam: University of Amsterdam Press and ISIM, Stanford (CA): Stanford University Press.

Bhan, G. and Shivanand, S. (2013) '(Un)Settling the city. Analysing displacement in Delhi from 1990 to 2007'. *Economic and Political Weekly*, 48(13): 54–61.

Bittar, J. (2011) *Morar Carioca. Rio de Janeiro*. Paper delivered 11 November 2011 at Clube de Engenharia: Rio de Janeiro.

Braathen, E. (2011) *Addressing sub-standard settlements, policy brief*. Chance2Sustain, Available at www.chance2sustain (accessed on 6 October, 2014).

Bredenoord, J. and van Lindert, P. (2014) 'Backing the self-builders. Assisted self-help housing as a sustainable housing provision strategy'. In J. Bredenoord, P. van Lindert and P. Smets (eds) *Affordable housing in the urban global South. Seeking sustainable solutions*. London: Earthscan (Routledge), pp. 55–72.

Cardoso, A.L. (ed.) (2013) *O Programa Minha casa Minha Vida e seus Efeitos Territorias*. Rio de Janeiro: Letra Capital Editora – IPPUR/UFRJ.

Cardoso, A.L. and Lago, L.C. (2013) 'O Programa Minha casa Minha Vida e seus Efeitos Territorias'. In A.L. Cardoso (ed.) *O Programa Minha casa Minha Vida e seus Efeitos Territorias*. Rio de Janeiro: Letra Capital Editora – IPPUR/UFRJ, pp. 7–17.

CEBRAP (2010) *Background Report: Brazil*. Chance2Sustain. Available at www.chance2 sustain (accessed on 6 October, 2010).

Charlton, S. (2009) 'Housing for the nation, the city and the household: Competing rationalities as a constraint to reform.' *Development Southern Africa*, 26(2): 301–15.

Coehlo, K., Venkat, T. and Chandrika, R. (2012) 'The spatial reproduction of urban poverty. Labour and livelihoods in a slum resettlement colony'. *Economic and Political Weekly*, 47(47 & 48): 53–63.

Department of Housing (2004) *Breaking new ground: A comprehensive plan for the development of sustainable human settlements*. 26 August, 2004. Pretoria: Department of Housing.

Dupont, V. (2011a) 'The dream of Delhi as a global city'. *International Journal of Urban and Regional Research*, 35(3): 533–54.

Dupont, V. (2011b) 'The challenge of slums and forced evictions'. In M.-H. Zérah, V. Dupont and S. Tawa Lama-Rewal (scientific eds) *Urban policies and the right to the city in India. Rights, responsibilities and citizenship*. New Delhi: UNESCO and Centre de Sciences Humaines, pp. 76–97.

Dupont, V. (2013) 'Which place for the homeless in Delhi? Scrutiny of a mobilisation campaign in the 2010 Commonwealth Games Context'. *South Asia Multidisciplinary Academic Journal*, 8: 2–18.

Dupont, V. (2014) 'Slums in Indian metropolises confronted with large-scale urban projects and real estate development: Recent trends in Delhi'. In N. Aveline-Dubach, S-C. Jou and H-H.M. Hsiao (eds) *Globalization and new intra-urban dynamics in Asian cities*. Taipei: National Taipei University Press, pp. 319–50.

Dupont, V. and Ramanathan, U. (2008) 'The courts and the squatter settlements in Delhi. Or the intervention of the judiciary in urban "governance"'. In I.S.A. Baud and J. de Wit (eds) *New forms of urban governance in India. Shifts, models, networks, and contestations*. New Delhi: Sage, pp. 312–43.

Fernandes, E. (2007) 'Constructing the "Right to the City" in Brazil'. *Social & Legal Studies*, 16: 201–19.

Ghertner, D.A. (2008) 'Analysis of new legal discourses behind Delhi's slum demolitions'. *Economic and Political Weekly*, 43(20): 57–66.

Ghertner, D.A. (2010) 'Calculating without numbers: Aesthetic governmentality in Delhi's slums'. *Economy and Society*, 39(2): 185–217.

Gilbert, A. (2004) 'Helping the poor through housing subsidies: Lessons from Chile, Colombia and South Africa'. *Habitat International*, 28: 13–40.

Gilbert, A. (2007) 'The return of the slum: Does language matter?' *International Journal of Urban and Regional Research*, 31(4): 697–713.

Goebel, A. (2007) 'Sustainable urban development? Low-cost housing challenges in South Africa'. *Habitat International*, 31: 291–302.

Hajer, M.A. and Wagenaar, H. (2003). 'Introduction' in M.A. Hajer and H. Wagenaar (eds) *Deliberative policy analysis: Understanding governance in the network society*. Cambridge: Cambridge University Press, pp. 5–37.

Harris, R. (1998) 'The silence of the experts: "Aided self-help housing", 1939–1954'. *Habitat International*, 22(2): 165–89.

HLRN-HIC (2004) *Acts of commission, acts of omission. Housing and land rights and the Indian State*. A report to the United National Committee on Economic, Social and Cultural Rights. New Delhi: Housing and Land Rights Network – Habitat International Coalition.

HLRN-HIC (2014) *Forced to the fringes. Disaster of 'resettlement' in India*. Report 1: *Savda Ghevra, Delhi*. Report 2: *Kannagi Nagar, Chennai*. New Delhi: Housing and Land Rights Network – Habitat International Coalition.

Holston, J. (2008) *Insurgent citizenship: Disjunctions of democracy and modernity in Brazil*. Princeton (NJ): Princeton University Press.

Hordijk, M. (2000) *Of dreams and deeds: The role of local initiatives for community based environmental management in Lima, Peru*. Amsterdam: Thela Thesis.

Hordijk, M., Sara Miranda, L. and Sutherland, C. (2014) 'Resilience, transition or transformation? A comparative analysis of changing water governance systems in four southern cities'. *Environment and Urbanisation*, 26(1): 130–46.

Huchzermeyer, M. (2001) 'Housing for the poor? Negotiated housing policy in South Africa'. *Habitat International*, 25: 303–31.

Huchzermeyer, M. (2004) *Unlawful occupation: Informal settlements and urban policy in South Africa and Brazil*. Eritrea: Africa World Press.

Huchzermeyer, M. (2006) 'The new instrument for upgrading informal settlements. South Africa: Contributions and constraints'. In M. Huchzermeyer and A. Karam (eds) *Informal settlements: A perpetual challenge?* Cape Town: UCT Press, pp. 41–61.

Huchzermeyer, M. (2011) *Cities with 'slums'. From informal settlement eradication to a right to the city in Africa*. Cape Town: UCT Press.

Huchzermeyer, M. (2014) 'Changing housing policy in South Africa'. In J. Bredenoord, P. van Lindert and P. Smets (eds) *Affordable housing in the urban global South. Seeking sustainable solutions*. London: Earthscan (Routledge), pp. 336–48.

Jain, A.K. (1990) *The making of a metropolis. Planning and growth of Delhi*. New Delhi: National Book Organisation.

Lalloo, K. (1998) 'Arenas of contested citizenship: Housing policy in South Africa'. *Habitat International*, 23(1): 35–47.

Li, T.M. (2007) *The will to improve. Governmentality, development and the practice of politics*. London: Duke University Press.

Mahadevia, D. (2009) 'Urban land market and access of the poor'. In Ministry of Housing and Urban Poverty Alleviation and United Nations Development Programme *Urban Poverty Report*. New Delhi: Oxford University Press, pp. 199–221.

Marais, L., Ntema, J. and Venter, A. (n.d.) *State control in self-help housing: Evidence from South Africa*. Bloemfontein: Centre for Development Support, University of the Free State.

Menon-Sen, K. and Bhan, G. (2008) *Swept off the map. Surviving eviction and resettlement in Delhi*. Delhi: Yodapress.

National Department of Housing (NDoH) (2000) *The User Friendly Guide to the National Housing Code*. Pretoria: Department of Housing.

Nuttall, J. (1997) *The first five years: The story of the Independent Development Trust*. Cape Town: Independent Development Trust.

Parnell, S. and Hart, D. (1999) 'Self-help housing as a flexible instrument of state control in 20th-century South Africa'. *Housing Studies*, 14(3): 367–86.

Parnell, S., Pieterse, E. and Watson, V. (2009) 'Planning for cities in the global South: An African research agenda for sustainable human settlements'. *Progress in Planning*, 72(2): 233–41.

Pelling, M. (2010) *Adaptation to climate change: From resilience to transformation*. London: Routledge.

Pithouse, R. (2009) 'A progressive policy without progressive politics: Lessons from the failure to implement "Breaking New Ground"'. *Town and Regional Planning*, 54: 1–14.

Priya, R. (1993) 'Town planning, public health and urban poor. Some explorations from Delhi'. *Economic and Political Weekly*, 28(17): 824–34.

Pugh, C. (1991) 'Housing policies and the role of the World Bank'. *Habitat International*, 15(1/2): 275–98.

Raman, N. (2011) 'The board and the bank: Changing policies towards slums in Chennai'. *Economic and Political Weekly*, 46(31): 74–80.

Risbud, N. (2009) 'The poor and morphology of cities'. In Ministry of Housing and Urban Poverty Alleviation and United Nations Development Programme *Urban Poverty Report*. New Delhi: Oxford University Press, pp. 177–98.

Roberts, D. (2010) 'Prioritizing climate change adaptation and local level resilience in Durban, South Africa'. *Environment and Urbanisation*, 22(2): 397–413.

Santos Junior, O. (2009) *O Fórum de Reforma Urbana: incidência e exigibilidade pelo direito á cidade*. Rio de Janeiro: FASE.

Souza, C. (2006) 'Desenho constitucional, instituições federativas e relações inter-governamentais no Brasil pós-1988'. In S. Fleury (ed.) *Democracia, Descentralização e Desenvolvimento: Brasil & Espanha*. Rio de Janeiro: Editora FGV, pp. 186–211.

Strauch, L., Takano, G. and Hordijk, M. (2015) 'Mixed-use spaces and mixed social responses: Popular resistance to a megaproject in Central Lima, Peru'. *Habitat International*, 45(3): 177–84.

Swilling, M. (2006) 'Sustainability and infrastructure planning in South Africa: A Cape Town case study'. *Environment and Urbanization*, 18(1): 23–50.

Swilling, M. and Annecke, E. (2012) *Just transitions: Explorations of sustainability in an unfair world*. Cape Town, Juta and Tokyo: United Nations University Press.

Tawa Lama-Rewal, S. (2011) 'Urban governance: How democratic?' In M.-H. Zérah, V. Dupont and S. Tawa Lama-Rewal (scientific eds) *Urban policies and the right to the city in India. Rights, responsibilities and citizenship*. New Delhi: UNESCO and Centre de Sciences Humaines: pp. 21–30.

Taylor, A., Cartwright, A. and Sutherland, C. (2014) *Comparison of climate change adaptation strategies of three South African municipalities*. Paris: AFD.

Tissington, K. (2011) *A resource guide to housing in South Africa 1994–2010. Legislation, policy, programmes and practice*. Johannesburg: Socio-economic Rights Institute (SERI).

Turner, J. and Fichter, R. (1972) *Freedom to build: Dweller control of the housing process*. New York: Macmillan.

UN-Habitat (2013) *A time to think urban*. Nairobi: United Nations Settlement Programme.

Vainer, C. (2011) 'Cidade de Exceção: Reflexões a partir do Rio de Janeiro'. *Proceedings of XIV Encontro Nacional da Anpur*. Rio de Janeiro: Anpur.

Ward, P.M. (ed) (1982) *Self-help housing: A critique*. London: Mansell.

4 Settlement stories I

A question of knowledge?

Settlement story 4.1 The challenges of communication and participation in slum rehabilitation: the Tehkhand and Kathputli Colony projects in Delhi

VÉRONIQUE DUPONT AND M.M. SHANKARE GOWDA

The current national policy for 'Slum-Free City Planning' in India, the *Rajiv Awas Yojana* programme, announced in 2009, asserts community participation as a requirement. For each slum identified, the decision-making process regarding its redevelopment plan 'should necessarily be done with the involvement of the community' and 'with the assistance from lead NGOs/CBOs' (GOI 2010: 18). A similar principle is also stated in the new strategy of in-situ slum rehabilitation under public–private partnership launched by the Delhi Development Authority (DDA) in the late 2000s (DDA 2007: section 4.2.3). A meaningful participation process is expected to imply, as a minimum, comprehensive and accurate information provided to the affected residents, and a fair and inclusive consultation process. It is thus directly related to the issue of knowledge management. The first two in-situ rehabilitation projects initiated by the DDA for squatter settlements occupying its land, the stalled Tehkhand project and the ongoing Kathputli Colony project, provide cases in point to examine these questions.

The stalled Tehkhand project

The DDA launched a first pilot project in Tehkhand, in the V.P. Singh Camp located on the southern periphery of the city, on land partly occupied by a squatter settlement. In 2006, it invited bids from private developers to construct 3,500 tenements for re-housing slum dwellers in five-storeyed apartment blocks. The developer had to provide physical infrastructure and basic social facilities, and was allowed, as an incentive, to construct and sell 750 high income-group apartments. Since the slum occupied only a minor part of the 14.3 hectare plot, there was no need to transfer its residents to a transit camp. Housing for the slum dwellers was to be subsidised by the DDA (as the land-owning agency), the Delhi Government and the Central Government. The rehabilitated families were expected to contribute their share through loan facilities.[1]

In 2008, the developer who won the auction started land levelling and excavation operations on the site adjoining the slum, in order to build a complex of luxury apartments. The complex was called 'Castlewood', and advertised on the furthest road from the slum, thus unnoticeable by its residents. Castlewood's lavish advertising brochure included appealing photos of the old Tughlaqabad Fort and green belt on the western side of the site, though no mention was made of features less attractive to the potential upper-class buyers. These included a large landfill, a disaffected cement plant, and the inland container depot entailing heavy truck traffic on the road bordering the site's northern side.

There was no opportunity to test the efficacy of the developer's advertising efforts – or, in other words, his ability to conceal certain information to the potential buyers. The project did not get clearance from the Ministry of Environment and Forests and was stopped in mid-2009. The site was located on the protected Aravalli Ridge, and the DDA had sold the land for residential purpose without the mandatory authorisations. The developer, who was not properly informed at the time of purchase, confronted the DDA through a litigation filed in the Delhi High Court.

Nevertheless, in V.P. Singh Camp, most residents were unaware of the DDA re-development project, let alone its terms. Though a few local leaders were informed through their contact with elected politicians, neither the DDA nor the builder had any procedure of information and consultation with the slum dwellers. Besides, informed leaders did not share the information within their communities. In short, the residents were kept apart from the plans affecting them. This case shows how the retention of information may occur at different levels, and be used by various stakeholders for their own interests.

Kathputli Colony: a slum rehabilitation project in slow progress[2]

The second pilot rehabilitation project undertaken by the DDA was presented as 'a benchmark for many such projects to follow to make Delhi a slum free state'.[3] It concerns Kathputli Colony, a forty-year old squatter settlement spread over 5.22 hectares in a centrally located and well-connected area. It houses around 15,000 people, among which are a large group of folk artists and craftsmen from Rajasthan who settled in this locality in the late 1960s. In fact, Kathputli Colony is named after the many puppeteers who live in the settlement. Since then, other groups of migrants from various regions have moved to Kathputli Colony. As a result, it became a heterogeneous settlement where varying housing conditions reflect socio-economic disparities. Like many squatter settlements in Delhi, Kathputli Colony is characterised by a lack of adequate infrastructure and amenities, and deficient public services.

The most active civil society organisations operating in Kathputli Colony are linked to its cultural professions. The first co-operative was formed in 1978 to defend the interests of street performers. It also provides space to artisans to pursue their activities, and its present president is a recognised leader among the Rajasthani community. In addition, two NGOs promoting the traditional artists and artisans have been particularly active in Kathputli Colony. One of them has made its presence particularly visible in the settlement. It also runs a primary school providing vocational training for artists' children, as well as a dispensary. However, competition and rivalries eventually developed between the two NGOs working in the same field, and with the same community. We shall see later the consequences of this rivalry.

The rehabilitation project was brought to the knowledge of the residents when the Ministry for Urban Development laid the foundation stone for a fourteen-storeyed housing complex of 2,800 two-room flats of 25 square metres in February 2009. This was the complex intended for the slum dwellers. The private firm who was awarded the development contract in October 2009 will use only part of the land occupied by the slum (60 per cent) to build, and deliver the blocks of flats along with mandatory amenities to the DDA free of cost. On the rest of the land, to make its investment profitable, the developer had an ambitious plan for a high-end 54-storeyed residential tower, as well as a commercial complex.

The project involves transferring the families to a transit camp, to be built by the developer, before construction work can start. Finding vacant public land in the vicinity was an important factor of delay in implementing the project. A significant obstacle was the mobilisation of various residents' and traders' associations *against* the location of the transit camp in their respective neighbourhood. Finally, the camp was constructed on a site located around three kilometres from the present settlement. Eligible Kathputli Colony residents will be accommodated in rows of pre-fabricated one-room tenements of 12 square metres per family, with shared bathing and toilet facilities. The construction of the camp was completed in March 2013, but until February 2014 no official notification was issued for the transfer.

A biased process of communication and consultation

The DDA's relationship with the Kathputli Colony residents was through one of the two prominent NGOs working with the artists, the most visible NGO in the settlement (as described above). Similarly, this organisation was also used by the DDA's private partners to communicate with the residents. Thus, initially the consultation procedure was mediated by this NGO. The latter acted as the main interlocutor with the DDA, the consultant appointed to prepare the detailed project report, and the developer. The NGO assisted the consultant to conduct a socio-economic survey, and public information meetings were held in the premises of its school. Moreover, its executive staff organised appointments between the local leaders and DDA officers.

We can understand the role of this NGO as ambiguous, and in line with the notion of a 'local knowledge broker' as discussed in Chapter 5. On the one hand, this association facilitated the DDA's interactions with the residents and allowed some degree of consultation – or at least information. Yet, on the other hand, it also introduced some bias in the consultation process, which resulted from the lack of consensus regarding this NGO's role in the preparatory phase of the project.

Its legitimacy in representing all the residents was contested by the other NGO, and the acute conflict between the two organisations led to direct altercation in the settlement. Subsequently, the mediating NGO withdrew gradually from its role, pushing the local leaders to organise themselves and interact directly with the DDA. In fact, the multiplicity of communities in the settlement would make it difficult for any single NGO to claim uncontested representativeness and play the role of a neutral and consensual agent.

The direct encounters between DDA officials, the developer and the residents took the form of different kinds of spaces, with different degrees of openness and control. The first information meetings were organised by the DDA, along with the consultant or the developer, and fits nicely with what Cornwall (2002) would label an 'invited space'. Later in the process, other public meetings were initiated by the residents' leaders who called DDA officials, and therefore constructed a kind of 'negotiated space' (cf. Baud and Nainan 2008) where the residents actively tried to promote their claims. Such meetings usually gathered from 50 to 100 residents, including local leaders, which is still a relatively low number in a settlement totalling around 3,000 households. In addition, many of the interactions with the DDA took place only with the local leaders, seen as representatives of their respective communities. However, the outcomes of these meetings were not communicated to all the residents, showing that the information flow can be blocked at different levels, including inside the settlement.

These spaces for resident participation were perceived very differently according to the local leaders, ranging from satisfaction to scepticism. Several denounced the lack of consultation on issues that concerned residents. These contrasting views echoed the various positions of the local leaders vis-à-vis the NGO that initially monitored the dissemination of project information. They also reflected the discrimination of some communities in the settlement, and revealed the absence of a systematic consultation procedure that would have ensured that all the groups of residents were taken into consideration. For instance, given the history of the settlement, the artists – especially the Rajasthani – thought initially that the rehabilitation project would be only for them. Thus, during our interviews, other communities complained that they were not invited to the discussions regarding the project. As they feared that they might be excluded, their leaders eventually became proactive to get information and follow the project.

Furthermore, the residents were not involved in the conception and design of the project, but informed only afterwards. In this regard, the episode of the show flat is significant. A show flat was built in the premises of the school run by the mediating NGO. For the DDA engineer interviewed,[4] the show flat was a way to explain the housing project to Kathputli Colony's residents. The explanations provided by a manager from the private firm stressed another point: the purpose of the show flat was to present it to the DDA for its approval, and not to elicit residents' views.[5] Indeed, the access to the show flat became one of the conflicting matters between the two rival NGOs. This escalated into a serious confrontation in front of the school, and eventually the flat was closed to the public. Hence, the rehabilitation buildings and flats were planned and designed without attempt to incorporate the perspectives of the people who would inhabit them. The same remark applies for the transit camp.

Incomplete information and non-participatory survey

Furthermore, despite meetings and recurrent requests, the DDA provided incomplete information to the residents. Five years after the project was launched, while the transit camp was ready for occupation, major issues were not clarified. Particularly pressing issues included an imprecise set of eligibility criteria determining who would access a flat in the re-housing scheme and, as a result, insecurity around the subsequent list of eligible families and the financial conditions tied to their eligibility. Despite four household surveys being conducted in Kathputli Colony between mid-2008 and January 2012 in relation to the project, the list of the surveyed households was not publicised by the DDA. The local leaders could access it only in January 2013, after repeated requests, including formal 'Right to Information' applications. Nonetheless, the list of households eligible for rehabilitation was not disclosed yet by mid-February 2014, until political events entailed new developments analysed below.

Identification surveys are central to DDA's approach to slum rehabilitation, and their results decide the fate of slum dwellers, as they are used to establish the list of households eligible for flats in the new housing complex. In other experiences of slum resettlement or rehabilitation, self-enumeration and participatory surveys have contributed to the empowerment of the affected communities (Appadurai 2001, 2012; Patel, d'Cruz and Burra 2002), although loopholes in this process have been also highlighted (Zérah 2009). In Kathputli Colony, the first surveys did not involve the community's participation, barring the assistance of some local leaders and residents to guide the surveyors in the web of narrow lanes criss-crossing the settlement. Eventually, the residents had little control on the way these surveys were conducted.

A challenge for participation is the fragmentation of the settlement into various communities living in distinct sections, with their own leaders and no unifying strong leadership at the entire settlement level. In addition, there is no consensual community-based organisation. Instead, competition and rivalries between the two main NGOs working in the settlement have created a new line of fragmentation. The conclusions drawn from a participatory water and drainage project in Kathputli Colony in the mid-1990s appear relevant even today: 'The conflicts between the two NGOs [. . .] have indirectly motivated the divisions within the community and disturbed participation in various stages of the process of settlement improvement' (Marulanda 1996: 10). In the context of the DDA rehabilitation project, mutual mistrust between these two NGOs has intensified. Thus, the results of the first survey, conducted in 2008 with the support of one NGO, were contested by supporters of the other NGO, who requested the DDA to undertake a fresh door-to-door survey, eventually conducted in 2010.

When the local leaders finally managed to get a copy of the list of the households surveyed in 2010, its scrutiny enabled them to point out many omissions. To avoid the exclusion of some families from the rehabilitation project, the local leaders realised, although belatedly, the importance of establishing their own list and collecting proof of residence for the families in their respective communities. This is what they did in May 2013 for those omitted from the DDA survey, and submitted these documents to the DDA.[6] In other words, they understood the potential power of community-generated knowledge for challenging the government's expert knowledge.

Recent turn: towards more participation and transparency?

Political events in February 2014 entailed a new turn for the Kathputli Colony rehabilitation project. Following the resignation of the Delhi state government, the president's rule was imposed in Delhi on 17 February, 2014. In substance, this means that the Delhi state came under the direct control of the central government. This created a new context for the DDA, which is an agency under the purview of the central government. Thus, the DDA took new initiatives to expedite its rehabilitation project in Kathputli Colony.

An order was issued on 22 February, 2014 for residents to begin 'registration' and move to the transit camp. Subsequently, several families moved there after signing a tripartite agreement with the DDA and the developer. By August 2014, approximately 500 families had resettled in the transit camp. However, large numbers of residents protested the proposed evacuation, and the majority continued to resist the move for at least another 15 months.

At the same time, around 21 February, a list identifying 2,641 eligible households was released on the DDA website, subject to final verification, after more than two years of pleas to do so. A website dedicated solely to the project was also launched,[7] including official notices and plans of the rehousing complex.

Threat of impending transfer to the transit camp and the contested household survey prompted the artists and artisans' co-operative and a group of residents including several leaders to file a writ petition in the Delhi High Court on 21 February, seeking that the project be stalled and that their alternative plan be considered. They were assisted by a prominent NGO working on housing rights that had recently got involved. The Court dismissed the case on 20 March, 2014, directing that a committee of residents be allowed to visit the transit camp and report any problems to the DDA and the developer; and that the latter consider the residents' suggestions regarding facilities required to be provided and deficiencies pointed out.[8] The DDA assured the Court that genuine households omitted from the survey might submit the requisite documents to the DDA for consideration. Incidentally, the NGO had already started a fresh survey to challenge the 2010 DDA survey and include the omitted households, this time in collaboration with the residents. The results of this survey, showing around 3,600 households in the settlement, were however rejected by the DDA, which again initiated a new identification survey in July–August 2014.

These recent developments indicated increased residents' participation as well as efforts towards transparency on the part of the DDA. In fact, the consultation between the three parties involved was arguably improved following the Court's directives. However, it may be too little and too late to overcome the residents' mistrust towards the DDA and the developer, and to ensure a smooth rehabilitation process.

Conclusion

The examination of the first steps of implementation of slum rehabilitation projects in Delhi underlines an authoritarian top-down approach with no proper space provided for the participation of the concerned communities. This lack of participation is noteworthy, as it contradicts the principles stated in the new national and state policies. Until January 2014, retention of information and opacity characterised the mode of governance in the two projects studied. As shown by fieldwork, the use of knowledge as power at different levels is detrimental to a fair participation process, within the settlement, as well as in the interactions between the concerned communities and the government. Case studies conducted in Delhi, as well as in Chennai, further evidence a double fracture in the politics of knowledge: the residents are not properly informed about the impending projects affecting them; and the government agencies have no proper knowledge about the needs and priorities of the people to be resettled and rehabilitated.

References

Appadurai, A. (2001) 'Deep democracy: Urban governmentality and the horizon of politics'. *Environment and Urbanization*, 13(2): 23–43.

Appadurai, A. (2012) 'Why enumeration counts'. *Environment and Urbanization*, 24(2): 639–41.

Baud, I. and Nainan, N. (2008) '"Negotiated spaces" for representation in Mumbai: Ward committees, advanced locality management and the politics of middle-class activism'. *Environment and Urbanization*, 20(2): 483–99.

Cornwall, A. (2002) 'Making spaces, changing places: Situating participation in development'. *IDS Working Paper 170*. Brighton: Institute of Development Studies.

DDA (2007) *Master plan for Delhi 2021*. Delhi Development Authority [As Notified on 7 February, 2007. Vide S.O. No 141 published in Gazette of India Extraordinary, Part II – Section 3 – Sub-Section (ii)].

Dupont, V., Banda, S., Vaidya, Y. and Gowda, S. (2014) 'Unpacking participation in Kathputli Colony Delhi's first slum redevelopment project, Act I'. *Economic and Political Weekly*, 49(24): 39–47.

GOI (2010) *Rajiv Awas Yojana. Guidelines for slum-free city planning*. New Delhi: Ministry of Housing & Urban Poverty Alleviation, Government of India.

Marulanda, L. (1996) 'Participatory experience in Kathpulti Colony, Delhi'. *Trialog*, 51: 5–10.

Patel, S., d'Cruz C. and Burra, S. (2002) 'Beyond evictions in a global city: People-managed resettlement in Mumbai'. *Environment and Urbanization*, 14(1): 159–72.

Zérah, M.-H. (2009) 'Participatory governance in urban management and the shifting geometry of power in Mumbai'. *Development and Change*, 40(5): 853–77.

Settlement story 4.2   Community knowledge and abandoned upgrading projects in Europe informal settlement

DAVID JORDHUS-LIER AND PAMELA TSOLEKILE DE WET

Europe is one of the four informal settlements in Cape Town that stretches across several kilometres on the south side of the N2 between the city and the airport. This settlement is situated in the predominantly black African township of Gugulethu. More than twenty years ago, people started to erect shacks on a municipal landfill site to form the informal settlements Kanana, Barcelona, Europe and Vukuzenzele.

Residents of the Europe settlement face poverty, and they are exposed to several socio-environmental risks. As it is located on top of a former landfill site (Old Nyanga Refuse Dump – 1956–87), the ground on which their shacks are erected is unstable. Furthermore, the land emits methane gases from the buried waste (Dayaram *et al.* 2011). The landfill site forms a ridge covered by an uncoordinated and increasingly dense cluster of shacks without proper drainage systems. Consequently as many as 82 per cent of Europe households have experienced floods (CORC 2010). These occur annually and force families to leave their homes, which require draining and frequent maintenance.

Moreover, service systems are very poor. The streets and the environment are littered with disposed materials and waste. The improvised collection points cause health hazards for the population. One former leader pointed out that the City of Cape Town's (CoCT) decision to outsource waste collection in Europe to a private company resulted in poor quality of the service. When community members complained to the councillor, they were told that after the CoCT had signed the contracts with the subcontractors, the service was 'out of her hands'. Similar to informal settlements in other settings, Europe does not have individualised toilets. The population has to rely on the bucket system and chemical toilets. Out of 896 toilets, 190 were non-functional at the time of enumeration due to vandalism and lack of maintenance (CORC 2010). There are no ablution facilities in the settlement. This makes personal hygiene after visiting the toilet a difficult exercise. Water service to the settlement is provided through eighteen standpipe water taps, and nobody pays for water or sanitation services (CORC 2010; Dayaram *et al.* 2011).

In a fashion typical for informal settlements across South Africa, the Europe settlement is tightly, albeit informally, organised by its own community members and 'led by a committee which oversees all issues concerning their settlement' (CORC 2010: 5). While the research team initially approached the Europe settlement to explore their political dynamics, we soon came to realise that many of the contestations shaping the politics of the settlement were in fact struggles over knowledge. In what follows we will discuss some of the most crucial issues in this regard.

Scientific knowledge and the suitability of the land

According to Baud *et al.* (2011), governments tend to give scientifically codified knowledge a privileged role in decision-making. The planned upgrading of Europe informal settlement was no exception. According to local government, the community had invaded land illegally. Since then, the City of Cape Town, as the owner of the land, relied mainly on the technical assessment done by engineers to test the feasibility of the land. Hence, early on in the N2 Gateway project, Europe and adjacent settlements were ruled out of the project given its location on unstable land.

The CoCT also considered the legal aspect of such occupation and assessed the financial viability of an upgrading solution. The CoCT did not seem to take into consideration the viewpoints of people who moved into the area due to socio-economic reasons, and their lived experiences were excluded from the knowledge system. Decisions were made by the City for the residents, but not *with* the residents. Conflict started when CoCT officials declared Europe uninhabitable and a danger to the health and safety of its residents. One of the city officials commented on the development of the site.

> To develop the site would present danger to the residents and the environment
> – water will be contaminated and the emissions of methane gas from the
> rubbish underneath would endanger people's lives. The City of Cape Town
> can be held liable. Lastly developing the land would cost the city a fortune.
> (Authors' interview, senior city engineer,
> April 2014)

Europe residents, on the other hand, did not see any threat or danger from living on this site. One of the community leaders expressed scepticism towards the scientific assessment of the site: 'I was born here in Europe; I have not seen nor experienced any threat from living in this area, except for flooding during the rainy season' (previous community leader, March 2013).

After talking to the representatives of provincial and local government, we also found diverging opinions concerning the assessment given above. Most government representatives seemed to argue that upgrading was unrealistic. However, in the opinion of the informal settlement dwellers, relocation was not an option either. One former community leader claimed that housing officials had identified areas in remote locations as potential relocation sites. Residents felt that they would lose any chance of finding employment if they had to move out of the city. Community residents justify in-situ upgrading on their twenty years of history in the area, and place great weight in access to schools, hospitals, transportation and other amenities.

Mapping exercises with expert communities

Around 2010, the community leadership in Europe and adjacent Barcelona settlement got actively involved in the Informal Settlements Network. This is a network of organisations based in informal settlements that is supported by organisations such as the Community Organisation Resource Centre (CORC) (both are part of the South African SDI Alliance). Slum Dwellers' International

(SDI) is a global network of CBOs that started in South Africa in 1996, but has since spread to thirty-three countries. It has a very strong presence in India. SDI has developed a holistic method towards slum dwelling (see Box 5.1). SDI favours incremental approaches with a high degree of participation and local learning. While SDI claims to be a bottom-up organisation, 'the SDI model' is increasingly being exported to new locations, and there is a constant negotiation between top-down policy transfer and bottom-up community engagement. Consequently, the SDI method plays out quite differently in different settlements and is sometimes contested by community members.

CORC embarked on a drainage project in Europe settlement, where a small individually based community investment (in the order of ZAR 5–15 per household) was to be supported by investment by a Community Upgrading Financing Facility (CUFF). However, after consultative meetings with community members, there remained insufficient 'buy-in' from residents as they did not feel that they would benefit from the intervention. Inevitably, this meant that those community members initiating the upgrading project did not manage to raise money or support from the entire community. The plans eventually fell through.

In Europe, CORC has used experts to work with the community, which has given residents the opportunity to learn and gain skills. This is a typical example of Epstein's (1996: 293) 'expertification of lay activists'. In this case, community leaders from grassroots organisations and street committees received training from organisations such as CORC. Through a process that included a so-called *enumeration*, community members in Europe were equipped with tools to help them participate in their own settlement planning for the upgrading and development of their residential area. This allowed them to report on the facts of their current living conditions in order to engage constructively with the state (CORC 2010).

Another spin-off from the CORC involvement was a community planning exercise involving community representatives, CORC facilitators and students from the Planning and Urban Development Department at the University of Cape Town. Community members who took the initiative to get Europe involved in community planning exercises explained that areas like the informal settlements along the 'N2 strip' have no proper plans, and that this is one of the main problems. The planning students actively engaged with community members through a six-week period, followed by a desk study resulting in several reports. These reports documented and mapped the physical, environmental and social make-up of the settlement. While this meeting between students and residents led to an increased understanding of the planning challenges of informal settlements, the plans did not lead to any concrete action. A CORC facilitator reflecting on this experience admits that the design phase was marked by insufficient community involvement, which in turn reduced the residents' sense of ownership in relation to the community plan.

One of the academics who facilitated the students' involvement critically reflected on this experience (Winkler 2013). To Winkler, the meeting between students and informal settlement residents was an encounter between conflicting rationalities. On the one hand, she identified community members whose lived experiences of poverty stretch back for more than twenty years and who are eager to see an improvement of their lives. On the other hand, she pointed to planners who conducted their risk and feasibility assessments under constant pressure. In this case, the strict deadlines varied from those that were imposed by municipal plans and budgets or, in the case of the students, by university semesters and exams. Winkler (2013: 216) asked a critical question: 'Who benefits from community–university partnerships?' While the students left with an experience for life, and valuable insight into the practical challenges of participatory planning, and the academic leading this learning experience obtained a publication out of it, the residents of Europe were left with maps and plans that could not be realised due to external factors. According to Winkler (2013: 225)

> the residents of Barcelona and Europe do not derive immediate benefits from knowing that issues pertaining to tenure security are not merely political issues. They therefore continue to fear evictions by the state. They also continue to live in shacks without adequate public services and infrastructure, on a contaminated site.

To them, the students represented yet another uncommitted approach by expert communities. In addition, Winkler (2013) claims that this particular engagement played a part in the ousting of the original leadership described above.

This background also represented a challenge for our own research in the settlement. While we had established a good relationship with the previous leadership who functioned as representatives of the CORC/ISN network in the settlement, other factions in the community viewed us with the same suspicion as local government officials and other NGO representatives. The leadership in Europe at the time of our research eventually came to the conclusion that they did not want further research to be conducted in their constituency. The leader of the adjacent settlement, Barcelona, who was also the *de facto* authority in Europe settlement during this period, said in a meeting 'We have been researched enough by UCT and CORC'. While this process was frustrating for our research team, it served as an indicator of the politics of knowledge in informal settlements. So-called 'research fatigue' has been documented elsewhere (e.g., Mandel 2003), and could be a particular challenge in a location where both local government and NGOs have failed to deliver tangible results amidst local expectations.

Who represents the knowledge of the community?

The local power struggles between different leaderships can also be read as a struggle over knowledge representation. Ambiguous responses by local government representatives regarding the prospects for upgrading in Europe have led different groupings to compete for recognition. The community leadership of Europe has changed three times since 2012, complicating the political dynamic. We can discern at least two competing narratives: one centring on mobilising the community to demand free services and houses from the government; another focusing on community organisation, local initiatives and engagement with NGOs and other non-state actors. While the latter approach characterised the leadership who had engaged in enumerations and other collaborative efforts with NGOs in 2010–11, this group was replaced by a young group of ANC Youth League activists in 2012 favouring a more political approach. This conflicts with the influence of the CORC enumeration report:

> The newly elected leadership was a group of young people, who were passionate about politics but did not have the vision, skills and knowledge to take the community to the next level of development. Hence they had to forge a relationship with the leadership in Barcelona [adjacent settlement]. Some of the leadership were politically aligned and were not in favour of the enumeration report.
> (Authors' interview, previous Europe leader, September 2012)

The 2012–13 leadership never got to know or understand the CORC enumeration report, a document that was supported and recognised by the previous leadership. The information in the report was not communicated down to the local residents. The use of English language and technical words meant this knowledge was easily lost in translation.

However, recently the original faction has re-emerged as a dominant force in the Europe community. This put pressure on the 2012–13 leadership to step down. Subsequently, CORC revived their engagement with Europe, initiating a plan for a new multi-purpose community hall. The current situation suggests that the residents have favoured a more pragmatic approach, and are critical of a rhetoric focusing on service delivery without tangible results. According to a community leader, this was also imbued with a gender dynamic: women in Cape Town's informal settlements are the main drivers of community organising. Men, on the other hand, seem more reluctant to participate in the meetings, and prefer to get straight to the practical tasks that require their manpower.

Another dilemma of knowledge sharing surfaced in the interaction between the Europe community and the CoCT. The SDI approach in South Africa encourages participating in knowledge exchanges with local authorities. This happened first through structured dialogue between the community and local government representatives, and second CORC initiated a series of partnership meetings in 2011–12. However, when the leadership who had forged ties with CORC were ousted in 2012, the new leaders alleged that the previous leadership withheld information with regards to the development of the area. The new chairperson also claimed that enumeration in Europe had been used by CoCT to identify newly built shacks and extensions for demolition in their area. Moreover, the partnership meetings with service departments in CoCT were treated with hostility. The new leadership came through political networks and suspected that the old leadership worked closely with the CoCT in all its capacities, including monitoring and governing the community. The fact that members of the community had failed to distinguish between the actions of the Anti-Land Invasion Unit and the interaction with ISN and the Informal Settlements Department through the project partnership meetings testifies to a high degree of mistrust and miscommunication.[9]

Leaders who had been in favour of structured talks with local government service departments were nevertheless staunchly against co-operating with politicians, even at a local level:

> We never involve the mayor, they always come to our communities with empty promises [. . .] Even councillors are clueless and often distant when it comes to our community issues. At the time I was a member of the sub-council, for me it was clear as how the informal settlement issues were never prioritised.
> (Authors' interview, previous Europe leader, September 2012)

This sums up one of the main differences between the two factions that came to dominate local politics in Europe during the time of our research. Whereas one group looked to the politicians (at least those in the ANC party) for solutions and viewed the local government bureaucracy with deep mistrust, the other group dismissed politicians as corrupt and chose to rely on a combination of self-organisation and partnership with NGOs and the service delivery departments.

One of the most striking features of the Europe settlement story is that, in contrast to many other cases presented in this book, the settlement has experienced little change in their living situation – neither of a progressive (i.e., upgrading) nor a repressive kind (i.e., forced resettlement). This has arguably marred many of the initiatives to engage in knowledge sharing and community mapping, as any expectations stemming from such initiatives have not been fulfilled. However, this story should not be used to discourage the mobilisation of community knowledge in cases where concrete results cannot be guaranteed. After all, had the community been more united behind one of the two approaches, the outcome could have been different. But it serves as a note of caution against reducing the problem of upgrading to the lack of 'knowledge flows'.

References

Baud, I.S.A., Pfeffer, K., Sydenstricker, J. and Scott, D. (2011) 'Developing participatory "spatial" knowledge models in metropolitan governance networks for sustainable development'. *Chance2Sustain Literature Review March 2011*, 1–20.

CORC (2010) 'Europe household enumeration report'. Gugulethu, October 2010, Cape Town: Informal Settlements Network, Europe Community Leadership and Community Organisation Resource Centre: 1–32.

Dayaram, C., Du Plessis, K., Joustra, A., Loubser, J., Mathee, E.J., Nell, D. and Reynolds, R. (2011) 'Interpretive mapping and analysis of Barcelona and Europe informal settlements (Western Cape) MCRP & MLA'. Cape Town, University of Cape Town, School of Architecture, Planning and Geomatics: 1–100.

Epstein, S. (1996) *Impure science: AIDS, activism, and the politics of knowledge*. Berkeley (CA): University of California Press.

Mandel, J.L. (2003) 'Negotiating expectations in the field: Gatekeepers, research fatigue and cultural biases'. *Singapore Journal of Tropical Geography*, 24(2): 198–210.

Winkler, T. (2013) 'At the coalface: Community–university engagements and planning education'. *Journal of Planning Education and Research*, 33(2): 215–27.

Settlement story 4.3 Community mapping exercise in Ocean Drive-In informal settlement, Durban

CATHERINE SUTHERLAND

The housing delivery process in South Africa has created a complex flow of knowledge between national, provincial and local state actors and the urban poor who are engaged in, or are recipients of, the state's housing process. The urban poor potentially have access to a wide range of information about the state's position on housing: through the statements of the ANC government about its housing goals and achievements; through councillors who reinforce the national or local position on housing; through contact with various NGOs and CBOs who challenge state policy; and through ordinary citizens transferring knowledge between themselves as they navigate the housing process. Evidence of the ANC government's large-scale roll out of so-called RDP housing across South Africa (see Chapter 3) reflects the state's policy discourse on housing delivery since apartheid. Rights to RDP housing are laid out in policy documents that provide the criteria an individual must meet to qualify for a state-subsidised house.[10] The ANC has also used promises of housing delivery as an electoral strategy. Hence, for many communities there is the strong expectation, and in many cases sense of entitlement, that the government will deliver houses to the poor. However, the challenges of housing a growing urban population has been far more complex and local governments have failed to deliver at the rate required to reduce the backlogs. After twenty years of RDP housing delivery there is also the recognition that this form of housing delivery may not be the best way of developing integrated human settlements that address poverty and provide people with access to the bundle of urban resources required to obtain a reasonable quality of life.

Formal policies aside, knowledge about the complex processes shaping housing implementation is transferred less easily and in many cases is hidden or retained at the local level. Local governments confront the challenges and conflicts associated with delivering housing with limited resources while at the same time facing a large, poor, expectant urban population. The shift in national policy in 2010 towards informal settlement upgrading as a solution to the housing crisis has been less well articulated to the public, as has the role of housing lists in allocating RDP housing in different cities and towns. State actors have adopted different strategies in sharing information and knowledge with the urban poor. For example, during the social protests in Durban in early 2013, it became evident that statements made by senior officials in the Housing Department were used to quell social protests at a time of crisis. Together with reports in the media,[11]

Figure 4.1 Residents of Ocean Drive-In showed their loyalty to and appreciation of the
government meeting its promise of formal housing to the poor by turning out
in ANC paraphernalia on the day the move to Hammonds Farm first started.

these ad hoc statements became the main mechanism used to clarify the housing process in the city in the absence of other, more established, knowledge processes.

One of the most contested issues is the allocation of housing when new greenfield projects come online. The Housing Department, through its Housing Settlements Committee, is responsible for allocating housing in eThekwini Municipality. This process is not transparent. Typically, information is neither shared with the public, those on the housing lists, nor those living in informal settlements. Hence, housing allocation becomes an intensely political process. The municipality has identified 167 settlements, known as 'priority settlements', that are deemed most at risk. These settlements are being relocated to greenfield sites as new housing projects are completed. The process of relocating informal settlers is managed through the allocation of housing numbers that are painted on the doors of informal houses. These numbers are obtained by individuals registering with the housing department once they have been informed that their settlement will be relocated to a greenfield site or upgraded (see Figure 4.2). Often, numbers are allocated years before the move or upgrading takes place and they are fiercely guarded by informal residents as this number signifies their 'right' to a formal house. The housing numbers with their associated 'owners' are kept on lists held by the municipality.

This case study reflects how a different form of knowledge, namely the production of a community-based map, has been used by the community of Ocean Drive-In informal settlement and supporting researchers (the Durban Chance2 Sustain team) as a means to hold 'rights' to a formal house in a resettlement process.[12] This was an attempt to ensure that all those who resided in the settlement, and that had been registered or recognised as legitimate claimants, would obtain housing in Hammonds Farm. The municipality has maps of all the informal settlements in the city. However, these maps are at the settlement scale and do not show the position of individual shacks, which comprise of both the main house of the owner (or renter) and the additional rooms constructed by tenants.

A community-based mapping project was instituted as part of the Chance2 Sustain research programme in Ocean Drive-In informal settlement in 2012 (Sutherland *et al.* 2013). Community-based mapping has emerged as a useful tool in participatory research. The goals of this form of mapping include producing indigenous maps for claims on ancestral lands (Massey and Jess 1995); ensuring access to and ownership of information (Elwood 2006); and fostering social learning between 'scientific experts' and communities (Chambers 2006). Community maps might also create legitimacy for local knowledge and generate a sense of confidence and self-determination (Hordijk 1999; Rambaldi *et al.* 2006). We instituted the mapping process in Ocean Drive-In in partnership with the community in order to explore the value of community-based mapping to informal communities in Durban.

By early 2012, the majority of the Ocean Drive-In community had been allocated housing numbers and was waiting to be relocated to Hammonds Farm. However, due to the delays in the move, many doubted that they would be

Figure 4.2 'Housing number' on the door of an informal house in Ocean Drive-In.

relocated to a formal house. This created a number of problems for the community, as they did not want to invest in or maintain their houses with the move to Hammonds Farm seemingly imminent. It also led to social protests as the community feared that 'their' houses in Hammond Farm would be allocated to other poor communities and individuals. Community members challenged the government about their 'place in the city', stating that the councillor and some officials had told them that they had no right to complain as their settlement was 'not on the map'. This statement seemed to contradict other municipal practices, as a local election polling station had been placed in Ocean Drive-In during the 2011 local government elections. Residents asked: 'If we are important enough to have a voting station, how can they tell us we are "not on the map"?' (Ocean Drive-In resident, June 2012).

Through a participatory research process the community and our researchers produced a community drawn and GIS map of Ocean Drive-In informal settlement (see Figures 4.3, 4.4 and 4.5).

The construction of the GIS maps by our research team revealed interesting politics of knowledge and information. Some community members initially hid their housing numbers using blankets on the day that we were using a GPS to geo-reference each house. These residents had not been involved in the initial drawing of the community maps and had not been informed by the sub-ward committee that represented the community about the mapping process. The mapping process was stopped as a result of this 'protest' and was only resumed once the community had been called to a meeting with the councillor and our team, and the purpose and ownership of the maps was discussed. Community members that covered their numbers had feared that we were from the municipality and were recording the numbers so as to 'steal them' and use them for somebody else. A large number of community members attended the formal meeting. One of the residents asked us: 'How will this map help us, of what use will it be to us?' We answered that there were many ways in which community maps support communities but we were unsure at this point about their value to the Ocean Drive-In community. However, we stated that if the community was prepared to join us in the journey of constructing a map, we could discover together what value it could have to Ocean Drive-In.

The process of developing the maps and the sharing of knowledge around the maps built trust and developed the relationship between the researchers and the community. In many subsequent visits to the community, we were identified and greeted by community members, or introduced as 'the people who made "i-map"'.[13] Many of the residents believed that the map and the research process had helped to facilitate some of the moves to Hammonds Farm, as they indicated that the moving process appeared to start up again each time the research outcomes were sent to the Housing Department. This is most likely co-incidental, but it meant that the mapping process and the maps provided the community with a sense of empowerment, suggesting that this knowledge-production process was making a difference to their lives.

Figure 4.3 A community member of Ocean Drive-In finalising her group's map.

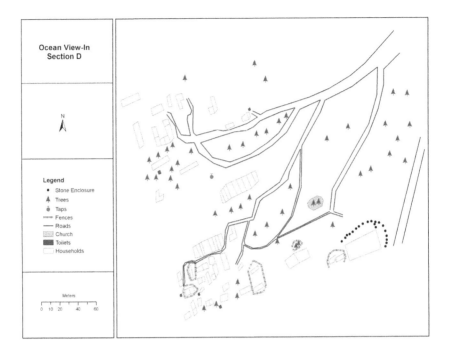

Figure 4.4 A digitised version of the community map.

GIS maps containing information about all the households and their numbers was completed prior to the incremental move to Hammonds Farm beginning on 7 November, 2012. These became an important source of knowledge that could be used by both the community and the Housing Department as they spatially reflected all the people living in Ocean Drive-In that were entitled to a formal house in Hammonds Farm. During the moving process a new committee had been established in the settlement to support those that were left behind, as the move progressed more slowly than planned. This committee took ownership of the map and has subsequently used it to hold the rights of the legitimate Ocean Drive-In residents to a house in Hammonds Farm. This map was also used in the negotiations between the community and the Housing Department over the seventy-three beneficiaries that were not registered by September 2013. As the move to Hammonds Farm had still not been completed by August 2014, the map remains a potential tool with which to demand rights to housing.

Mapping can form bonds between people but it can also exclude people who do not have spatial literacy. Once the community maps are reproduced as GIS maps, then the data is rendered technical, which can result in distancing and alienation. However, the so-called 'ground-truthing' workshops that were held with community members to verify the maps, provided much excitement and joy as residents located their houses and names and found themselves, their families and their friends 'on the map'.

Figure 4.5 A map produced by the Chance2Sustain researchers using a GPS to geo-reference each house in the settlement.

The development of this community-based knowledge was initially produced by the community and researchers as an open 'social learning' process with no fixed outcomes. The map was completed a few weeks before the move to Hammonds Farm. When the relocation process started the community members and the researchers initially felt that the only value the map had was to show that the recorded and mapped individuals once lived there. However, no one expected that the move would take so long and as the relocation process dragged on, making those left behind more vulnerable, the map began to be used by both the community and ourselves to hold the 'right' of people of Ocean Drive-In to formal housing in Hammonds Farm. The production of community-based spatial knowledge can therefore contribute to the inclusion of different forms of knowledge in contested participatory processes. The development of a community-based map for Ocean Drive-In informal settlement provides an example of how both expert and lay knowledge can be identified, produced, recognised and integrated to produce a map that enables communities to participate in, and secure their right to, the city. Community-based maps are formed outside of the invited spaces and knowledge forms constructed by the state. Such mapping also enables tacit knowledge to be transferred to formal or codified knowledge, thereby transforming the everyday lived spaces of ordinary people into an abstract spatiality that can be used to inform decision-making. In this case, a university-based research group became the 'brokers' between community knowledge and the 'outside' knowledge of the state. Maps can therefore act as vehicles for spatial learning, discussion, information exchange, joint analysis and decision-making and advocacy. They also facilitate communication between representative insiders (the community) and resourceful outsiders (researchers, government officials) (Rambaldi *et al.* 2006), as this story has tried to show, and can therefore be important in the social mobilisation of the urban poor.

References

Chambers, R. (2006) 'Participatory mapping and geographic information systems: Whose map? Who is empowered and who disempowered? Who gains and who loses?' *The Electronic Journal of Information Systems in Developing Countries*, 25(2): 1–11.

Elwood, S. (2006) 'Negotiating knowledge production: The everyday inclusions, exclusions, and contradictions of participatory GIS research'. *The Professional Geographer*, 58(2): 197–208.

Hordijk, M. (1999) 'A dream of green and water: Community based formulation of a Local Agenda 21 in peri-urban Lima'. *Environment & Urbanization*, 11(2): 11–30.

Massey, D. and Jess, P.M. (1995) *A place in the world? Places, cultures and globalization.* Oxford: Oxford University Press.

Rambaldi, G., Chambers, R., McCall, M. and Fox, J. (2006) 'Practical ethics for PGIS practitioners, facilitators, technology intermediaries, and researchers'. *Participatory Learning and Action*, 54(April): 106–13.

Sutherland, C., Scott, D., Buthelezi, S., Njoya, S. and Hordijk, M. (2013) 'Community mapping in the uncertain times of urban restructuring: The case of Ocean Drive-In in eThekwini Municipality'. Paper presented at the Society of South African Geographers Conference, September 2013, Stellenbosch.

Settlement story 4.4 The 'counter-knowledge alliance' in Vila Autódromo, Rio de Janeiro

EINAR BRAATHEN

The recent history of a Brazilian urban community is presented here with an emphasis on the role of knowledge in the community's struggle against collective eviction.[14] Vila Autódromo lies in front of the beautiful Lake Jacarépagua and between two avenues, 'Abelardo Bueno' and 'Salvador Allende', in the western zone of Rio de Janeiro, at least one hour drive from the city centre. According to the 2010 census (IBGE) it had 1,252 inhabitants, of which only 10.5 per cent did not own the house they lived in (Vainer *et al.* 2013). The village was named after a Formula 1 race track, the *autódromo*, located next to it. The race track itself was demolished in 2012 to give way to the so-called *Parque Olímpico* ('Olympic park'), with new sports venues planned for the 2016 Olympic Games. Vila Autódromo has for a long time been under tremendous pressure from real estate developers and the municipality. The plans for the 2016 Olympic Games constantly threatened the remaining 450 families of the community with forced removal. As pointed out in an international report,

> Vila Autódromo has a dual handicap [. . .]: not only does it occupy prime real estate but it is also perceived as a *favela*, the loaded Portuguese word for an informal settlement, in a metropolis long notorious for its contentious relationship with the poor.
>
> (Vale and Gray 2013: np)

The formalisation of an informal settlement

Vila Autódromo was a fishing village. It has been in existence since 1967 and is described by its residents as 'peaceful and orderly' (AMPVA 2012). It was transformed into a working-class neighbourhood during the construction of an upper-middle-class boomtown, Barra de Tijuca, in the 1970s. The community is socially organised and has been represented by the Association of Residents and Fishermen of Vila Autódromo (AMPVA) since 1987. The residents' association has organised a range of voluntary work initiatives, *mutirões*, and installed electricity, piped water, septic tanks and public telephone lines – all without any government assistance. The association has provided legal registration of the fishermen and helped to construct churches. And, more importantly, the association managed, by political and legal recognition, to turn Vila Autódromo into a 'formal' settlement.

The land belonged to the state of Rio de Janeiro. In 1989 the Vila Autódromo community accommodated and helped resettle victims of floods in a nearby community. In total 354 households in the community received land tenure from the state in the 1990s (Vale and Gray 2013). In 2005 the city declared part of the community to be a 'Special Zone of Social Interest', and this was an additional legal assurance against evictions (AMPVA 2012: 8). It meant the community was part of the new city Master Plan and thus a priority area in the urban upgrading programmes. This outcome was due to well-prepared technical inputs from the community.

Municipal mobilisation of knowledge – against the community

Although municipal law prohibits the eviction of any *favela* except in the case of physical risk due to land conditions, there have been a string of initiatives from the Municipality of Rio de Janeiro to remove the Vila Autódromo community. It started in 1992 when it stated that the community would cause 'esthetical and environmental damage' (AMPVA 2012: 8). Before the 2007 Pan-American Games, strong community resistance fought back plans for real estate development linked to the event (AMPVA 2012: 9). The pressure on Vila Autódromo escalated after Rio de Janeiro won the Olympic bid in October 2009. The discourses shaping the decision-making process for Vila Autódromo frequently shifted. These discourses drew on a variety of knowledge bases.

In the way of transport

In 2008 the municipality had its urban and environmental legacy plan for the Olympic Games. (Municipality of Rio de Janeiro 2008). It announced that more than 3,500 families in six communities, one of them being Vila Autódromo, had to be removed due to public works for the Olympics. Vila Autódromo was to be demolished because of the needed extension of the two adjacent avenues (AMPVA 2012: 10). These plans were part of the final Olympic bid and pledged a 26 km Bus Rapid Transit (BRT) line, known as *TransOlímpica*, connecting competition venues and existing transportation networks across the city.

From being at risk . . .

In December 2009 the Municipal Strategic Plan 2009–12 was presented by the mayor. It included the goal of 'reducing by 3.5 per cent the area covered by *favelas* in Rio' in order to 'protect the environment'. A few months later, in June 2010, city planners announced another plan: 119 *favelas* were to be entirely removed by 2012 because they 'were located in areas of risk of landslides and flooding'. Vila Autódromo was on that list (Bastos and Schmidt 2010). Residents and supporters mobilised in front of Rio City Hall, demanding stronger representation and formal documentation of the environmental claims. Nevertheless, in February 2011 a judge ordered the removal of all houses in Vila Autódromo that lay within 25 metres of the lagoon, citing federal legislation that requires a buffer between construction and any body of water (Magalhães 2011).

Around that time the city also revoked the community's Special Zone of Social Interest status in order to strengthen the rationale for resettlement. This move was arbitrary and probably illegal (Gaffney and Melo 2010: 20), and meant the community was no longer a prioritised area for urban upgrading projects. In March

2010 community leaders met with representatives from city government, the state housing secretary, public defenders and activist groups. City officials reaffirmed the plan for resettlement, now justifying it as a suggestion from the International Olympic Committee. However, they offered the community an opportunity to devise an alternative.

. . . to being a risk

The municipality continued to use the Olympics as an excuse to remove the community. In March 2010, the special secretary of Rio 2016 introduced a new rationale: 'Safe conditions should be secured through the creation of an open space around the perimeter of the race track and a strip around the edge of the Jacarepaguá lagoon' (AMPVA 2012: 10). As commented by two foreign urban development experts, 'the meaning of "safety" now teetered ambiguously between safety *for* residents and safety *from* them' (Vale and Gray 2013).

The residents' association responded:

> We are not a threat to the environment, neither to the landscape nor to the security of anybody. We are a threat only to those who do not recognize the social function of property and the social function of the city.
>
> (AMPVA 2012: 11)

Planning an Olympic Park

Rio 2016, the private organisation in charge of hosting the Olympic Games, together with the Brazilian Institute of Architects, launched a formal competition in May 2011 for the Olympic Park. The park was to harbour main sports venues as well as apartment buildings (*condominios*) for the Olympic delegations. The proposal contained a site plan that virtually deleted Vila Autódromo from the map. The boundaries of the site plan cut through the village and divided it in two sections: the lagoon strip of solidly built houses was encompassed within the territory of the Olympic Park. The more informally constructed parts were outside the boundary. The competition was won by the international firm AECOM. Its bid was marked by 'admirable professionalism' (Vale and Gray 2013). AECOM chose to preserve the inland part of Vila Autódromo. In its winning plan, the community would remain not only for 2016 but also in the 2018 and 2030 'legacy' projections, by which time the majority of the Olympic Park would presumably be sold to private developers to create a new urban district. However, the rules of the competition provide that the winning proposal can be adapted at the discretion of the Rio 2016 committee. This is common procedure for competitions, to be sure, but it stacked the game against Vila Autódromo. Within a month of the announcement of the winning scheme, Vila Autódromo had again been erased from the plans (Vale and Gray 2013). In October 2011, the Rio newspaper *O Globo* reported that Vila Autódromo would be removed by 2013 (Magalhães 2011).

In the meantime, the construction of the Olympic Park was subject to a public tender. The winner was the consortium *Rio Mais*, consisting of three of the major building corporations in Brazil: Odebrecht, Andrade Gutierrez and Carvalho Hosken. They had built the original race track (*autódromo*) and the Athletes Village for the 2007 Pan-American Games. The contract for the Olympic park amounted to USD 1.1 billion (Mais Democracia, 2013). As the concessionaries of the Olympic Park, the consortium was permitted to use 75 per cent of this public land to accommodate luxury gated communities (*condomimios*), which they could sell or rent after the Olympics (Vainer *et al.* 2013).

Counter-hegemonic knowledge: people's planning

To strengthen their struggle against this powerful coalition, and to pass from a defensive strategy to a more proactive one, the leaders of the residents' association developed contact with some well-known academics in September 2011. They had met each other through the city-wide People's Committee on the World Cup and Olympics. Jointly they started the project of formulating a *Plano Popular*, a 'People's Plan', for upgrading the community.

The plan was to be elaborated by the community itself, but with qualified professional advice from urbanists, architects, social scientists and economists, among others. In total more than forty professionals and academics were involved, based in two research groups in the region: a group at the Institute for Urban and Regional Research and Planning, Federal University of Rio de Janeiro (UFRJ), and the group for urban studies and housing projects at Fluminens Federal University (UFF) (Vainer *et al.* 2013). A total of 100 residents participated in the workshop's preparing plan. First, there was a 'diagnostic workshop' on 19 November 2011. They mapped out the physical points of concern that the plan had to address, through a 'popular cartography'. On the air photo map the participants marked places of flood risk, existing playgrounds in a precarious state and places where garbage heaped and mosquitoes were breeding. They also identified places where they wished to have a crèche, a bus stop, street lighting, a pedestrian crossing with traffic lights for school children, a closer health post and a drainage canal.

During the following weeks studies were carried out in the field and perusing documents to analyse the points of concern raised in the workshop. Then there was a new workshop on 3 December, 2011 to discuss solutions. The proposals were presented to an assembly for the whole community on 18 December, 2013, and the assembly approved a preliminary plan. It also elected a council to discuss and elaborate the plan further. In February 2014 they carried out joint voluntary work, *mutirões*, to deal with immediate and manageable problems revealed by the preliminary plan. These problems included the treatment of solid waste, action against mosquito breeding spots and improvement of basic sanitation.

Then followed committee and assembly meetings to discuss final proposals for the respective four sections of the plan: a housing programme; a programme for sanitation, infrastructure and environment; a programme for improved public services; and a programme for community and cultural development. The housing programme was particularly detailed with a budget attached to it. Here, 82 new homes within the community site would be allocated to people who had to evacuate their houses, at the cost of USD 6 million. On 5 August, 2012, the final People's Plan for Vila Autódromo was approved with simple drawings to illustrate the changes. In this way, the process had exposed that 'urban planning is transformed from being a monopoly of politicians and technocrats into being an instrument of people's struggle' (AMPVA 2012: 15).

On 16 August, 2012, the plan was delivered to the mayor of Rio de Janeiro, Eduardo Paes, one month before the municipal elections. The mayor, campaigning to be re-elected, promised that he and his Housing Department would need only 45 days to review the plan. However, it took exactly one year for the Mayor to report back to the community.

Competing plans, negotiations and new conflicts

In the meantime, the municality pushed its own plan, *Parque Carioca*, which was announced as the new 'home' of the Vila Autódromo residents. The construction of 920 housing units, of which 450 were earmarked for residents from Vila Autódromo, had started on a location one kilometre away. The Mayor repeatedly claimed that the majority of residents wanted to leave, and at a meeting on 1 July, 2013, he claimed that 70 per cent had already signed a contract with the municipality.[15] By that time, several homes spread out throughout the community were marked for removal. Scattered removal has been a well-known psychological weapon adopted to weaken resistance in Rio's *favelas*.[16]

Those tactics had to change in the time following the street demonstrations in June 2013, the largest in Brazil's political history (see Box 7.2). Vila Autódromo residents took an active part in these demonstrations. With their allies, they organised a march from the community through the surrounding area on 20 July, 2013, showing continued community opposition to the threat of eviction among other issues. The date 9 August, 2013, represented a turning point for the residents of Vila Autódromo. After 20 years of resisting the threat of removal, the Mayor Eduardo Paes committed to a solution that could guarantee the permanence of the community. The mayor acknowledged that there had been errors in the treatment of the community and said he was willing to initiate a round of negotiations based on the permanence and in-situ upgrading of Vila Autódromo.

The same day the Residents' Association released a public note stating that: 'After years of resistance and struggle, Vila Autódromo achieved a commitment from the Mayor: Vila Autódromo and its residents will not be removed.' A series of 'technical' meetings followed where negotiations between the residents, accompanied by advisors, and the municipality took place. The municipality presented their revised plan: removal of 'only' half of the community (278 families) in order to provide elevated access for athletes and journalists onto the Olympic Park. In response, the team behind the People's Plan issued an updated design that met the requirements for the access roads and pedestrian bridge. The

People's Plan added the relocation of 30 more families in available space within the community. However, the municipal delegation did not make any efforts to meet the residents halfway and no agreement was made.

Throughout 2014, demolitions continued to take place in Vila Autódromo. Bulldozers rolled through the streets like war tanks and demolition crews have marked their permanence by setting up offices in containers at the community entrance. By residents' own estimates, more than the half of the families had left the community, the majority opting for resettlement in the *Parque Carioca* housing complex and the rest accepting financial compensation (Steiker-Ginzberg 2014).

Concluding remarks

In spite of several setbacks and losses, a significant portion of the Vila Autódromo residents have been able to hold the fort. Their struggle has resembled a Gramscian 'war of positions', a type of stalemate where the cultural and knowledge-related hegemony of the establishment has been countered. The municipality, on the other hand, over time concluded a full circle of arguments, ending with the same type of reasons for removing the residents as presented in the first place: Vila Autódromo was in the way of the new transport system. Instead of extension of adjacent avenues they finally held that they had to build access roads to the Olympic Park across the village. For each wave of new arguments from the municipality, the residents' association produced legal or technical counter-arguments, which forced the municipality to come up with new justifications.

The residents' association and its 'counter-knowledge alliance' was able to prevent forced evictions and demolition of Vila Autódromo for five years, from 2009 to 2014. Time will tell whether they will succeed in defending the remaining residents. Faced by ever new technical arguments the residents' association responded: first, by mobilising judicial knowledge and building on its accumulated capital of legal rights; second, by politicising the conflict and mobilising external support; and third, by trying to solve the conflict through community-based urban planning and offering cost-efficient technical solutions. After some time, the activists learned to combine these approaches into a coherent three-pronged strategy.

References

AMPVA (2012) 'Plano Popular da Vila Autódromo'. Associação de Moradores e Pescadores da Vila Autódromo (AMPVA)/Vila Autódromo Residents' and Fishermen's Association, August 2012.

Bastos, I. and Schmidt, S. (2010) 'Prefeitura removerá 119 favelas até o fim de 2012'. *O Globo*, 7 January, 2010.

Gaffney, C. and Melo, E.S.O. (2010) *Mega-eventos esportivos no Brasil: uma perspective sobre futures transformações e conflitos urbanos*. Rio de Janeiro: Observatório das Metrópoles, FASE –IPPUR/UFRJ.

Magalhães, L.E. (2011) 'Minuta de edital prevê remoção de favela Vila Autódromo até 2013 para obras do Parque Olímpico'. *O Globo*, 4 October, 2011.

Mais Democracia (2013) *Who runs Rio?* Instituto Mais Democracia: Rio de Janeiro.

Municipality of Rio de Janeiro (2008) 'O Plano de Legado Urbano e Ambiental Rio 2016'. Office of the Secretary of Urbanism, October 2008.

Steiker-Ginzberg, K. (2014) 'Diverging paths: Vila Autódromo residents resist, move on, await'. Published on 11 August, 2014. Available at www.rioonwatch.org/?p=17177 (accessed on 28 January, 2015).

Vainer, C., Bienenstein, R., Megumi, G., Oliveira, F.L. and Lobino, C. (2013) 'O Plano Popular da Vila Autódromo. Uma experiência de planejamento conflitual'. In: *XV Encontro Nacional da ANPUR (Desenvolvimento Planejamento e Governança)*, Recife.

Vale, L. and Gray, A. (2013) 'Displacement decathlon. Olympian struggles for affordable housing from Atlanta to Rio de Janeiro'. The Design Observer Group. Available at http://places.designobserver.com/feature/displacement-decathlon-atlanta-rio-olympics/37816/ (accessed on 28 January, 2015).

Settlement story 4.5 The role of knowledge and information management in organising collective resistance to a mega-project in Lima[17]

LISA STRAUCH AND MICHAELA HORDIJK

With a population aspiring to 9 million, the Peruvian capital city Lima has increased nearly nine-fold in population size since 1950. This rapid urban growth has been dominated by two different spatial logics. One is the supposedly 'formal' development of the city's higher income areas led by the real estate market. The other is the 'informal' urbanisation process, shaped by the collective action of the poor, who have incrementally built and upgraded their own neighbourhoods. While these two logics, though spatially segregated, have always co-existed, the subtle balance has increasingly gravitated in favour of the latter.

A new urban development dogma

Since the 1950s Peruvian governments have permitted the occupation of public land by the urban poor and promoted incremental home building as a way to cope with the huge housing deficit that resulted from rapid urban growth. Today, however – in the words of a former city councillor – the new urban development dogma reads as: 'Growth through investment, not through invasion' (Romero Sotelo 2006). Increasingly, urban planners seek to modernise the city through large-scale development projects. In this process, the private sector has come to play a key role. The private sector has been included through the development of public–private partnerships (PPPs), particularly through the granting of road infrastructure concessions. The easing of existing bureaucratic rules and regulations has allowed multinational corporate actors to become influential decision-makers in urban governance.

Efforts to modernise the city through public–private mega-projects have, however, reinforced spatial inequalities in the city. Large-scale projects require the redevelopment of spaces typically inhabited by low-income residents, entailing the displacement of people. However, the capacity of affected communities to negotiate their fate in the displacement process is often seriously hampered by their deliberate exclusion from decision-making in mega-projects. Information tends to be strategically hidden from them as their interests and concerns go against powerful interests.

This case study reflects on the politics of knowledge in community resistance against a mega-project. It does so by analysing the social contestation of the 'Vía Parque Rímac' mega-project currently under construction, displacing some of Lima's oldest *barriadas* along the river Rímac. It is based on an in-depth case study in the settlements affected by the project, including 90 open interviews with residents and their leaders and ten with government officials, representatives from the company executing the mega-project and civil society activists. The research was carried out in 2012–13 as part of a master's thesis project (Strauch 2013).

'Vía Parque Rímac' and the settlements along the bank of the river Rímac

In March 2009, the Brazilian construction company OAS submitted an unsolicited bid for a USD 571 million mega-project involving the construction of an inner-city toll highway to the municipality of Lima. The project – in its initial phase designated *Línea Amarilla* ('yellow line') – offered a complementary transportation axis to a part of the currently heavily congested *Vía Evitamiento* expressway. It included the redevelopment of the existing highway, and the construction of a new highway component. The latter included 9 km of new road construction along the river Rímac and the construction of a 2 km tunnel underneath the river. The primary motivation for OAS was the profits it would obtain from a 30-year concession of the highway's tolls, including a concession of the existing toll system from the Vía Evitamiento, considered the most profitable in the country.

The project is emblematic of the expanding role of the private sector in urban planning and the increasingly undemocratic governance mechanisms this entails in several ways. The municipality of Lima approved the project in June 2009, however, without subjecting it to proper political or public discussion, as information was kept secret in the name of commercial confidentiality (see Strauch, Takano and Hordijk 2014 for a detailed analysis). Moreover, the mega-project entailed vast social implications that had not been communicated to affected communities before approval. The planned new highway ran though the low-income settlements of the *Margen Izquierda* and *Margen Derecha del Río Rímac* (MIRR and MDRR, translated: left and right bank of the river Rímac), displacing at least 1,350 families.

The MIRR and MDRR constitute an area of approximately 50 settlements and are home to more than 80,000 people (INEI 2007). The settlements located along the river Rímac are some of the first settlements that evolved through land invasion and collective action in Lima. In contrast to many other poor settlements that emerged on desert land in the periphery, the MIRR and MDRR are located right next to the historical centre of the city. Many of the initial squatter settlements have achieved access to basic services though collective action. Makeshift shelters have long been replaced with constructions in durable materials. Most houses have also incrementally expanded to multi-family apartments housing third- and fourth-generation urban dwellers. Still, despite these advances, there are settlements that have existed for years in spaces difficult to upgrade, such as on top of sanitary landfills and on the steep banks of the river. Over time, erosion of the riverbank has put houses at serious risk of collapsing into the river. These neighbourhoods show a certain level of consolidation of the individual dwellings but still lack access to basic infrastructure. Overall, the conditions across and within these settlements are very diverse, depending on location and exposure to different risks.

Social contestation and redesign of the project

When the municipality of Lima publicly announced the project, it was met with dismay from affected communities. Not only had they neither been informed nor consulted, the compensation schemes were also insufficient for buying alternative housing. The contract considered compensating the affected families, but it established a differentiated scheme for tenants and holders of a legal property title: USD 70 and USD 200 per square metre, respectively. Residents without a title, a majority of those concerned, were to be compensated for their plot through a one-time payment of USD 5,000. Furthermore, in 2007 the municipality of Lima had changed the zoning of the MIRR, declaring the area destined for constructing the highway as a high-risk area due to its proximity to the riverbank, prohibiting any residential use. Activists and residents alike suspected that the mega-project and the ordinance were linked as it legitimated the eviction politically and significantly lowered the market price of the dwellings. In response to the perceived threat of the mega-project, the communities mobilised and took to the streets (see also Settlement Story 6.4).

Given the pending social conflict, the *Línea Amarilla* project became a hotly debated topic throughout the municipal election campaign in 2010. The mayoral candidate, Susana Villarán, opposing the incumbent government that had approved the project, made the issue central to her electoral campaign. She declared to the protesting communities that if elected she would suspend the project. However, when she was elected and took power in January 2011, she could only cancel the contract at high political, and eventually financial, cost.

Villarán re-negotiated the contract with OAS and redesigned the project. In June 2011 she announced the modification of the project and renamed it 'Vía Parque Rímac'. The new project reduced the number of affected families in the MIRR and MDRR by modifying the original roadway, and improved the economic conditions of the compensation scheme. It established that all residents would be compensated with a minimum of USD 30,000 for each dwelling and that the amount for compensation would be calculated by a valuation of the dwelling's market price. However, the housing re-allocation scheme offered to the affected households did not improve. As under the previous administration, the project offered a housing unit of 60 square metres in an apartment block in the MIRR built by the concessionaire. In addition to the compensation scheme, the contractor was obliged to invest USD 2.5 million into urban upgrading projects in the MIRR and MDRR to benefit families not directly affected by displacement. Additionally, the new contract included two important campaign promises from Villarán: a connection of the most populated district San Juan de Lurigancho and the city centre at an extra cost of USD 20 million, and the inclusion of the *Río Verde* ('green river') project into the construction. This included the canalisation and greening of 6 km of riverfront and the construction of a 25 ha metropolitan park close to the city centre at a cost of USD 80 million.

With these changes the project became a mixed-use project that, as Lehrer and Laidley (2009) indicate, is more difficult to contest because they appear to advance a multitude of urban development goals, i.e., integrating the development of infrastructure with the construction of social housing and urban green spaces.

The politics of knowledge in resistance

When in November 2009 the local government signed the contract for the execution of the mega-project, the families to be displaced from the MIRR and MDRR had never been consulted nor informed. Given the lack of interaction between project authorities and people affected, the majority learned about the project just like every other citizen of Lima: via public media. Through newspapers and television residents were confronted with the design of a highway that ran through their self-constructed settlements, facing the fact that they had been completely excluded from the planning process. As many residents argued:

> The authorities must inform us before creating this project, first talk to us as inhabitants, inform us about what they will do. Yet we found out through the media, through the television we learned that they would carry out a mega-project. In fact, at first I didn't think it would be realised. We said: How is it possible? What do we do? How had our presence been considered in this project? How had they considered the houses? Was there going to be a relocation or a resettlement?
>
> (Authors' interview, 20 October, 2012)

The secretive planning nature of the project and the exclusionary management of information soon ignited resistance. Once the majority of the population became aware of the project, their loosely organised response took the form of requesting dialogue and information. Nevertheless, when formal processes for demanding information (such as writing letters) did not yield results and project personnel responded evasively, resistance quickly took a more activist stance. In spring of 2010 community members staged two street marches, the main objectives of which were to demand transparency and access to information.

> We did the marches because the municipality did not inform us at all. Therefore we as neighbourhood leaders decided we are doing a march directly to the company. With the march we wanted to know what the cause of this project was and we made them listen to us, they opened us the doors, we had a meeting in the centre with the company, they invited all the leaders and they informed through videos about everything of the project and about the compensation that they were going to give. With the march we managed to get information because [the former mayor] made the project without any consultation of the people, not even of those affected.
>
> (Authors' interview, 23 October, 2012)

Besides the highly visible street protests, communities engaged in generating their own knowledge and information as a means of resistance. For example, two neighbourhood councils got involved in surveying their settlements. With the survey they aimed to determine what the demands of the population were and which forms of relocation they wanted to fight for. Given the lack of information provision from the project authorities, neighbourhood leaders were often the main channels through which residents obtained information about the project. To inform residents, they organised workshops and invited lawyers and politicians to assemblies where residents could voice their concerns and ask questions. Neighbourhood leaders also used blogs, Facebook pages and mailing lists to publicise their demands and communicate dates for marches and protests. However, lack of internet access circumvented the active engagement of many community members within these media spaces.

The most prominent form of communication and knowledge dissemination in the settlements remained face-to-face communication through general assemblies. But also community newspapers and leaflets served as tools for generating community-driven information about the project. The company, however, partially co-opted local media channels by funding the publication of a monthly paper normally published by a group of residents from the MIRR. Through the newspaper it advertised its social activities and promoted the new housing blocks constructed for resettlement.

'Invited spaces' for participation

Even after the re-design of the project, no meaningful dialogue was established between residents, the municipality and project authorities. Given the communities' demands for information and dialogue, the municipality set up an office that organised informative workshops and offered advice to residents about their compensation and relocation. With this 'invited space' for participation (cf. Miraftab and Wills 2005), the municipality claimed to have met the residents' 'right to participation and information' and to have eased the 'atmosphere of tension and distrust' by providing a space for 'permanent dialogue with the affected residents'. In fact the space only provided information about decisions already taken and did not allow for meaningful debate. This concern was echoed in many interviews with residents:

> They are treating us with indifference. They only offer us a compensation of 30,000 USD or an apartment in Patio Unión, which they're advertising everywhere – but this is a unilateral agreement! And they are coming, offering, they are trying to encourage the neighbours to accept these apartments but we already have said publicly that we reject it.
>
> (Authors' interview, 20 October, 2012)

Furthermore, interviews conducted in the settlements in 2012–13 revealed that the lack of information was still the top concern of all residents. A list of affected households had not been disclosed implying that nobody knew who was definitely affected.

> In fact, until now the municipality has never come here to say: you know what? You will be evicted. They didn't send us any notification, nothing at all. The municipality has never told us that we will be relocated. They should come here and talk to the people, have a dialogue, that is what we want, but they don't come.
>
> (Authors' interview, 24 November, 2012)

> When we asked for information about the project they always said that they didn't have the completed study yet and that therefore they cannot inform, what are they hiding?
>
> (Authors' interview, 15 January, 2013)

While lack of information was the main reason why communities mobilised in the first place, it was also the reason why the resistance was difficult to sustain. Even though residents were aware of the mega-project, they often lacked concrete knowledge about compensation schemes, options for relocation or even about whether their house was affected or not. This generated uncertainty and led to desperation and inaction, and had direct effect on people's capacity to organise resistance.

To be sure, neither public nor private project authorities were eager to change this. Overall, they tried to deny the existence of social conflict in the area. Rather, resistance was seen as transitory, something that would pass with time:

> In the beginning some leaders of some neighbourhoods made some activities, like some street blocks but those were temporary things, not massive – eventualities
>
> (Interview, 29 October, 2012, Municipality of Lima official)

The municipality and company rhetorically framed the settlements as spaces of disorder and risk in need of intervention and the mega-project as a socially viable project that represented an opportunity to improve the living conditions of the people from the Margen Izquierda del Río Rímac. The media echoed this discourse and hence the social implications of the project were largely absent in the public debate. While there has been sporadic media coverage of communities' protests activities, these did not translate into a critical engagement with the mega-project. Media coverage rather tended to delegitimise the protesters' cause. While media narratives foregrounded the modernising part of the project – such as the construction of a tunnel underneath the river – they placed social implications in the background. Affected communities were portrayed as beneficiaries of the project that were given the opportunity to escape from their precarious living conditions at the 'edge of the abyss'. Protesters, on the other hand, were framed as irrational, ungrateful rebels (*La Republica* 2013).

Conclusion

The centrality of knowledge issues in processes of social mobilisation was evidenced in how the lack of information and transparency was the primary reason that communities along the river Rímac chose to organise themselves in 2009. Paradoxically, this same lack of information had a demobilising effect in the longer run. It is difficult to sustain collective action if nobody knows for sure what will happen when, and who will be affected in which manner. Media could have acted in support of these communities, yet they were not only absent, they even strengthened the narrative that authorities wanted to spread. Neighbourhood leaders – experienced in engaging with local authorities – now had to deal with private developers, with whom they had no prior experience. Due to the socially constructed blockages to inclusive knowledge management by project authorities, such as the lack of transparency and the fragmented provision of information, affected communities saw their capacity to negotiate their fate reduced to a minimum.

References

INEI (Instituto Nacional de Estadística e Informatica) (2007) *XI censo de población y VI de vivienda.*

La Republica (2013) 'Del borde del río al condominio soñado'. 2 June, 2013. Lima: La Republica.

Lehrer, U. and Laidley, J. (2009) 'Old mega-projects newly packaged? Waterfront redevelopment in Toronto'. *International Journal of Urban and Regional Research*, 32(4): 786–803.

Miraftab, F. and Wills, S. (2005) 'Insurgency and spaces of active citizenship: The story of Western Cape Anti-Eviction Campaign in South Africa'. *Journal of Planning Education and Research*, (25): 200–17.

Romero Sotelo, M.E. (2006) *El arquitecto desarrollador. Retornado al territorio productivo y a las ciudades humanizadas.* Lima: Universidad San Ignacio de Loyola.

Strauch, L. (2013) 'Seeking spatial justice in Lima – a case study of resistance mobilisation to an urban megaproject from Lima's *barriadas*'. UvA Master Thesis. Available at: http://dare.uva.nl/en/scriptie/454385 (accessed on 31 January, 2015).

Strauch, L., Takano, G. and Hordijk, M. (2014) 'Mixed-use spaces and mixed social responses: Popular resistance to a megaproject in Central Lima, Peru'. *Habitat International*, 45(3): 177–84.

Notes

1 At the time of the interview with the concerned DDA officer (27 February, 2008) the financial modalities for the eligible families were still under discussion.
2 This section draws on Dupont *et al.* (2014).
3 Source: 'Raheja bags Delhi first slum redevelopment project', *Impression Quarterly Newsletter*, Vol iv, Issue 1, New Delhi, January 2010. Available from Raheja Developers' website at www.raheja.com (accessed on 18 November, 2014).
4 Authors' interview (3 November, 2012).
5 Authors' interview (2 November, 2012).
6 Authors' interviews with various local leaders in May and June 2013.
7 Available from www.kathputlicolonydda.com/index.asp (accessed on 18 November, 2014).
8 Bhule Bisre Kalakar Co-operative vs Union of India, WP(C) 1290/2014.
9 ALIU is organised under the Informal Settlements Department, which goes some way in explaining why people have associated the exchange of information with the department with the demolition of shacks.
10 In Durban these criteria tend to be overridden by the relocation of all residents from informal settlements on the municipality's priority list. Living in a settlement on the municipality's priority list often determines the delivery of subsidised housing, rather than the national criteria.
11 In response to the social unrest related to housing during 2013, eThekwini Municipality placed a full page information sheet in the *Sunday Tribune* Newspaper titled 'Facts about housing delivery' endorsed by the City Manager to communicate its position on dealing with the housing backlog and service delivery (*Sunday Tribune*, 20 October, 2013).
12 Hammonds Farm is a low-cost housing project that was developed for the relocation of this informal settlement of 725 households, as well as others from elsewhere in the Municipality, as part of the delivery of formal housing to the poor.
13 This is the colloquial Zulu word used to describe the map.
14 This report is based on fieldwork carried out in April and May 2012, which started with a long interview with community leaders in Vila Autódromo on 26 April, 2012, followed up by new field visits in September 2013 and in March–April 2014.
15 OsteRio, 1 July, 2013. Available at www.iets.org.br/article.php3?id_article=2048 (accessed on 28 January, 2015).
16 Professor Carlos Vainer. Author's interview 20 March, 2014.
17 This text draws on and contains extracts from the following published article: Strauch, L., Takano, G. and Hordijk, M. (2015) 'Mixed-use spaces and mixed social responses: Popular resistance to a megaproject in Central Lima, Peru'. *Habitat International*, 45(3): 177–84.

5 Knowledge and power in upgrading and resettlement initiatives

*David Jordhus-Lier, Einar Braathen,
Véronique Dupont and
Catherine Sutherland*

Introduction

In this chapter we explore the politics of informal settlements by considering how knowledge is produced, used, shared and contested. Open flows of knowledge in general, and the inclusion of community-based knowledge and the knowledge generated by social movements in particular, have been highlighted as important pre-requisites for participatory public interventions in housing for the poor (McFarlane 2006, Huchzermeyer 2011). In the following chapter, we examine the flows of knowledge in informal housing processes, reflecting on how openings and blockages enable and constrain the attempts of urban dwellers to meaningfully engage in interventions affecting their lives.

Interventions in informal urban areas bring together multiple actors, including urban planners, developers, communities and a range of other experts and non-experts whose knowledge determines what is possible or desirable in an upgrading process. The motivation for choosing to apply a knowledge perspective on urban informality is twofold. First, informal settlements, by their very definition, challenge the ways knowledge is being managed in urban environments. Informal settlements by their nature do not fit easily into the bureaucratic practices of planning authorities, local political structures and public service providers, and hence knowledge about informal settlements in the formal state apparatus is often limited and erroneous. Hence, Roy frames the challenge of informality as an epistemological challenge for planners (Roy 2005). Second, and following from this, generating knowledge about informal practices is often highly contested. State agencies need a knowledge base to govern informal areas, as they tend to escape various forms of bureaucratic data collection. Attempts to monitor and map informality by the state are often challenged by alternative forms of knowledge generation by representatives of the communities affected, or by dissident experts (NGOs, academics and social movements) both as a means of providing a counter-discourse on informality, and as a way of protecting the rights of informal settlers.

This chapter starts with a discussion of knowledge concepts and definitions, where we contend that urban political analysis requires a definition of knowledge that explicitly acknowledges power dynamics, lived experiences and social relations. We then show how local, community-based forms of knowledge can challenge traditional governing practices, creating a counter-discourse, with reference to relevant academic literature and to our case studies. Finally, we identify three critical challenges that have emerged from our empirical research, all of which threaten the participation and empowerment of marginalised communities in upgrading and resettlement initiatives.

Defining knowledge: practiced and relational

Although no single definition of knowledge exists, we can make a heuristic distinction between *knowledge, information* and *data*. Whereas data refer to the multitude of facts and evidence that surrounds us that has not yet been interpreted, we use the concept of information on data and facts that are organised, and often codified, in certain ways. In the context of settlement upgrading, such information could include budgets and technical plans. It could also mean 'knowing what the formal rights of beneficiaries are' or even 'when the next meeting is scheduled?'

Information only becomes knowledge 'when it is put into a larger context' or set of meanings (Bruckmeier and Tovey 2008: 316). While it is often assumed that there is a linear development from data, via information, to knowledge, Bruckmeier and Tovey (2008) argue that this can go both ways – as data might emerge only once knowledge is generated. The distinction between the three is still useful, however, as they imply different levels of embeddedness in a social reality. Knowledge entails understanding processes, relationships and procedures. For instance, rather than simply knowing one's rights, one has to understand *how* these rights can be realised – through the legal system, through obtaining access to public services, through self-organisation, or through political mobilisation. Knowledge, understood in this way, combines information and experience.

Knowledge is a socially embedded phenomenon. Bruckmeier and Tovey's (2008) *relational knowledge* concept builds on Haraway's (1988) notion of 'situated knowledges' but refers more specifically to how the generation of knowledge cannot be separated from the interaction between the social actors who produce it. Put differently, knowledge is interwoven with power. Studies of knowledge processes that fail to acknowledge the power dynamics conditioning them will therefore only generate a shallow understanding of knowledge.

In sociology and political science, we find classical contributions to 'the rationalist reading' of power and knowledge. According to Robert Dahl (1957), power is exercised by certain people who control resources that give them power over other people by forcing them to do things they otherwise would not have done. Technical knowledge (or skills and know-how) is one of these resources. A fair society must constantly redistribute these resources. A more radical approach looks at power as management of meaning, hegemonic ideas and cultural manipulation (Lukes 1974). This type of power is exercised to prevent conflicts, grievances and demands from arising, for instance by legitimising certain types of knowledge and delegitimising others. A Foucauldian approach is even more radical by challenging any instrumentalist understanding of power. Power is structured in networks of social relations and discourses that capture advantaged and disadvantaged alike (Foucault 1980, 1982). Those trying to pull these strings of power do not necessarily produce the desired outcomes. Instead, all actors are subjected to 'disciplinary' power, a prevailing web of power relations that resides in every perception, judgement and act.

Braathen, Attwood and May (2012) try to combine these readings into a multi-dimensional approach when they discuss knowledge, power and empowerment in relation to South African telecentres. They argue that power is shaped along all four dimensions introduced above: by privileged actors' ability to (i) control resources, (ii) control the processes of decision-making, and (iii) control meanings, as well as (iv) being subject to discursive relations that discipline the conduct of power. Knowledge plays a role in all four dimensions, of course, and attempts to empower marginalised groups and actors without acknowledging the importance of these forms of power and the role of powerful actors who control how knowledge is produced are likely to fail.

McFarlane's (2006) introduction of a post-rationalist approach to knowledge can further add to this discussion. Exploring knowledge views in development, he explicitly distances himself from what he understands as the rationalist position of the World Bank and their mantra 'Knowledge for Development'. Rather than thinking of knowledge as something that can travel in a linear fashion, being applied to local settings to foster development, a post-rationalist reading sees knowledge as always 'in translation'. Because knowledge is always situated in specific places, and is formed by interaction between particular actors and learned through concrete practices, it 'always changes as it moves' (McFarlane 2006: 299). The assumption that knowledge management can build 'resilience through innovation, communication and knowledge services', as the World Bank (2013) puts it, fails to move beyond a rationalist knowledge concept. By extension, this means that talking about knowledge as allocated or distributed is problematic, and even Bruckmeier and Tovey's (2008: 316) descriptions of knowledge as 'socially distributed in different and unequal forms' veer close to a rationalist reading of knowledge, as warned against by McFarlane.

To follow up on McFarlane's point, while knowledge has come to the fore in development discourse and in urban studies, the way knowledge is understood often rests on a top-down approach. A critical approach to knowledge management needs to be aware that using such buzzwords indiscriminately can serve to further a depoliticised development discourse. MacKinnon and Derickson (2013: 263) use a knowledge lens to critique the resilience paradigm currently dominant in urban planning that, in their view, is based on a conservative concept – 'externally defined by state agencies and expert knowledge'. They rather propose the alternative concept 'resourcefulness' (MacKinnon and Derickson 2013: 264), which 'emphasizes forms of learning and mobilization based upon local priorities and needs as identified and developed by community activists and residents.'

Our findings underpin the need to infuse the study of knowledge with an explicit power analysis. For instance, MacKinnon and Derickson identify 'access to knowledge' as an immediate challenge facing individuals and organisations in their activism. Furthermore, they argue for the acknowledgement of 'folk knowledge' as an important mobilising factor and stress the importance of equipping local communities with a certain level of technical knowledge in order to be resourceful (MacKinnon and Derickson 2013). This latter point is particularly relevant to our research as presented in Chapter 4, as local knowledge and expert knowledge across our settlement stories are often kept away from each other due to an absence of participatory planning, entrenched social exclusion, low levels of education and, in many cases, linguistic barriers. The following sections explore this discussion of knowledge based on both a reading of relevant academic contributions and on findings from our own research.

Knowledge forms: distinct types or overlapping characteristics?

Before we start discussing how to bridge the knowledge gap between informal settlements and formal authorities, it is worth asking whether this gap is created by differing *knowledge levels*, or whether it is a matter of different *knowledge forms*. In fact, several scholars have argued that knowledge appears in different forms. For instance, van Ewijk and Baud (2009) distinguish between three different types of knowledge in urban governance: tacit, contextual-embedded and codified forms of knowledge. Whereas tacit knowledge is experiential, practised and non-codified at an individual level, contextual-embedded knowledge refers to other forms of shared, non-codified knowledge practised through institutions and social networks. Contextual-embedded knowledge hence enjoys a different kind of legitimacy. Codified knowledge, on the other hand, is typically written – often in digital form.

If knowledge indeed appears in different forms, what is it that appears to lend more legitimacy to certain forms than others? Their format and availability

	Tacit	Contextual-embedded knowledge			Codified knowledge
		technical, economic	community-based, social	political and network levels	(analytical, regulatory, standards, etc.)
Actors	Individuals with experience	Professional knowledge belonging to sector professionals	Community knowledge spread by social networks	Political knowledge within political and social networks	Academically and professionally taught and diffused

Figure 5.1 Types of knowledge.
Source: Baud *et al.* 2011: 8.

certainly play a role. Scientific knowledge very often appears as codified know-ledge. While statistics, GIS, planning tools and juridical procedures enjoy a high social status, they are at the same time inaccessible to many ordinary people as they require technical training to be understood and made use of.

Not surprisingly, scientific knowledge has often led to political contestation and mistrust between the 'knowledge holders' and those implicated and affected by this knowledge. Whether it relates to medical treatment and vaccinations, climate change or genetically engineered foodstuffs, scientific knowledge is often challenged 'on the ground' with reference to people's lived experiences (Epstein 1996, Fischer 2000, Leach and Scoones 2007). In our research, this is evident in how informal settlement residents make sense of concepts of technical planning, such as noise contours and soil assessments, which inform explanations of inter-ventions that affect them. Fischer (2000) states that truths, including the claims of science, are social constructions heavily reliant on public credibility (cf. Epstein 1996), and not simply based on systematic verification. Illustratively, the responses from the citizenry to scientific truths are more reflexive than often assumed. Silence is often assumed to imply acceptance of, or even trust in, scientific explanations. Fischer, however, argues that people often keep ambivalence to themselves and find their own ways of making sense of conflicting claims. Silence might rather imply alienation, or that people, regardless of whether they agree or not, feel compelled to act as if they trust experts because they stand in a relation of dependence to knowledge institutions (e.g., academia and health institutions).

It could be argued that certain contributions to the study of knowledge have relied on essentialising notions of distinct knowledge forms. For instance, McFarlane's (2006: 295) otherwise sophisticated account states that codified knowledge is easily expressed in written form, while tacit knowledge is char-acterised as 'difficult to communicate and does not travel well'. This implies distinct categories or knowledge types with particular characteristics. But the validity of such generalisations depends on whose vantage point one takes. In fact, some of our research shows how codified knowledge in development projects does not always travel easily to key audiences, such as affected resident groups. Vice versa, tacit knowledge can often be communicated between actors if the methods used to exchange knowledge are well suited to this purpose.

On a related note, knowledge categories might be less clear-cut in practice than indicated above. Fischer also draws on Lindblom and Cohen (1979) when he asserts that both experts and lay people base most of their beliefs on *ordinary knowledge*, in other words knowledge that is neither scientifically scrutinised nor verified. Fischer (2000) advocates a form of deliberation that seeks solutions to problems by juxtaposing *expert knowledge* with *local knowledge*, and the ordinary knowledge of all involved (expert and lay) citizens. Not only should there be room for competing scientific paradigms but also for different forms of knowledge. Importantly, the act of communicating different forms of knowledge is also dependent on the professional identities of experts involved in the projects. In our cases, we have met planners, engineers and managers expressing a range of professional identities: from activists with firm beliefs in participatory processes to individuals assuming a managerial role relatively detached from the social dynamics in the affected areas.

Mosse (1994) goes even further in blurring the boundaries between different knowledge categories. His contribution to the debate precedes most other sources reviewed here, but he holds some important insights that tend to have been overlooked in recent discussions. Taking an explicitly problem-focused approach to how knowledge is managed in participatory rural appraisals, Mosse ascertains that knowledge is always mediated by power relations, which in turn shapes how it differs in form and character. But rather than making a strict analytical distinction in the form of a typology, he claims that knowledge is differentiated by degree and is '*more or less* public, "official", codified, agreed, recognized as such, and accessible to outsiders' (Mosse 1994: 518, our emphasis). He also identifies some relationships between these characteristics. For instance, in contexts where gender and social status might discourage marginalised subjects from speaking up, the more 'public' the setting of knowledge exchange, the more exclusionary it might appear.

Appropriate knowledge and active citizens

Leaving the focus on knowledge and urban informality for a while, there is a broader argument to be made about the importance of knowledge in contemporary politics. Fischer (2000), for instance, describes an increasing complexity in the governing of modern societies. This complexity has led us to a heavy reliance on scientific expertise. Fischer (2000: 49) draws on Beck's (1992) notion of the risk society, where 'the dark side of progress increasingly comes to dominate social and political debate'. In other words, the scientific knowledge that came to dominate governance throughout the twentieth century also created new risks. Here, Fischer sees a dilemma: to combat risks such as climate change, environmental degradation or biomedical hazards, which in part have been caused by scientific knowledge, we cannot rely on scientific knowledge alone. What is proposed is the need for *appropriate knowledge*. Appropriate knowledge is not limited to scientifically verifiable explanations of causes and consequences but includes ways of communicating scientific facts to affected publics and, vice versa, ways of incorporating the experiences and explanations of people affected by risks in scientific accounts and political processes. The main task is then not to transmit expert knowledge to lay people, but to find ways of applying, translating and making different forms of knowledge usable to solve particular problems. Put differently, appropriate knowledge is appropriated knowledge by relevant actors.

Fischer (2000: 2) calls for 'new approaches to bringing citizens and experts together', and while he acknowledges the strengths of advocacy research and the politics of counter-expertise (cf. Epstein 1996), he finds that the main shortcoming in contemporary knowledge regimes is their lack of citizen participation. Advocacy research is socially committed research by scientists who simultaneously act as activists. While they often champion issues of social and environmental justice, and give scientific credibility to the viewpoints of marginalised groups, they often fail to do so on the terms of those they claim to represent, argues Fischer. Citizens need to be viewed as active and reflexive agents in knowledge production, not simply an audience who needs to be educated. In a truly participatory model, scientists and other guardians of scientific knowledge should act as 'specialised citizens', according to Fischer (2000), on premises and in processes set up in collaboration with affected citizens. In the various case studies presented in this volume, NGO representatives, committed academics and community representatives who have been allotted the role of 'knowledge brokers' (see below for a discussion) all inhabit intermediary roles between informal settlement dwellers, on the one hand, and formal authorities on the other. Thus they can be argued to take on the role of 'specialised citizens' as called for by Fischer.

Contesting credibility

At times, resisting an intervention requires the mobilising actors to directly contest scientific or technical claims. Some of the more thought-provoking contributions to studying the politics of knowledge have focused on highly contested political issues such as environmental degradation (Fischer 2000), climate change (Lidskog and Elander 2007) and the AIDS epidemic (Epstein 1996). For instance, Epstein (1996) states that the presence of activists in scientific debate has served to yoke together moral-political arguments with epistemological claims, creating a more holistic understanding of the problem in question. Likewise, the ways in which planners, developers and authorities employ supposedly scientific and technical justifications for evictions and relocations are often disputed by local residents and their allies. We argue, based on a reading of the literature and with reference to our research, that in order to effectively challenge the credibility of powerful state and corporate actors, two dimensions are particularly important. First, local actors must be able to build knowledge alliances to engage with different forms of appropriate knowledge and to construct legitimacy for their claims. Second, and simultaneously, their knowledge must remain embedded in local communities and maintain their legitimacy with community members.

Challenging power through knowledge alliances

Jacobs (2013) argues that in struggles over scientific legitimacy, communities often form strategic knowledge alliances with experts or civil society organisations (CSOs), such as legal advisors during court cases. While social movements seem to have a critical role to play in credibility struggles over knowledge, Scoones (2005: 1) points out that in studies of social movements 'the politics of knowledge is however often underemphasised'. Leach and Scoones (2007) have studied how scientific knowledge has been challenged by various political actors, and they claim that social movements must be understood as

> knowledgeable actors [. . .] engaged in political processes, which involve contestations between knowledge claims linked respectively to particular political and social commitments and cultures.

> (Leach and Scoones 2007: 27)

Leach and Scoones draw on Epstein's (1996) thinking to create a typology of the different, yet related, ways in which political actors and social movements challenge science: by disputing particular scientific claims; by seeking to acquire scientific authority by aligning with scientific expertise; by rejecting scientific epistemology on a more fundamental basis; and, finally, by challenging the ways science is produced and by whom it is controlled. A case in point is the slum dwellers who were evicted from the bank of the Yamuna river following an order by the High Court of Delhi, described in Box 5.3. Here, NGOs and human rights organisations sympathetic to slum dwellers disputed the scientific basis for the eviction, by referring to statistics from the Central Pollution Control Board to document how the informal settlement dwellers contributed only minimally to the river's pollution. We find similar patterns in the other cities. An alliance of residents in Vila Autódromo and sympathising academics also produced a set of 'technical counter-arguments' to challenge the decision to relocate the community in preparation for the 2016 Olympic Games in Rio de Janeiro (see Settlement Story 4.4).

While networks of activists can generate an impressive knowledge base through their activism – what Epstein (1996: 350) refers to as 'building lay expertise' – their lack of formal credentials means that they first and foremost base their credibility on being spokespeople of groups directly affected by the contested issues. For instance, AIDS activists represented people who participated in clinical treatment experiments. Scott and Barnett's (2009) study of environmental activism in South Durban shows how particular policy issues, environmental politics being among them, have become 'scientised'. In other words, the authority of science in certain political processes forces any attempt by citizens to mobilise against state policies or corporate conduct to engage with scientific claims. Scott and Barnett (2009: 374) observe how civic science – a popular engagement with science that includes 'gathering, analyzing, interpreting and diffusing scientific information' – and lay knowledge was employed as a main strategy by a community-based organisation to reframe a debate around local pollution.

Scientific knowledge is often fragmented and partial, and so is the lay expertise of those who get involved in knowledge contestation. For lay experts, there are also risks involved which relate to conflicting credibilities. For instance, they might feel caught between the requirements of movement building and popular legitimacy, on the one hand, and their participation in expert communities on the other. Moreover, Epstein (1996: 352) aptly notes that 'knowledge hierarchies are rarely "accidental" in their origins'. Class, education, race and gender help determine who become these privileged knowledge bearers and representatives of lay constituencies in the realm of science.

Epstein (1996) hails the emergence of activists in contested scientific debates for their potentially democratising influence. Similarly, Corburn (2003) argues that the inclusion of local knowledge in planning processes enhances procedural democracy, although this is wholly reliant on whether the actors who represent communities are legitimate and representative. Our research reveals that, in some cases, the inclusion of community actors might serve to empower particular individuals rather than the community at large. Typically, these are individuals whose legitimacy to a large extent is based on their privileged role in planning and community liaison, and not derived from democratic elections.

Local knowledge and spatialised epistemologies

Based on the discussion above, we adopt a relational view of knowledge in our study of the politics of informal settlement upgrading and relocation. In other words, we understand knowledge as expressed to different degrees as formal/informal, or codified/non-codified, and always bound up in relations between social actors. Knowledge is not a thing that can travel or be distributed, but rather represents contextualised meanings and capabilities that all people need – to make sense of their world, and to change it. While such a definition of knowledge is both relational and post-rational, it is not (yet) spatially sensitive. The spatialities of knowledge warrant some reflection, given that much of the literature above explicitly emphasises *local* knowledge (Geertz 1983, Fischer 2000). Also, many of our study sites are areas defined by their informality, implying that there is a particular value in including knowledge from these areas, which previously have been marginalised in knowledge production.

Corburn identifies particular ways in which local knowledge can contribute epistemologically to urban planning. He suggests that scientific knowledge tends to generalise and aggregate information in a way that 'tends to miss local particularity' (Corburn 2003: 428). While Pfeffer *et al.* (2012: 261) support this notion, they argue that the 'inclusion of community-based or tacit knowledge can be done locally, but requires upscaling and embedding in wider institutional processes in order to become recognized and accepted' – to which we may add '*by* powerful actors'. We contend that the inclusion of community-based knowledge can potentially strengthen the legitimacy of local processes without being upscaled, and hence it has value in its own context.

While Fischer (2000) does not make this very explicit, his framing of local knowledge does have a spatial dynamic. With inspiration from Haraway (1988), who claims that all knowledge is grounded in its *position*, Fischer states that knowledge cannot simply be valued according to certain objective criteria. Rather, its validity must be understood according to *whose viewpoint* it presents and *from where* it is presented. Such a view openly acknowledges what we refer to as spatialised epistemologies, which can be elaborated in several ways. First, all knowledge is tied to, or embedded in, particular places with their unique set of social relations. This might seem like an obvious point, but it is still worth iterating. Local knowledge draws its legitimacy from the fact that it reflects the experiences and viewpoints of citizens affected by a particular problem or process. While expert knowledge often presents solutions to these problems, it tends to lack embeddedness. Hence, expert knowledge requires a deliberative process in order to become operational. Second, the places and landscapes where knowledge is produced hold different positions in social hierarchies. A university institution, or a downtown government office, tends to be imbued with a different credibility than local residential committees, particularly when those living there are marginalised groups in society. However, credibility is relational, depending on who is concerned, and deep chasms of mistrust might develop between expert communities such as universities and groups in society. Third, places of knowledge production are to different degrees and in different ways connected to other places. For instance, universities are part of a global academic knowledge community, while local community knowledge might be fragmented and detached even from the knowledge production of neighbouring communities. Moreover, attempts to scale up or connect fragmented local knowledge production into city-wide or trans-local networks might simultaneously serve to reduce the legitimacy of such actors in the eyes of their respective constituencies. Fourth and last, most forms of knowledge inhibit their own spatial representations. The knowledge of planners, as it is transformed into maps, portray urban space as compartmentalised, manageable and orderly – as seen from above. Other forms of knowledge – that of a community member, or a visiting journalist – might portray urban informal spaces in very different ways, as narratives, for instance. This becomes evident in Settlement Stories 4.2 and 4.3, where the contrast between community maps and the maps of urban planners are discussed.

Local knowledge not only adds to planning and governance processes 'because it is local', but because it reflects the viewpoints of localities that have previously been excluded. Roy's (2005: 152) notion of policy epistemologies suggest that local knowledge disrupts 'models of expertise, making it possible to generate knowledge about upgrading and infrastructure from a different set of experts: the residents of informal settlements'. The international network Slum Dwellers' International (SDI) and the discourse that has developed around this organisation is firmly based on this notion, epitomised by slogans such as 'documenting the undocumented' and 'knowledge is power'. SDI has become a main vehicle championing the inclusion of community knowledge in upgrading initiatives in many countries (Patel and Baptist 2012, Patel, Baptist and d'Cruz 2012).

When knowledge is spatially coded, for instance by producing maps, social inequalities and the unevenness of socio-economic development is laid bare in a way that ultimately can counteract spatial injustices that otherwise would go unnoticed. Pfeffer et al. (2012: 277) argue that the use of participatory spatial knowledge management tools (including participatory GIS and community mapping) holds a particular promise in 'produc[ing] new knowledge, incorporating tacit, practice and community knowledge, reflecting lived urban realities to a much greater degree'. Of course, as the authors explicitly acknowledge, the introduction of such tools creates certain thresholds to participation in terms of digital access and literacy. As an example, Skuse and Cousins' (2007) ethnographic study of an informal settlement in Cape Town vividly illustrates how the communications infrastructure of an informal settlement can be innovative and highly dynamic, but at the same time represent a huge barrier to interactive technologies. This is important, because it highlights that the notion of 'knowledge flows' is not just complicated by power imbalances, but also by the uneven access to technologies and means of communication that are the results of disempowerment.

Experiences with community-based knowledge

Alternative knowledge production might be conducted through surveys or counts and be spatially visualised through maps. In some cases, this knowledge production follows a standardised 'model', such as the one developed by SDI (see Box 5.1 on 'the SDI model'). In other cases, it may be borne out of local interactions between community members, often in collaboration with some facilitators with access to resources, tools or specialist knowledge.

Through such exercises, local community representatives with few prior skills in constructing systematised knowledge accounts might acquire skills and experience that they can use to further the interests of their community without external assistance. This is what Epstein (1996) refers to as the 'expertification of lay activists'. This might involve these individuals acquiring specialist expertise. However, it can also refer to a process where local activists obtain the communication skills to champion the lived experience of community members as 'experiential expertise'. In other words, we are not simply looking at how communities generate alternative forms of knowledge, but also how they legitimate this knowledge as equally valuable to scientific knowledge.

One of the most encouraging examples of this community-based knowledge generation is to be found in Settlement Story 4.3, where Sutherland describes an academic-community knowledge exchange in the Ocean Drive-In informal settlement in Durban, in which a team from the University of KwaZulu-Natal (UKZN), including the author, were involved. A community-based mapping project was initiated to enable Ocean Drive-In residents to be informed about a planned resettlement to a formal housing project, Hammonds Farm. Community members had been allocated housing numbers in preparation for an anticipated move, but due to the delays many doubted that they would be allocated a formal house. This created uncertainty and social protests as the community feared that 'their' houses in Hammonds Farm would be allocated to others. Community members, through the research team, challenged the government to recognise their 'place on the map' through a participatory research process generating community-drawn and GIS-coded maps of their settlement. The process of developing the maps and the sharing of knowledge about the maps also built the relationship between the researchers and the community. The GIS map became an important source of knowledge to the community, and was used in the negotiations between the community and the Housing Department over beneficiaries.

While the empowerment potential of community mapping that Arputham (2012) discovered in the 1970s (see Box 5.1) can be discerned in some of our case studies, the contrasting experience of Europe informal settlement in Cape Town provides less cause for optimism (Settlement Story 4.2). Throughout the last five years, the residents of Europe have been involved in several community-mapping exercises, including an enumeration by a SDI-affiliated NGO and the involvement of planning students at the University of Cape Town. Whereas both these initiatives generated in-depth spatial knowledge about the socio-environmental condition of the settlement, the residents' experience with these

Box 5.1 The 'SDI model' and the Mumbai experience

David Jordhus-Lier

The literature on informal settlement upgrading seems to agree on two insights. One, there is a gradual understanding that authorities must leave a notion of 'eradicating slums', or targeting 'cities without slums', and rather acknowledge that slums are there to stay. As a consequence of this, the 'rules' that apply in cities' urban planning regimes need to be radically altered to deal with informality. Second, there is an increasing consensus on the need for community participation. Realising the ideals of pro-poor development entails residents themselves collecting spatial knowledge about their own communities and, relatedly, organising collectively to be able to use this knowledge to implement real change. The fact that community participation has become a catchphrase in the literature also testifies to the success of 'scaling up' this model from local communities to national and international arenas.

The Slum Dwellers International (SDI) is the embodiment of the approach outlined above. But while this network of community-based organisations is now a global force in its own right, its origins are embedded in particular urban environments. The movement started in the Indian city of Mumbai, where the NGO the Society for the Promotion of Area Resource Centres (SPARC) was established in 1984 as a network of social work professionals working on urban poverty issues. SPARC formed an alliance with a national network of slum dwellers and a local women's savings organisation and has since then achieved significant leverage over informal settlement policies in Mumbai and globally. The Shack/Slum Dwellers' International was established in 2006 by eight national federations, of which the Indian and South African affiliates have been key drivers. Activists involved in, and sympathetic to, SPARC and SDI have been actively publishing articles outlining the rationale of this particular approach to informal settlement upgrading, which we can refer to as the 'SDI model'.

Political neutrality and engagement

Certain key features can be argued to characterise the 'SDI model', all of which can be traced back to the initial experience in Mumbai. First, the network was built on a principle of political neutrality. Successfully avoiding the partisan politics of civil society in the city, the alliance managed to defend their neutrality. This meant 'working with whomever is in power' (Appadurai 2001). In Mumbai, this could even mean co-operation with the right-wing, Hindu party Shiva Sena. By contrast, in South Africa, which is otherwise completely dominated by the African National Congress (ANC), this approach could entail working with the Democratic Alliance-led administration in Cape Town. Appadurai (2001: 29) describes the network as 'fundamentally populist and anti-expert in strategy and flavour'. This also meant building strong links to existing leadership to ensure that activism was built on active participation by residents (Arputham 2012). Political neutrality facilitates engagement with authorities, which is another important characteristic of this model. In contrast to many of the more confrontational political strategies employed by slum dwellers around the world, the 'SDI model' is based on the notion that more can be achieved by co-operating with authorities than by sheer resistance. This is a contested principle that often clashes with the reality on the ground, during phases of high tension and low degrees of trust between citizens and the state.

Community-generated spatial knowledge

Second, the entire methodology of the SDI alliance relies on community-generated spatial knowledge. The key tool for generating this form of knowledge is the so-called *enumeration*. The first enumeration took place in Janata Colony in Mumbai as far back as 1975. Arputham (2012), who was involved in this groundbreaking exercise, vividly describes the method, combining a more expert-led settlement profile with a household survey conducted by the community members themselves. The enumeration filled two different purposes, Arputham argues. On the one hand, it forced the authorities to recognise the existence of these urban dwellers, their numbers and their location in the city. The survey also showed the authorities the legality of a purportedly illegal settlement (Arputham 2012: 27):

> Each telephone pole shows you are an established settlement. Every telephone pole has an official address – a district, an area. So it means that the settlement too has an official address. When the government says you do not have any documentation, we can show how many telephone poles or electricity poles we have and these have addresses.

On the other hand, the enumeration served to unite the Janata Colony and prove to residents that they do not have to depend on outsiders to create knowledge about themselves. This is described as a first step to more efficient forms of organising, which is another important part of the 'SDI model'. Community-generated spatial knowledge can be both descriptive, as in the enumerations, or normative and visionary, through community development plans or surveys of vacant land to prepare for establishing new settlements (Patel, Baptist and d'Cruz 2012).

Community organisation

The network has, since its origins in Mumbai, developed into a large international federation where local and national organisations of slum dwellers engage with authorities, from global development institutions to local governments, about 'changing the rules' of urban development. This has only been possible due to a third principle in the 'SDI model', namely the emphasis on community organisation. Of course, community organisation has a strong local dimension. Arputham described how the enumeration in Janata showed the aggregate amount of money flowing into the settlement, thus helping residents to realise that if they joined forces, they could co-ordinate a collective savings and investments scheme. Of course, organising is also decisive to give slum dwellers leverage when faced with local authorities. But as each settlement tended to lose out in political battles around evictions and upgrading, the need to scale up their politics soon emerged. A vehicle that has allowed the network to scale up is institutionalised *exchanges*, horizontal learning programmes where community members go from one settlement to another to meet with peers and learn from each other's experiences. In the SDI network, they also facilitate national and international exchanges. Representatives in the SDI network explain how these exchanges allow lessons learnt in one location to travel to another location, and for different actors to develop a common agenda.

Critique of the 'SDI model'

None of the characteristics of the 'SDI model' described above are uncontested. In fact, despite its global success (or possibly because of this), the 'SDI model' has received criticism both from activists in the various locations where it has been implemented and by academics who study their politics. This book presents several case studies where the principles of political neutrality and engagement have been questioned, and where the emphasis on savings and incremental development has been left in favour of more political strategies. The ideal-type planning and development tools of the 'SDI model' can sometimes clash with political traditions and culture in slums. Slums are often well organised, although there are also examples of marginal and recent slums with low levels of organisational life. Often, settlement leadership may be connected with strong political external organisations and parties. One paradox can be found in how attempts to nurture 'development-oriented' leadership in slums can actually undermine legitimate leadership positions in settlements.

From the academic side, several points of concern have been raised. Roy (2009: 166) has, in an otherwise sympathetic reading of SPARC's role in upgrading in Mumbai, questioned how the organisation 'rejects rights-based approaches to inclusion that seek to confront the state'. Huchzermeyer (2011) echoes this critique based on her analysis of the SDI experience in South Africa, and criticises how the network has favoured alliance building with national political agendas over grassroots activism.

Points of criticism notwithstanding, the 'SDI model' continues to wield great influence over the urban development agenda, from global actors such as the

World Bank's Cities Alliance to numerous pilots and partnerships in metropolitan areas across the world. In the context of this book, this model represents one form of knowledge-based mobilisation that, at particular times and in particular places, might offer informal settlement residents real, transformative opportunites, but at other times are abandoned in favour of protest, court cases or individual coping strategies.

References

Appadurai, A. (2001) 'Deep democracy: Urban governmentality and the horizon of politics'. *Environment & Urbanization*, 13(2): 23–43.

Arputham, J. (2012) 'How community-based enumerations started and developed in India'. *Environment & Urbanization*, 24(1): 13–26.

Huchzermeyer, M. (2011) *Cities with 'Slums': From informal settlement eradication to a right to the city in Africa*. Claremont, SA: University of Cape Town Press.

Patel, S., Baptist, C. and d'Cruz, C. (2012) 'Knowledge is power: Informal communities assert their right to the city through SDI and community-led enumerations'. *Environment & Urbanization*, 24(1): 13–26.

Roy, A. (2009) 'Civic governmentality: The politics of inclusion in Beirut and Mumbai'. *Antipode*, 41(1): 159–79.

Box 5.2 Technical decisions and the politics of relocation: the King Shaka Airport noise contour in Durban

Catherine Sutherland

Housing policy and practices in Durban have shifted away from the eradication of informal settlements, reflecting a growing recognition that informal residences are part of the solution to housing the poor. Given the substantial housing backlogs and the need for more flexible and adaptive solutions to the housing challenge, in-situ upgrading is now considered to be the most appropriate approach for people residing in informal settlements. However, this is highly dependent on land issues as informal settlements will only be upgraded on sites where the land is owned by the state or can be bought at an affordable price. However, for this to happen, land has to be deemed suitable for upgrading, by being free from human-induced and environmental hazards, and not holding alternative economic value.

Large-scale projects in the north of Durban

Residents of the Ocean Drive-In informal settlement (see Durban fact sheet in Chapter 2) had initially been informed that their settlement would be upgraded, even though it was located on private land. This land was situated in the valuable coastal corridor, but it did not have high economic value due to lower levels of development in the northern zone of the municipality. However, the decision to relocate the airport to the north of the city and to develop Dube TradePort around the new King Shaka Airport in 2007 raised land value in this area. The new airport was rapidly developed, so as to be ready for the 2010 FIFA World Cup. This mega-project is now being framed as an 'aerotropolis', with plans being developed for land adjacent to the site to support economic growth in the area. Ocean Drive-In, therefore, became a settlement on strategic and valuable land, rather than a settlement on land that was deemed upgradable. The settlement lends itself to upgrading as it is located close to transport and work opportunities, which is critical to the livelihoods of its residents, many of whom work informally or in casual employment. The settlement is not dense and residents make use of the environmental services offered by the site, such as open plots for urban agriculture and trees that offer shelter and protection from the elements.

Relocating the residents of Ocean Drive-In

However, a decision was taken to relocate residents of Ocean Drive-In to Hammonds Farm, rather than upgrading the settlement. Given that these informal settlers are recipients of a state intervention that will have a significant impact on their lives, it is important to question how information and knowledge flows between the community and the municipality around a relocation project. The eThekwini Municipality, as with all other municipalities in South Africa, is comprised of politicians (councillors) and officials. The relationship between the political and technical arms of the municipality is defined by the institutional structures of the local state. Officials present technical reports and policy to Council and politicians make decisions based on these proposals. This process of decision-making can be confusing to communities as they are often informed by councillors that the politicians make the decisions in the city, while at the same time they deal with officials on the ground, who are responsible for housing registrations and information and 'rules' about how relocations will take place.

Justifying the move

So how does knowledge and information travel between the state and its citizens and to what degree are decisions debated and negotiated at the ground level? In the case of relocations there is little negotiation between the local state and communities. In some informal settlements in the city, such as Kennedy Road in the inner city, the slum dwellers' movement *Abahlali baseMondjolo* has successfully challenged the decision of the municipality to relocate this settlement, using resistance and protest, insurgency and legal action to do so. However, these are exceptions.

In the case of Ocean Drive-In, residents had expressed the desire to remain on the site and have it upgraded as they valued its location. They knew that the move to Hammonds Farm would impact on their work opportunities as many of them walked to work in the nearby coastal zone, where they could obtain piecemeal jobs or where some of them worked permanently. Their children attended local schools and they benefited from the support they received from a private school immediately adjacent to the settlement, which sponsored the crèche in the settlement. They also knew that in their present location they were one of a few small informal settlements in a relatively wealthy coastal corridor. This meant less competition for the valuable resources that emerged through voluntary social giving and for employment. In Hammonds Farm they would be located in a large area of low-income housing, having to compete with much larger numbers of the urban poor for opportunities.

Residents were informed in 2009 by the councillor and the sub-ward committee that they would be relocated to Hammonds Farm, rather than having their site upgraded. According to one of the residents, they had been told this was because Ocean Drive-In was located on 'private land owned by a wealthy man that now lives in America' (Personal communication, June, 2012). Some residents had discussed this matter with the 'street level bureaucrats' that visited Ocean Drive-In from the municipality to update the housing registration process and to paint the housing numbers on the doors. They had informed the residents that they would be moving because the owner now wanted to sell his land for development associated with Dube TradePort. Officials in the Housing Department indicated that the settlement would be relocated because it was on private land in the high-income coastal corridor and that eThekwini Municipality did not want informal settlements located in this development zone.

The noise contour

However, a discussion with a senior housing official revealed that a noise contour of the new airport had been used to make the final decision to relocate Ocean Drive-In to Hammonds Farm. Decisions to relocate informal settlements are always intensely political and hence it is easier to make and implement these decisions when they are 'rendered technical'. The construction of the new airport had introduced a new 'line' to control development in the north of the city, the so-called 55 decibel (dB) noise contour. In July 2010, eThekwini Municipality issued a regulation based on the Record of Decision of the Environmental Impact Assessment for the King Shaka Airport, that no residential development would be permitted within the 55 dB noise contour of the airport. According to Sutherland, Sim and Scott (2015: 189):

> questions have been raised about the extent to which the 55 dB noise contour has become a convenient technical tool for controlling housing

development in the north of the city. This contour line, in precluding the original extent of land for housing, serves to open up more land for industrial and commercial development, which is not restricted by noise impacts.

The 55 dB contour had been used to defend the decision about relocating Ocean Drive-In, shifting it away from a political process of negotiation and participation, to one that was based on the 'rules of the game' of the airport EIA. Interestingly this information has not been communicated to residents of Ocean Drive-In, as they have no knowledge of the 55 dB noise contour. They have often raised the issue of the noise of aircrafts, the way they shake their shacks as they fly over to land, and their fear of aeroplanes crashing on their homes, but they have never been part of a discussion as to whether they wanted to trade-off the impacts of the airport against other important benefits they gain from living in Ocean Drive-In. These informal settlers were in fact living in this zone prior to the airport being built, and so technically the upgrade of the settlement should not be considered as a 'new residential development within the 55 dB noise contour'. And yet this is how the settlement has been constructed by the Housing Department in their decisions. What is important here is that this matter has never been discussed with the community and so they have been excluded from any debates about the validity of a noise contour in a city desperately needing land for housing. The noise contour has also impacted on the amount of land available for housing in the large-scale Cornubia housing project, which is now more about commercial land than housing (Sutherland *et al.* 2015).

In this case of relocation, the flow of knowledge has been controlled by the councillor and the officials so as to present a clear and uncontested reason for the 'move' to Hammonds Farm. A political decision had been rendered technical. The 55 dB noise contour has been used to deny other options being explored for the possible upgrading of Ocean Drive-In, thereby undermining the policy that informal upgrading should be prioritised over relocations in eThekwini Municipality. The value of the land, which is privately owned, and the economic development goals of the municipality in the northern corridor are no doubt the main reasons for relocating the settlement, but it is the noise contour that has been used to defend the decision. It is a technical concept that is being employed in the north of the city, as it reduces political contestation and negotiation on the ground, even though it is being debated and challenged by planners working in the municipality, based on its exclusionary principles.

Reference

Sutherland, C., Sim, V. and Scott, D. (2015) 'Contested discourses of a mixed-use megaproject: Cornubia, Durban'. *Habitat International*, *45*(3): 185–95.

Box 5.3 Contested knowledge – the pollution of the Yamuna river in Delhi as a cause for slum eviction

Véronique Dupont

In the decade after the turn of the millennium, massive demolition drives affected the squatter settlements located along the Yamuna river (Dupont 2008). The river flows across Delhi from north to south. In 2004 alone, 40,000 homes were demolished within a few months, with only a minority of the evicted families being resettled to distant relocation sites. Slum clearance was followed by dramatic transformations in the large riverbed and embankment zone. Transport infrastructure and redevelopment projects were further boosted by the preparation for the 2010 Commonwealth Games after Delhi won the bid to host this international sporting event in November 2003. However, the implementation of urban renewal projects was not the direct cause for most of these evictions. What prompted them were orders by the High Court of Delhi, in a Public Interest Litigation filed by a NGO, Wazirpur Bartan Nirmata Sangh, against the Union of India in order to remove squatters and encroachers from the public land. The Court used two main arguments to justify the removal of all slum clusters located along the river: first, that they constituted encroachment on the riverbed and, second, that they were polluting the river.

In its last order, dated 3 March, 2003, the Court observed:

> River Yamuna which is a major source of water has been polluted like never before. Yamuna Bed and both the sides of the river have been encroached by unscrupulous persons with the connivance of the authorities. Yamuna Bed as well as its embankment has to be cleared from such encroachments [. . .] Yamuna River has been polluted not only on account of dumping of waste, including medical waste as well as discharge of unhygienic material, but the Yamuna Bed and its embankment have been unauthorisedly and illegally encroached by construction of pucca [consolidated] house, jhuggies [huts] and places for religious worship, which cannot be permitted any more [. . .]
>
> In view of the encroachment and construction of jhuggies/pucca structure in the Yamuna Bed and its embankment with no drainage facility, sewerage water and other filth is discharged in Yamuna water. The citizens of Delhi are silent spectators of this state of affairs. No efforts have been made by the authorities to remove such unauthorised habitation from Yamuna Bed and its embankment.

Subsequently, the following order was passed:

> We, therefore, direct all the authorities concerned [. . .] as well the Central Government to forthwith remove all the unauthorised structures, jhuggies,

places of worship and/or any other structure which are unauthorisedly put in Yamuna Bed and its embankment within two months from today.[1]

The argument of unauthorised occupation of public land was, however, applied with discrimination: whereas the removal of the poor's habitation was expedited quickly and brutally, many other unauthorised constructions, which should have been also affected by the court order, were protected from demolition. This anti-poor bias was denounced by several activists and researchers (see, for example, Dewan Verma 2004, Bhan 2009, Ramanathan 2006). These voices pointed out the number of illegal structures already built or under construction in the same non-constructible zone, including the Secretariat of the Government of the Capital Territory of Delhi and the Metro Depot by the Delhi Metro Rail Corporation. These and other public projects started in violation of development and environmental laws, yet they eventually benefited from ad hoc regularisation in the revised Master Plan and Zonal Development Plan (DDA 2007 and 2008; see also Follman 2014).

As for the accusation that the slums were polluting the river, this was also challenged by several NGOs and human rights organisations. Thus, a Joint Urgent Action Appeal by two prominent NGOs,[2] underlined that this argument ignored available evidence from a report on pollution[3] that documented that the 300,000 residents living on the banks of Yamuna river 'accounted only for 0.33% of the total sewage released into the river' (OMCT/HIC-HLRN 2004: 2). Indeed, a study by the Central Pollution Control Board showed that the untreated domestic sewage discharged in the river was generated by the residents of planned and regularised colonies, not by those who live in slums and unauthorised settlements without sewage systems (Baviskar 2011). These criticisms implied that the decisions of the court were not supported by robust empirical evidence.

This court case exemplifies how, in the 2000s, slums were portrayed as a nuisance, and this 'new nuisance discourse' was used as 'the primary mechanism by which slum demolition [took] place' (Ghertner 2008) – in Delhi especially. It further illustrates a broader context of what Baviskar (2002) labels a 'bourgeois environmentalism' and 'its hostility to the poor in pursuit of a "clean and green" environment' (Baviskar 2011: 50). From this viewpoint, argues Baviskar, the presence of the poor becomes synonymous with pollution.

In this case, we also see two types of knowledge confronting each other. On the one hand, a popular form of knowledge, based on perception and prejudices that associate slum dwellers with unhygienic practices, and on the other hand a technical form of knowledge based on various statistical data. Paradoxically, it was the first one that was promoted by the judges in the court, hence acquiring an official, legitimate status. The second one had to be promoted by civil society organisations denouncing the evictions. This knowledge was not audible in the court, and hence not considered as legitimate. Through its validation by the court, the popular form of knowledge proved to be more powerful than that of experts, at the expense of vulnerable slum dwellers.

References

Baviskar, A. (2002) 'The politics of the city'. *Seminar* – 'Shades of Green: A symposium on the Changing Contours of Indian Environmentalism', 516(August): 40–2.

Baviskar, A. (2011) 'What the eye does not see: The Yamuna in the imagination of Delhi'. *Economic & Political Weekly*, *46*(50): 45–53.

Bhan, G. (2009) ' "This is no longer the city I once knew": Evictions, the urban poor and the right to the city in millennial Delhi'. *Environment & Urbanization*, *21*(1): 127–42.

DDA (2007) 'Master plan for Delhi 2021'. As Notified on 7 February, 2007. Vide S.O. No. 141 published in *Gazette of India* Extraordinary [Part II – Section 3 – Sub-Section (ii)]. Delhi: Delhi Development Authority.

DDA (2008) *Draft zonal development plan for River Yamuna/River front, Zone 'O'*. July 2008. Delhi: Delhi Development Authority.

Dewan Verma, G. (2004) 'Illegal I-T-Park on river bed'. Available from http://architexturez.net/doc/az-cf-22781 (accessed on 29 January, 2015).

Dupont V. (2008) 'Slum demolition in Delhi since the 1990s. An appraisal'. *Economic & Political Weekly*, *43*(28): 79–87.

Follman, A. (2014) 'Yamuna Urban mega-projects for a "world-class" riverfront – The interplay of informality, flexibility and exceptionality along the Yamuna in Delhi'. *Habitat International*, *45*(3): 213–22.

Ghertner, D.A. (2008) 'Analysis of new legal discourses behind Delhi's slum demolitions'. *Economic & Political Weekly*, *43*(20): 57–66.

Hazard Centre (2004) 'Yamuna Pollution and Prejudices', Hazard Centre Report No. 29. Delhi: Hazard Centre.

OMCT/HIC-HLRN (2004) 'Joint urgent action appeal. Over 300,000 people to be forcefully evicted from Yamuna Pushta in Delhi: 40,000 homes demolished so far'. Case IND-FE050504, 5 May 2004. Delhi, Geneva, Cairo: The Habitat International Coalition-Housing and Land Rights Network (HIC-HLRC) and the World Organisation against Torture (OMCT).

Ramanathan, U. (2006) 'Illegality and the urban poor'. *Economic & Political Weekly*, *41*(29): 3193–7.

'mapping exercises' stand in contrast to the story of Ocean Drive-In in Durban. Two factors stand out. First, due to the authorities' assessment of the unsuitability of the land, the residents' participation did not lead to an experienced change in their living situation, hence any expectations stemming from these initiatives were eventually unfulfilled. Second, rivalry between local leaders politicised the role of the enumeration and the community plans, circumscribing their influence.

Another experience to draw lessons from can be found in Vila Autódromo in Rio de Janeiro (see Settlement Story 4.4), where the alliance between residents and academics described above led to the formulation of a *Plano Popular*, a

'People's Plan', for upgrading the community. The plan was developed by the residents in various working groups. They were supported by a group of scholars and students from the two federal universities of the Rio region. They produced an integrated plan for housing upgrading, for sanitation/infrastructure and environment, for public services, and for the economic as well as cultural development of the community. The overall impression from our research is that attempts to generate community-based knowledge through knowledge alliances do hold potential, but are too often circumscribed by factors that they cannot control, and often cannot be sustained. In the next section, we will discuss these challenges in more detail.

Challenges to participatory knowledge practices

While the achievements of Slum Dwellers' International (SDI) and similar move-ments, such as Project Preparation Trust (PPT) in Durban, are considerable and have produced a series of constructive engagements with local authorities, they have a long way to go in changing the *modus operandi* of urban governance worldwide. Therefore, it comes as little surprise that our findings from the case settlements only show glimpses and isolated instances of inclusive knowledge management and participation. Moreover, the SDI model has itself received criticism for disciplining opposing views, 'co-opting community knowledge' and promoting co-operation with authorities at the expense of autonomy and self-determination (see Box 5.1). In the last part of this chapter, we employ an intentionally problem-oriented analysis of our case findings and identify a series of challenges to participatory knowledge practices.

Across the six cities discussed in this volume, we have studied many settlements that are identified as informal or illegal by their respective authorities. This status puts these settlements, and their residents, in a weak position in the face of powerful developers, investors and state authorities who might view the land on which they reside as valuable and strategic for urban development, or land uses other than housing. Even through many of the contested interventions claim to have various degrees of 'participation' in their decision-making, we found that in most cases affected communities experience these interventions as exclusionary. We highlight three critical dimensions that we have observed across the case studies, namely: retention of information, belated exchange of knowledge, and the ambiguous role of knowledge brokers.

Retention of information

While shared knowledge flows and the incorporation of different forms of knowledge has been highlighted as empowering (Baud *et al.* 2011, Kennedy *et al.* 2011), our findings more often depict blockages to these flows. It is worth reflecting on whether even the notion of flows, as well as the rather technical notion of 'incorporation', implies a fairly apolitical understanding of knowledge management.

Depending on the national and local contexts studied, transparency and the right to access information might be enshrined constitutionally or through other legal and contractual frameworks. Hence, various actors involved in an urban intervention might be formally obliged to share specific kinds of information. Still, they might choose to retain this knowledge to particular publics and might be able to maintain this practice due to their powerful, privileged position. This is the case in several of our studies, where allocation lists, spatial plans and time frames are deliberately kept away from the public. Sometimes, as evident in the Settlement story 4.5 from Lima, pretexts such as 'corporate confidentiality' can be used to legitimise secrecy, even with people whose lives are directly affected by interventions. Importantly, retention of information and deliberate exclusion of knowledge can also occur between elite actors, as shown in the case of the Tehkhand project in Delhi in Settlement story 4.1, as well as in Jacobs' (2013) study of the various contractors and public agencies involved in the N2 Gateway project in Cape Town.

Retention of information can have severe effects on the strategic possibilities of various actors, but those who stand with the most to lose are poor communities. First, it is very difficult to meaningfully engage in a process on which those affected have limited and insufficient information. Second, when information on selection and time frame is retained, it can fuel rumours and mistrust between people or increase insecurity. The experiences of the residents of the V.P. Singh Camp squatter settlement in the southern periphery of Delhi (see Settlement story 4.1), show how a project presented as a benchmark for consultative rehabilitation in fact left most slum dwellers unaware of the plans for the project, and the terms on which these poor residents were to be included. Another project presented in the same Settlement story, the Kathputli Colony rehabilitation project, depicts how local leaders in 2010 attempted to access a household survey conducted by the Delhi Development Authority, but had to go through repeated requests and appeals, and were not able to access this information for three years. Even after this, a final list of eligible households continued to be contested and kept away from the scrutiny of residents.

Interestingly, community actors might also be protective about their own knowledge. In fact, given the tendency of the formal governance and planning apparatus to incorporate community knowledge in ways that might be against the interests of local communities, local actors might choose to retain information from the hands of decision-makers. Skuse and Cousins (2007: 980) found this to be an active strategy among informal settlement residents in Nkanini in Cape Town:

> [T]hose staking a claim to informal urban space actively resist 'being known' or 'understood' by local authorities. 'Being known' is often viewed by residents of informal settlements and their community leaders as counterproductive to the promotion of coherent 'informal settlement discourses'. . .

This resonates with the settlement story from Ocean Drive-In in Durban, where residents were hiding the number on their front doors from government officials, as they feared these would be 'taken from them' and the new houses would be allocated to others. The case of Europe, Cape Town is another example of how factions in the community express reluctance to share information about their community. While proponents of the 'SDI model' argued that knowledge exchange could facilitate upgrading, their opponents fear that this would rather be used to their disadvantage, for instance as a basis for identifying shacks and extensions to be demolished.

Belated exchange of knowledge

When the timing is wrong, either deliberately or through particular circumstances, the sharing of knowledge fails to empower. In upgrading and resettlement processes, options and plans are often already meticulously defined by various 'experts' before any engagement occurs. What is left for residents is that they are included in consultation at a late stage in the process, if at all. This point was made very clearly by Piper (2012) in his review of an upgrading project in Cape Town. The Violence Prevention through Urban Upgrading (VPUU) programme had been widely touted as a democratic and participatory success by city authorities. However, Piper argues that it was only in the implementation phase that VPUU has allowed for participation from ordinary residents. The failure to include community knowledge in the planning phases of housing 'mega-projects' in Salvador, Brazil and in Durban and Cape Town, South Africa has also been documented in three separate studies (Somers 2012, Jacobs 2013, Sutherland, Sim and Scott 2015). Similarly, in the above-mentioned Kathputli Colony rehabilitation project in Delhi, residents were not involved in the conception and design of the project, but only informed afterwards. This is also mirrored in Settlement story 4.5, where residents facing relocation in preparation for the grandiose Línea Amarilla/Vía Parque Rímac project in Lima were not consulted in the planning stages, and were only allowed token consultation thanks to a shift in the political administration.

In other words, the timing of knowledge-sharing practices has bearings on the level of participation. The degree of participation can be arranged along a continuum from substantial delegation of decision-making power to outright manipulation under the guise of participation (cf. Arnstein 1969). In such a continuum, mere consultation with excluded groups, typically only once during a process, 'prevents the possibility that investigation and action over time may lead to a change in the knowledge of people themselves' (Gaventa and Cornwall 2006: 127). Similarly, inclusion of community knowledge in the late stages of implementation tends to be experienced as token participation or 'rubber stamping' by local communities. From the outset, it is likely that project managers, city officials, community leadership and ordinary residents have quite different views of what 'participation' means. When such buzzwords are used uncritically, false expectations and a sense of disappointment are likely to develop among community members who thought their views would shape decision-making in the upgrading of their settlements.

One reason why politicians and project managers might be reluctant to embark on truly participatory processes to harness local knowledge is that they are time-consuming, messy and unpredictable – like democracy in its essence. Van Donk (2011: 18) captures this well when she states that

> local communities may be consulted, as legislation necessitates, but they are not routinely equipped with relevant information and insights to participate in a negotiated process of determining priorities and trade-offs.

As the settlement stories illustrate, when participation is limited, it tends to trigger resistance and tension, threatening to delay any ambition of speedy implementation. In fact, the lack of information and consultation is identified as the main cause for resistance in several of our case studies. This serves to show how fast-track alternatives to 'meaningful participation' are not necessarily quicker options, at least not without the use of force and authoritarian state repression.

The ambiguous role of local knowledge brokers

Through our research, we were made aware of how power asymmetries are not only manifest in the relationship between local communities and the state. They are also evident within community formations, in particular during external interventions. As we have stated in the section on knowledge alliances above, expert actors and organisations might play an important role in bridging community experiences and legal or technical knowledge. We use the term 'knowledge brokers' to encapsulate the role of these actors (a term originally used in management studies, see Hargadon 1998, but brought into the development discourse by the World Bank). By being knowledge brokers, NGOs and academics both translate and legitimise different forms of knowledge in communication with different groups. But these knowledge brokers in turn draw heavily on selected community representatives who are chosen to engage with external 'expert communities', while at the same time being seen as legitimate representatives of the community.

These individuals (or 'local knowledge brokers') become privileged knowledge bearers. For instance, during the planning stages of a project, local knowledge brokers are typically informed about what is possible from an engineering or planning point of view. The same individuals will also learn who the powerful gatekeepers in government are, and what language is understood by the decision-makers. They also know how to access critical information, and with this knowledge comes power. Once they are informed about plans and lists, the knowledge brokers possess the power to selectively and strategically share this knowledge with the community, or with chosen individuals. They also have the power to retain information from fellow community members.

This was the case in the Joe Slovo informal settlement in Cape Town (see Settlement Story 6.3). In 2006, a Task Team was elected to be responsible for the community's involvement in the large-scale housing project, N2 Gateway.

This group has since held an increasing influence on knowledge exchange between project management and the community. While many residents feel that they are well represented by the Task Team, these tend to be those individuals who have been allocated houses in the new development. For some of the so-called 'non-beneficiaries', who have not been deemed eligible, the Task Team is not seen as representative in the same way. Moreover, residents we interviewed expressed distrust towards the ability of the Task Team to share knowledge and relevant information. Once the development and the allocation of houses started taking place, these residents claimed that the exchange of knowledge became reliant on clientelist networks. As is explained in Settlement story 6.3, the Task Team's role has triggered resistance from other organisations claiming to represent the community, and from women who felt excluded from representation in the Task Team.

The case of the Kathputli Colony in Settlement story 4.1 is another tale of local knowledge brokers, as one NGO assumed a key position in communicating with authorities, private contractors and community members. When many settlement residents, and a rival NGO that was also based in the settlement, felt that this NGO did not sufficiently represent the population of Kathputli Colony, it became clear that the consultation process between authorities and the different groups in Kathputli Colony was hampered by a bias. As alluded to above, it is impossible to discuss community participation without simultaneously considering the concept of representation. This is because not even in the most democratic, participatory processes is everybody involved in every stage of decision-making. There is always somebody who speaks *on behalf of* somebody else. By inviting communities into a participatory process, there might be formally elected leaders, traditional leaders, informal authorities, political movements and a rich associational life that might claim to represent the community. Once some actors are entrusted responsibility for co-ordinating community responses, relaying messages and distributing information and resources, power dynamics in local communities are irrevocably changed. In Piper's (2012) study of the VPUU, he argues that this might in fact be a good thing, as responsibility for upgrading is shifted from rent-seeking local politicians to community representatives that are trained through the project (he labels them 'development trustees'). In other cases, however, people who had questionable legitimacy in the community in the first place might become even more illegitimate in the eyes of the local community, as they are perceived to misuse the information and resources with which they have been entrusted.

Conclusion

By juxtaposing a growing literature on knowledge in urban politics with our empirical research material, we believe this chapter has bolstered the assertion that upgrading and relocation of informal settlements across the urban South represents a contested politics of knowledge. To analyse our settlement stories, we have also been compelled to work through the various definitions of knowledge existing in the literature. In the settlement stories of Chapter 4, we have not approached knowledge as a thing that can be owned by particular actors. Rather, in the upgrading, rehabilitation and resettlement projects presented here knowledge is always subject to power relations, and what is worth knowing depends on who you are and what your agenda is. Upgrading and relocation initiatives bring local residents, their representatives and various professional experts into contested engagements where the flow of knowledge, the credibility of different forms of knowledge, and the ownership of knowledge emerge as particularly challenging issues. In some of the cases, the bone of contention has been the retention of information, either from formal authorities or knowledge brokers in the community. In others, certain technical judgements have been challenged, or seemingly apolitical justifications have been sought to be re-politicised. Fischer's notion of appropriate knowledge is useful here, we argue, as the interventions at the heart of these contested politics quite often represent technical solutions to urbanisation and urban sustainability at a metropolitan scale, but are lacking in credibility among citizens directly affected by them. Hence, to a certain degree, appropriate knowledge equals locally embedded knowledge that actively draws on the participation of people whose lived experience is based in the communities and areas targeted for intervention.

This being said, our case studies have also served to problematise a naïve notion of community knowledge and participation sometimes visible in academic studies and policy documents. Rather than treating community knowledge and scientific knowledge as separate forms of ideal-types, these knowledges overlap in reality. When and if the knowledge of affected communities is incorporated in planning processes, it is often subjected to the power of experts or disciplined in the 'invited spaces' (see Chapter 7, p. 196 for a discussion) of state authorities and developers. Moreover, as the communities themselves are often fragmented there is no such thing as a neatly defined 'community' whose knowledge can be included. Our research has also shown how the fragmentation of communities can be directly related to the way in which knowledge is shared in development interventions.

Both encouragement and notes of caution can be drawn from the cases presented. Most importantly, exchanges of community knowledge and expert knowledge require a level of trust that can only be achieved through long-standing meaningful engagements with the people concerned. This trust cannot emerge if affected residents experience the retention of information, or unacceptable delays in knowledge exchange, or if the role of local knowledge brokers is seen as not having legitimacy. The establishment of alternative sites of knowledge generation, for instance through community-mapping, can help to rebuild trust. But even such engagements carry their own risks, as our cases have shown. By way of conclusion, we uphold that while participatory approaches hold great potential in creating social inclusion in urban informal areas across the global South, knowledge exchange *in itself* is not the solution to empowering marginalised communities. Attempts to redress knowledge inequalities will remain flawed as long as power imbalances remain neglected. Transparency in knowledge flows must be accompanied by community mobilisation if marginalised citizens are to have a meaningful say in processes that affect them.

Notes

1   High Court of Delhi, *Wazirpur Bartan Nirmata Sangh* versus Union of India (CWP 2112/2002), 3 March, 2003.
2   The Habitat International Coalition-Housing and Land Rights Network (HIC-HLRC) and the World Organisation against Torture (OMCT).
3   The report was written by the Hazard Centre (2004), an NGO working on urban issues, such as land and housing.

References

Arnstein, S.R. (1969) 'A ladder of citizen participation'. *Journal of the American Institute of Planners*, 35(4): 216–24.
Arputham, J. (2012) 'How community-based enumerations started and developed in India'. *Environment & Urbanization*, 24(1): 27–30.
Baud, I., Pfeffer, K., Sydenstricker-Neto, J. and Scott, D. (2011) 'Developing participatory "spatial" knowledge models in metropolitan governance networks for sustainable development'. Chance2Sustain Literature Review, March 2011. Bonn: EADI: 1–19.
Beck, U. (1992) *Risk society: Towards a new modernity*. London: Sage.
Braathen, E., Attwood, H., and May, K. (2012) 'The role of politics in telecentres: Cases from South Africa'. *International Journal of E-Politics*, 3(3): 1–20.
Bruckmeier, K. and Tovey, H. (2008) 'Knowledge in sustainable rural development: From forms of knowledge to knowledge processes'. *Sociologia Ruralis*, 48(3): 313–29.
Corburn, J. (2003) 'Bringing local knowledge into environmental decision making: Improving urban planning for communities at risk'. *Journal of Planning Education & Research*, 22: 420–33.
Dahl, R. (1957) 'The concept of power'. *Behavioral Science*, 20: 201–15.
Epstein, S. (1996) *Impure science: AIDS, activism, and the politics of knowledge*. Berkeley (CA): University of California Press.
Fischer, F. (2000) *Citizens, experts and the environment: The politics of local knowledge*. Durham (NC): Duke University Press.
Foucault, M. (1980) *Power/knowledge: Selected interviews and other writings 1972–1977*. Brighton: Harvester Press.
Foucault, M. (1982) 'The subject and power'. In H.L. Dreyfus and P. Rabinow (eds) *Michel Foucault: Beyond structuralism and hermeneutics*. Brighton: Harvester Press, pp. 208–26.
Gaventa, J., and Cornwall, A. (2006) 'Challenging the boundaries of the possible: Participation, knowledge and power'. *IDS Bulletin*, 37(6): 122–8.
Geertz, C. (1983) *Local knowledge: Further essays in interpretive anthropology* (Vol. 5110, third edn). New York: Basic Books.
Haraway, D. (1988) 'Situated knowledges: The science question in feminism and the privilege of partial perspective'. *Feminist Studies*, 14(3): 575–99.
Hargadon, A. (1998) 'Firms as knowledge brokers'. *California Management Review*, 40(3): 209–27.
Huchzermeyer, M. (2011) *Cities with 'slums': From informal settlement eradication to a right to the city in Africa*. Claremont, SA: University of Cape Town Press.
Jacobs, F. (2013) 'The challenge of housing the poor: Stakeholders, politics and knowledge use in decision-making processes for the N2 Gateway Housing Project in Cape Town'. Unpublished master's thesis, Master of International Development Studies, University of Amsterdam: 1–93.

Kennedy, L., Robbins, G., Scott, D., Sutherland, C., Denis, E., Andrade, J., Miranda, L., Varrel, A., Dupont, V. and Bon, B. (2011) 'The politics of large-scale economic and infrastructure projects in fast-growing cities of the South'. Chance2Sustain Literature Review, March 2011. Bonn: EADI: 1–23.

Leach, M. and Scoones, I. (2007) 'Mobilising citizens: Social movements and the politics of knowledge'. IDS Working Paper, 276: 1–37.

Lidskog, R. and Elander, I. (2007) 'Representation, participation or deliberation? Democratic responses to the environmental challenge'. *Space & Polity*, 11(1): 75–94.

Lindblom, C. and Cohen, D. (1979) *Usable knowledge: Social science and social problem solving*. New Haven (CT): Yale University Press.

Lukes, S. (1974) *Power: A radical view*. London: Macmillan.

MacKinnon, D. and Derickson, K.D. (2013) 'From resilience to resourcefulness A critique of resilience policy and activism'. *Progress in Human Geography*, 37(2): 253–70.

McFarlane, C. (2006) 'Knowledge, learning and development: A post-rationalist approach'. *Progress in Development Studies*, 6(4): 287–305.

Mosse, D. (1994) 'Authority, gender and knowledge: Theoretical reflections on the practice of participatory rural appraisal'. *Development & Change*, 25: 497–526.

Patel, S. and Baptist, C. (2012) 'Editorial: Documenting by the undocumented'. *Environment & Urbanization*, 24(1): 3–12.

Patel, S., Baptist, C. and d'Cruz, C. (2012) 'Knowledge is power: Informal communities assert their right to the city through SDI and community-led enumerations'. *Environment & Urbanization*, 24(1): 13–26.

Pfeffer, K., Baud, I., Denis, E., Scott, D. and Sydenstricker-Neto, J. (2012) 'Participatory spatial knowledge management tools'. *Information, Communication & Society*, 16(2): 258–85.

Piper, L. (2012) 'Development trustees, not rent-seeking deployees: The designed meaning of community upgrading in the Violence Through Urban Upgrading Project, Cape Town'. African Centre for Citizenship and Democracy Working Paper 11: 1–22.

Roy, A. (2005) 'Urban informality: Toward an epistemology of planning'. *Journal of the American Planning Association*, 71(2): 147–58.

Scoones, I. (2005) 'Contentious politics, contentious knowledges: Mobilising against GM crops in India, South Africa and Brazil'. IDS Working Paper, 256: 1–52.

Scott, D. and Barnett, C. (2009) 'Something in the air: Civic science and contentious environmental politics in post-apartheid South Africa'. *Geoforum*, 40(3): 373–82.

Skuse, A. and Cousins, T. (2007) 'Spaces of resistance: Informal settlement, communication and community organisation in a Cape Town township'. *Urban Studies*, 44: 979–94.

Somers, K. (2012) 'My house, my life: Decision-making processes and local citizen participation in housing project Minha casa, Minha vida in Salvador da Bahia'. Unpublished master's thesis, Master of International Development Studies, University of Amsterdam: 1–81.

Sutherland, C., Sim, V. and Scott, D. (2015) 'Contested discourses of a mixed-use megaproject: Cornubia, Durban'. *Habitat International*, 45: 185–95.

Van Donk, M. (2011) 'Tackling the "governance deficit" to reinvigorate participatory local governance. Putting participation at the heart of development – Putting development at the heart of participation'. Cape Town GGLN and Isandla Institute Working Paper: 10–27.

Van Ewijk, E. and I. Baud (2009) 'Partnerships between Dutch municipalities and municipalities in countries of migration to the Netherlands: Knowledge exchange and mutuality'. *Habitat International*, 33(2): 218–26.

6   Settlement stories II
Communities' responses

Settlement story 6.1 Ups and downs in Rio de Janeiro: the changing phases of mobilisation in Morro da Providência

EINAR BRAATHEN[1]

Morro da Providência is the first settlement in Brazil called *favela*. It is a self-built informal settlement dating back to 1893 (Gonçalves 2010). The *favela* has been affected by the large urban renewal programme for the old port area of the city, *Porto Maravilha*, which is linked to the development plans for the 2016 Olympic Games. The *favela* took a direct part in a grand upgrading programme for the *favelas* of Rio de Janeiro, *Morar Carioca*. These and other public interventions have recently provoked social mobilisation among the residents.

Social and political background

The *favela* is located along the slopes close to the old port area, in the central part and historical downtown of the city of Rio de Janeiro. According to Brazil's 2010 census its population was 3,777, of which 28 per cent were categorised as extremely poor (living in households with income less than half of the minimum wage). The *favela* is supplied by water and electricity, but there is no public sanitation system. The average school attendance was six years. In the early stages of the settlement the majority of the residents were afro-descendant, while in recent times the majority has origins in the North East of Brazil.

In 1968 a neighbourhood association, *Associação de Moradores*, was created in Morro da Providência. Through collective efforts the residents supported victims of a landslide (1968) that killed fifty-eight persons. The association paved access paths (1970) and connected houses to a water reservoir (1974). Methodist Church missionaries from the USA assisted in these and other collective self-help activities. Ever after the 1968 landslide the public authorities have considered most of Morro da Providência a 'risk area' (vulnerable to natural disasters), and relocation of the community has become a public policy issue. The democratisation process in the 1980s created politicians who, for electoral reasons, pledged urban upgrading instead of demolition of the *favelas*. Therefore, close links were established between the elected politicians (governor and mayor) and the leaders of the neighbourhood association who managed to attract public funds and projects to the community.

Rio's power supply company came and brought electricity connection to the houses. The *Favela-Bairro* project, co-ordinated by the Municipal Board of Housing (SMH) and funded by the Inter-American Development Bank (IDB), started in 1994 and aimed to implement urban infrastructure, services, public facilities and social policies in the communities. In 2007, another upgrading project (*Cimento Social*) was introduced, patronised by one of the city's federal senators. Due to these efforts, the *favela* reached a relatively decent level of urban infrastructure services. However, the price was to be paid on election day. Clientelist politics had captured the *favela*. Self-help and self-organising capacities were devalued. At the same time drug traffic was on the rise, partially compensating for the increasing unemployment, particularly among young men. Drug traffickers controlled the economic, social and even political life of the community, including the neighbourhood association.

Nonetheless, an era of periodic social (re)mobilisation – and social-political transformation – was soon to emerge. Two issues triggered the social mobilisation: security and urban renewal.

Lack of security: constant source of mobilisation and demobilisation

In 2008 the 'war on drug trafficking', declared by the governor of the state of Rio de Janeiro (Sérgio Cabral) and supported by the federal government, reached the community. A special battalion from the Brazilian Armed Forces was deployed to bring peace and order to Morro da Providência.[2] Three boys from the community were killed by a rival drug trafficking faction after they had been handed over by the military intervention force. The community protested against this unlawful way of securing 'law and order' (Bautès, Dupont and Landy 2014).

In 2010 a unit from the new community policing programme of the state, UPP (*Unidade de Policia Pacificadora*), was installed in the *favela*. This event paved the way for a string of public works. There were hopes that UPP could wipe out, in co-operation with the community itself, the power of the drug-trafficking gangs. The drug barons had taken control of the dilapidated port zone and many *favelas* elsewhere in Rio ever since the 1980s, when the economic and employment crisis took its toll on Brazil. The drug barons offered to some extent both protection and social assistance to the community. The neighbourhood association in Morro da Providência became a dead duck, and independent social mobilisation was quelled, partly because the gangs were connected with the political rulers of the city.

Unfortunately, UPP's success was only partial. In March 2013, the Public Prosecutor of Rio ordered the arrest of twenty-one UPP policemen in Morro da Providência, who were suspected of having connections with traffickers. In addition, twenty-five alleged traffickers were arrested. In June 2013 the chief of the drug traffic in Morro da Providência was shot dead in a confrontation with the cleansed UPP police. Other traffickers then imposed a mourning period in the community, forcing all stores to remain shut inside and around Morro da Providência. Those who did open their stores reported to have received a visit from two traffickers who threatened to burn their stores down if they refused to follow orders. As these incidents show, the drug trafficking continued to operate in the community and weakened its voice and capacity for social mobilisation.

Mobilisation against 'marvellous' urban renewal

After 2010 the residents of Morro da Providência faced the combined impacts of two major urban development programmes. First, there was the urban renewal programme for the port area, *Porto Maravilha* (Marvellous Port). Based on private–public partnership, its mandate was to convert the port area into a fancy waterfront recreation area and a media centre for the 2016 Olympic Games. Second, there was the cross-city programme to upgrade the *favelas*, *Morar Carioca*. Through participatory on-site *favela* upgrading and with a budget of almost USD 4 billion (BRL 8 billion), the programme pledged to integrate every *favela* into the formal city by the year 2020 (Steiker-Ginzberg 2014). It was to become the lasting 'social legacy' of the 2016 Olympic Games. The large-scale works would include the improvement of sanitation systems, installation of water drainage systems, street lighting, road surfacing, the construction of public green spaces and recreational areas, improvement of transportation networks, and the construction of social service centres.

The *favela* 'renewal' plan was presented ready-made to the community in January 2011, however, without any prior consultation or participatory process. The residents, therefore, organised several spontaneous protests, for example raising banners and posters with hand-written messages to the municipal secretary when he addressed a public information meeting in the *favela*. Their rage was directed against the priorities and contents of the programmes, in particular the plan to build a huge station for a cable-car network and a funicular. These works would occupy the main public spaces in the *favela*, and dozens of houses had to be demolished to give space to the new public installations. The critique escalated when hundreds of houses had suddenly been numbered, literally speaking; the municipality had painted a number on houses it claimed were part of a 'mapping' of dwellings located in 'risk areas'. The municipality later on admitted that 832 houses were to be demolished – nearly half of the homes in the *favela*.

A residents' action committee was swiftly organised. The activists feared that the municipality had embarked on a project for the beautification and gentrification of the *favela* – or 'social cleansing' as they saw it. They did not want the *favela* to become a tourist resort, *para inglês ver*, 'for the British to see' as they put it, with a popular Portuguese metaphor.

In the heated debate in 2011 the neighbourhood association distinguished itself by its total silence, for reasons mentioned above. The residents' committee therefore sought support from a wider network established to fight *Porto Maravilha*, the plan for the old port area. The cable car was supposed to link the central train/metro station and the renewed 'marvellous' port, with one station on the way – in Morro da Providência with a terrific view. The wider resistance network was called *Foro Comunitario do Porto*, Community Forum of the Port. It was initiated by cultural activists centred on a cultural heritage site called *Quilombo da Pedra do Sal*, Rio's first community of runaway slaves and the cradle of the Rio-type samba. The Community Forum was also supported by urban human rights activists, progressive NGOs who fought for 'the right to the city', and city councillors belonging to the left and green opposition parties. A partisan politicisation of the struggle was in the air. However, the forum's activists managed to avoid that by turning to the Public Defenders Office (the ombudsman) of the State of Rio de Janeiro. A more technical and judicial type of struggle took the upper hand.

Judicial and technical battles

In mid-2012, the public works started without the residents' consensus. Henceforth, the residents were helped by the Public Defenders to file a case against the municipality, accusing it of neglecting the residents' constitutional rights – mainly the right to housing and of popular participation in urban planning. Other more specific laws had been flawed as well, e.g., the right to information about the necessity of demolishing one's home, and the right to adequate resettlement in a nearby area.

Initially, the municipality stated that families had to be displaced because of environmental risks. The residents themselves, however, hired engineers and independent experts, who provided a counter-report proving that the vast majority of the houses in Morro da Providência were *not* in areas of landslide or other risks. To handle disagreements, a joint mediation commission was set up by the residents and the city government alike, on the initiative of the Municipal Council of Housing where half of the members are civil society representatives. By late 2012, the number of families threatened by displacement was reduced to 671, of which 475 had still not agreed to leave (Antunes 2013).

Moreover, a victory for the co-operation between the residents and their outside supporters was celebrated in December 2012. The residents of Providência obtained an injunction, granted by the Judge Maria Teresa Bridges Gazineu, who suspended the works of *Morar Carioca* in Morro da Providência due to the lack of fulfilment of public audience requirements before the construction began. Only the construction of the cable car could proceed (Antunes 2013). The injunction entailed a momentary relief to the residents that were threatened with displacement.

The municipality's strategic shift

In hindsight one can see that the injunction coincided with a shift in the overall development strategy of the city. This shift took place after the Mayor, Eduardo Paes, was safely re-elected in October 2012 with promises of delivering the houses of the *Morar Carioca* programme. The city management realised that they had to prioritise the Olympic Games in 2016 and the required infrastructure projects. The construction of the cable car across Morro da Providência was among the priorities. The large-scale housing and social investments of *Morar Carioca* were no longer a priority.

The municipality could therefore take a more flexible approach to the 475 families who had refused to leave their houses. The Municipal Secretary of Housing insisted that the works were progressing 'in rhythm' with the negotiations and that 'there is no pressure, there is dialogue'. On the other hand, we could observe municipal agents arranging meetings in small groups in an attempt to persuade residents who were not aware of the court proceedings, and who lived near the public work sites, to sign up for replacement housing. Moreover, the municipality did not follow up its earlier pledges to open a process of participatory dialogue with the community, recommended by the Brazilian Institute of Architects (IAB). In January 2013 the municipality cancelled a contract with a progressive NGO, iBase, supposed to facilitate the dialogue process. In addition the municipality launched a judicial offensive: it appealed the injunction decision and brought the matter to the Civil Chamber of the Court of Rio de Janeiro. Morro da Providência was again hit by frustration and social demobilisation.

However, the street demonstrations in June 2013 – the largest ever in Brazil's history (see also Box 7.2 by Braathen) – changed the mood completely in Morro da Providência.

After June 2013: The echo of 'the voice of the street'

The demonstrations started in São Paulo as claims for free public transport. In the social media, cell-phone cameras showed the police using excessive force against the demonstrators. Then was the kick-off of the Confederations Cup in football, the rehearsal of the FIFA World Cup 2014. Hundreds of thousands of people filled the streets, claiming not only cheaper and higher quality public transport, but also improved public services in general, end to police violence, eradication of corruption, inquiries into the excessive costs of the stadiums built for the football tournament, and last but not least a moratorium on forced evictions in the wake of the public works for the mega-sport events. 'The voice of the street' became a key reference point in the public debate in Rio de Janeiro and Brazil for the next six months or so.

A new generation of activists were networked in the various mobilisations dominating Rio de Janeiro for the rest of 2013. In the old port area, they met in weekly assemblies and in August organised a local march starting from a building squatted by young anarchists and ending in Morro da Providência. People in the Community Forum of the Port were more than willing to hand over the leadership of the struggle to younger community activists, who also participated in all-city networks such as the city-wide People's Committee of the World Cup and the Olympics, *Comité Popular da Copa e das Olimpíadas*.

On 28 August, 2013, the sixth Civil Chamber of the Court of Rio de Janeiro considered the appeal put forward by the municipality. The court upheld the decision to freeze the *Morar Carioca* works. The city was authorised to continue the work on the cable car only, for which a station had already been built. Following the court decision, and not least the street demonstrations, the mayor sent his right-hand advisor to the community of Morro da Providência and offered talks to reach a consensus about the upgrading of the *favela*. By the end of 2013, this consensus was still an unfinished process. However, the community's activists were more self-reliant and participated in all-city networks of *favela* activists not seen in Rio de Janeiro since the democratisation years of the 1980s.

2014: *The People's Cup out-manoeuvred*

In the run-up to the FIFA World Cup in June and July 2014, the Residents' Committee of Morro da Providência participated in *Copa Popular*, a people's football cup organised by communities threatened to be displaced for the sake of the mega-sport events. By June 2014, twenty-nine communities and 4,772 families had been displaced in Rio de Janeiro due to World Cup or Olympics-related development projects. 4,916 other families from sixteen communities were at risk of eviction, according to the Comitê Popular (2014).

On 2 July, 2014, while Brazil was still optimistic about its chances to become the world champions in football, Mayor Paes and Governor Pezão opened the cable car of Morro da Providência. 'Today we are not only gaining an urban mobility service for the residents, but we are also gaining a new touristic service for the city', the Mayor pointed out. This and other events during the World Cup were heavily policed. Attempts by protest demonstrations were promptly dissolved by force.

Of the almost USD 90 million (BRL 163 million) invested in Providência, the cable car accounted for nearly half the spending at BRL 75 million. The remaining was mainly spent on compensation homes for the displaced families. Almost nothing was left for community upgrading, such as improvement of sanitation systems, installation of water drainage systems, and the construction of public green spaces and recreational areas (Steiker-Ginzberg 2014). A wide array of legal requirements, above all those of participatory planning and decision-making, were ignored without consequences for city rulers.

By way of a conclusion, we have observed that the struggle in Morro da Providência led to a partial victory for the residents – a strongly reduced number of evictions. But they were not able to stop a prestige project of the municipality – the cable-car system. The social mobilisation against the municipality involved a gradually smaller portion of the settlement. Demobilisation has been a chronic aspect due to the legacy of clientelism and drug barons. Yet, with time, the mobilisation of a community minority became more intensive and was part of city-wide mobilisations, thus more politicised. Support from activists and civil society organisations outside the *favela* compensated for the indifference shown by those *favela* dwellers who did not feel direct threats from the municipal interventions. The linking-up with technical and juridical counter-expertise – even based in the state apparatus such as public universities and Public Defenders (ombudsman) – has been important. Protests and street demonstrations have been followed by engagement and dialogue.

The mobilisations evolved through three stages, each with its ups and downs (signs of demobilisation): first, a very localised and spontaneous struggle against the top-down intervention of the municipal urban upgrading programme, *Morar Carioca*; second, as part of the Community Forum of the Port mobilisation against the mega-project linked to the Olympic Games, *Porto Maravilha*; third, as part of city-wide and national demonstrations for improved public services and substantive citizenship in the wake of the mega-sport events. The people's social mobilisation had to give way to the government-FIFA World Cup mobilisation. Nonetheless, there are strong indications that social movements centred on housing issues will re-emerge as powerful actors in Brazilian urban politics.

References

Antunes, C. (2013) 'Os Descontentes do Porto'. Revista Piauí, 76, January 2013. Available from http://revistapiaui.estadao.com.br/edicao-76/questoes-de-politica-urbana/os-descontentes-do-porto (accessed on 2 October, 2014).

Bautès N., Dupont, V. and Landy, F. (2014) 'Acting from the slums. Questioning social mobilization and resistance movements'. In F. Landy and M.-C. Saglio-Yatzimirsky (eds) *Megacity slums. Social exclusion, urban space and policies in Brazil and India.* London: Imperial College Press, pp. 363–407.

Braathen, E., Sørbøe, C. M., Bartholl, T., Christovão, A.C. and Pinheiro, V. (2013) *Rio de Janeiro: Favela policies and recent social mobilizations.* NIBR-Working Paper 2013: 110. Oslo: Norwegian Institute for Urban and Regional Research.

Comitê Popular (2014) *Megaeventos e Violações dos Direitos Humanos no Rio de Janeiro.* Rio de Janeiro: Comitê Popular da Copa e Olimpíadas, June 2014. Available from https://comitepopulario.files.wordpress.com/2014/06/dossiecomiterio2014_web.pdf (accessed on 12 January, 2015).

Gonçalves, R.S. (2010) *Les favelas de Rio de Janeiro – histoire et droit, XIXe et XXe siècles.* Paris: L'Harmattan.

Machado da Silva, L.A. (2008) *Vida Sob Cerco. Violência e Rotina nas Favelas do Rio de Janeiro.* Rio de Janeiro: Nova Fronteira.

Steiker-Ginzberg, K. (2014) 'Morar Carioca: The dismantling of a dream favela upgrading program'. Available from www.rioonwatch.org/?p=17687. Published on 10 September, 2014, accessed on October 2, 2014.

Settlement story 6.2 The trajectories of social mobilisation in two informal settlements in Durban

CATHERINE SUTHERLAND

Social mobilisation around the right to adequate housing follows many different trajectories in Durban,[3] from intense social protests to the mundane, everyday forms of resistance that the poor engage in to secure their 'right' to the city. It is fragmented, localised and sporadic, assuming many different forms. The 'leadership' in different settlements mobilise their citizens differently, as a result of each settlements' typology, context and history and the varying practices and responses of the state in each setting.

Social mobilisation in Durban takes place within a relatively stable political context as the three tiers of government (national, provincial and local), which exercise power over the municipality, are led by the African National Congress (ANC). This political alignment increases the power of the local state, influencing its response to social movements. Since 2005, *Abahlali baseMjondolo* (AbM), a radical national social movement that emerged from the Kennedy Road informal settlement in Durban, has challenged the state's policy of 'slum elimination'. It has used powerful social protests and the slogan of 'no house, no vote' to shift the practices of the state. Its most significant legacy is the legal action that it has employed to secure broader rights to housing. However, AbM also engages with the state. Negotiations between the shack dwellers' movement and the eThekwini Municipality in 2009 led to the signing of an agreement that three informal settlements would be upgraded in-situ and that a further fourteen settlements would obtain basic services in line with the principles of the 2004 Breaking New Ground Policy. There has been a significant increase in social protests around housing in Durban since January 2013, revealing the political struggles over the right to housing in the municipality and the increasing tension between AbM and the ANC-led local government over housing provision.

Two informal settlements in Durban, one in the north of the city on the urban edge known as Ocean Drive-In, and another Cato Crest, which is located in the central area of the city, are used here as lenses to explore social mobilisation in response to relocation projects in the municipality.

Ocean Drive-In informal settlement

Ocean Drive-In informal settlement has been in existence for over thirty-two years. It is located on private land in the north of the city, in close proximity to the Dube TradePort mega-project, which includes the new King Shaka Airport. In 2012 Ocean Drive-In was home to 1,420 people who lived in 796 houses, many of whom participated in the circulatory migrant labour system of South Africa (Posel and Marx 2013). The settlement has a long history of social mobilisation, from Mama Shabalala and her women's committee marching to the Tongaat Town Council in the 1990s to protest against the lack of water in the settlement, to darker moments when the Inkatha Freedom Party (IFP) leader of the settlement and his family were burnt to death in their shack in 1985. Here the ANC members in the settlement mobilised and took control of the settlement as part of the political violence that spread across South Africa in the late 1980s, just prior to the end of apartheid.

Ocean Drive-In is one of five smaller informal settlements along the wealthy coastal zone, and hence community members have good access to a wide range of employment and social network opportunities. Up until November 2012, the sub-ward committee, which reports to the ward committee and the councillor of Ward 58, was the main political and social organisation within the settlement.

The relationship between community members and the local state is defined and controlled by the ward councillor. An independent committee was established in Ocean Drive-In in 2012 by those who believed that their views were not being represented by the ANC dominated sub-ward committee and the ANC councillor in municipal meetings. The policing committee also has a strong influence on the community, dealing internally with issues of conflict and crime.

Ocean Drive-In residents initially believed that their settlement would be upgraded. However, in 2009 they were informed by the municipality that they would be relocated to a formal low-income housing project, Hammonds Farm, 16 km inland of Ocean Drive-In. As a result of this impending relocation, services and facilities in the settlement were not upgraded and community members stopped investing in upgrading their homes. The delays and uncertainty around the relocation process resulted in a number of different forms of social mobilisation. The informal settlement had become a 'community-in-waiting', resulting in tension between the community, the ANC ward councillor and the municipality. The community mobilised themselves in different ways in response to the relocation process, which had been imposed on them by the Housing Department of the municipality.

Resistance

Quiet resistance is most strongly evident in the mundane and everyday practices of informal settlers as they struggle to secure their right to the city. Quietness is not, however, exclusive of creativity. For example, elderly people covered the doors to their houses with blankets on the day a community mapping process started when researchers from the Chance2Sustain project were recording house numbers with a GPS. This was a form of resistance and a strong statement that no one should 'steal' and misuse their house number. This resistance forced the engagement between the local state, the researchers and community members (as developed in Settlement story 4.3). It is also evident in the resistance shown by some community members who refused to register for a housing number until they had more 'secure' knowledge about their relocation to the resettlement project and the conditions of that relocation. Part of this quiet resistance was underpinned by their desire for their settlement to be upgraded, rather than relocated. One of the ways they expressed this was by remaining 'outside' of the formal relocation process by 'quietly' refusing to register.

Social protest

Ocean Drive-In residents have staged a number of protests on a busy road that runs adjacent to the settlement. Some of these protests were organised by the independent committee, while others were orchestrated by community members, frustrated with the lack of clarity about the move to Hammonds Farm. Two of the protests took place immediately after the state failed to meet the deadline of the proposed move to Hammonds Farm, including a large protest on 7 July, 2012.

Protests involve *toyi toying*,[4] road closures, the burning of tyres and marches. In most cases these protests resulted in the councillor of Ward 58 arriving with the police to disperse the protestors. In the case of the 7 July protest, community members demanded the keys to their houses at Hammonds Farm. The councillor immediately organised to take some members of the community in a taxi to the formal housing project to show them that the houses they had been allocated had not been occupied by someone else, and that the relocation process was being delayed as a result of the provision of services to the new project. These community members then reported back to the rest of the community that the houses were still empty.

The councillor arranged a formal meeting in Ocean Drive-In for the following Sunday to address the community on issues related to the relocation process. This revealed the success of the protest in obtaining the attention of the councillor, forcing him to respond. However, this meant that the protesters had to channel their concerns through the political, rather than technical or bureaucratic structures of the state, as the ward councillor took control of the protest, giving him more power over the community in the relocation process. The protest, an invented space of participation, was therefore captured and re-embedded in the invited spaces of participation of the local state and its ward committee system. The ward committee system was established by the Municipal Structures Act (1998) to ensure that community concerns are channelled through ward committees to the councillor, who then has the responsibility to report to other municipal politicians and officials. It therefore defines the relationship between citizens and the state.

The community meeting held by the councillor in response to the protest revealed a different agenda on the part of the councillor, as the meeting was politicised, with the ANC using it as a platform to retain party support in the community. The councillor presented himself as a decision-maker and allocator of resources (in this case housing). This led the community to believe that he was responsible for decisions related to the allocation of housing to Hammonds Farm, when in fact the municipality's Housing Department make these decisions and are responsible for the relocation. Through the control of the councillor, the community was distanced from the officials in the municipality, although they understood that municipal officials would deal with the bureaucratic matters associated with the move. The councillor also used the support of the police to deal with the event, which is significant, as many community members across Durban indicate that they do not protest, as they are fearful of the councillors and the police, and they do not want to participate in illegal strikes.

Engagement and partnership

The relocation of households to Hammonds Farm has been a slow process. By October 2014, half the residents of the original settlement were still waiting to be moved. As each household is relocated to Hammonds Farm, the shack they lived in is demolished by municipal workers, so as to prevent further invasions.

The new Ocean Drive-In committee, which was established once members of the sub-ward committee were unsurprisingly moved first to Hammonds Farm, engaged directly with municipal officials to improve the quality of life of those left behind. They developed a state-citizen social contract at the micro-scale by creating a process that became known as 'house swapping'.

'House swapping' occurs when residents in poor quality shacks are given permission by the municipality to move in to shacks that are of a higher quality, or located on a better site, that are vacated by those being relocated to Hammonds Farm, taking their housing numbers with them. This process requires a significant level of trust from both the state and residents of Ocean Drive-In. The remaining resident moves the number from their shack door to the vacated shack door, thereby stopping it being demolished and formally legitimising the 'house swapping' process. This process reflects a positive outcome of direct engagement between the new committee, community members and local state officials. It has had a significant impact on the quality of life of residents who are still waiting to be relocated. This process of engagement occurred outside of the formal political structures of the state in a space of participation constructed through the innovative action of community members around issues related to their everyday lived worlds. This example also reveals that residents have shown 'agency in times of constraints' (Bayat 2010: ix).

Demobilisation and fragmentation

It has been argued that many communities in South Africa have been de-mobilised through the political structures of the state, most notably the ward committee system (Pithouse 2009). In the case of Ocean Drive-In, community members have been de-mobilised through the control of the councillor. Residents of Ocean Drive-In have indicated that they cannot access services or employment (in state or public–private developments) without obtaining 'permission letters' from the councillor. Community members do not engage directly with the local state on important matters related to services and housing, even though these state-citizen engagement channels exist, as they have to report issues, and gain legitimacy to exercise their rights, through the sub-ward committee and the councillor.

The politics in the settlement is not homogenous. Ocean Drive-In has a long history of conflict between ANC and IFP party members. This conflict has been less apparent in recent years, although it simmers below the surface, being acted out at the individual level. The control of the settlement by the ANC councillor has meant that independent organisations, such as the independent committee, have emerged to reduce the influence of the ANC in Ocean Drive-In. Community members argue that meetings are always politicised and that the councillor only wants to talk politics and not address community issues, which residents believe should transcend party politics.

Ocean Drive-In is aligned with the other small informal communities along the coastal belt, but they do not form part of a broader network of informal settlements in the city. AbM representatives have visited the community but they were not welcomed back as a result of the decision by the sub-ward committee and the councillor to exclude them from engaging with the community.

The community displays a complex mix of unity and fragmentation. Ocean Drive-In is home to a community dominated by the sub-ward committee that was well recognised and respected within the community, resulting in the unification of the community around critical issues. However, it also has fragmented alliances created by the long-established policing committee and the emergence of the independent committee. Moving the majority of the sub-ward committee members to Hammonds Farm in the first round of relocation de-mobilised and fragmented the community further. This has had a significant impact on the large number of households who are still waiting to be moved.

Residents of Ocean Drive-In have adopted a wide range of strategies to mobilise around their poor living environment and the insecurity related to the relocation process. These strategies reflect the particular historical, political and social context of Ocean Drive-In. At times the community acts in a unified manner and at other times the dynamics of political mobilisation fragment the community, reflecting the divisions within it.

Cato Crest

The increase in social unrest, associated land invasions and the demolition of shacks under court order in Cato Crest in 2013 reveals the pressure on housing provision in the municipality. This case study is employed to reveal how social mobilisation intensifies when communities are displaced by in-situ upgrading or relocation projects. All registered residents of Ocean Drive-In have been allocated houses in Hammonds Farm, whether they are shack owners, renters or lodgers. However, in Cato Crest, an upgrading project led to the displacement of a large number of shack dwellers. This led to widespread mobilisation at a large spatial and political scale, revealing tensions around housing in the municipality.

Over 1,000 renters and lodgers who had been displaced from Cato Crest invaded land near the Cato Crest Stadium in March 2013. They symbolically named the area Marikana after the 2012 Lonmin mine massacre where police shot thirty-four striking mine workers. Through the invasion they demanded a response from the municipality to the housing crisis they found themselves in. This invasion was followed by large protests. This led to violent engagements between the police and informal residents, which impacted on the functioning of the city. An invented space of participation on the streets of Cato Manor and Cato Crest had been created. These protests were widely reported in the press.

The social mobilisation in Cato Crest differs considerably from that in Ocean Drive-In. First, the community structures in Cato Crest that led the protest reflect a more complex political arrangement. They reflect the tensions between AbM and the ANC in Durban, as well as tensions between different committees within the settlement. AbM is not active in many informal settlements in Durban as a result of particular ANC councillors and ward committees firmly stating that AbM is not welcome in their communities. Unlike Ocean Drive-In, where community concerns and social protests are addressed by the councillor, the intensity and political significance of the Cato Crest protests, as well as the significant impact of AbM on the mobilisation process, resulted in the protest being scaled up. Senior managers from the municipality, including the Head of the Housing Department Nigel Gumede, were called in to address the crisis and meet with the protestors. Second, the protest was associated with a large-scale land invasion that forced the municipality, including both politicians and officials, to react. Third, the protest was a direct challenge on the ANC and the head of the Housing Department, with both AbM and Cato Crest community demanding that Gumede resign. The assignation of an ANC ward committee member who had been engaging with the municipality and leading the protests on 15 March, 2013 reveals the politicisation of the housing crisis in Cato Crest.

One of the outcomes of the events in Cato Crest was that the malfunctioning of the housing allocation system for informal communities was exposed. The process of housing allocation in the municipality is indeed not transparent and there is very limited participation by ordinary citizens in the state's 'invited spaces' of housing allocation. These decisions are made by officials in the city's Human Settlements Committee. Many councillors claim that they influence housing allocation decisions. They use the housing allocation process both as a means of gaining favour with their constituents and of controlling them, which is problematic.

Protestors had demanded to know why they had not been allocated houses even though they had been on the state housing lists for many years. The housing lists had been created post-1994 as a way of allocating RDP houses to those who were eligible for state subsidised housing in a fair, timely and transparent manner. Informal settlers, residents of transit camps and peri-urban dwellers applied to the Housing Department to be registered on the housing lists, which in the past meant they would be allocated a RDP house when houses became available and their name reached the top of the list. As a result of the Cato Crest protests, Gumede revealed that the municipality had not used the 'housing lists' to allocate houses since 2007. Many of the urban poor have been waiting patiently for formal housing, believing their turn would come when they reached the correct place on the list, and hence this statement was met with disbelief and anger. However, it was a positive outcome as the state had been forced to be more transparent about how it allocates housing in the city. The myth of the housing lists had now been publically addressed. The discourses used by some of the senior managers of the Housing Department at the time of the Cato Crest protests, which continued through 2013, have been strongly criticised by AbM as they reflect a repressive state that is blaming migrants for the housing crisis in the city, thereby inciting xenophobia. According to an AbM spokesperson 'Gumede thinks that the land and housing crisis can be dealt with by more security, more evictions and more repression. However it is clear that the only solution is more land and more housing' (AbM, 19 March, 2013). In protest against these discourses and approaches, AbM continued to mobilise communities in the Cato Crest area during 2013, calling on the court to halt illegal evictions.

Conclusion

Social mobilisation in Durban reflects resistance and protest, engagement and partnerships, demobilisation and fragmentation, and legal action. National and local political structures, leadership and the political and social context of each settlement shape the trajectories of social mobilisation, as these case studies reveal. Social mobilisation is also shaped at the city scale by AbM and to a lesser degree Slum Dwellers International (SDI). Social movements are difficult to sustain due to power struggles and political competition within settlements; the power of councillors in controlling resistance; and as a result of NGOs providing unequal support to ensure that their own interests are met (Huchzermeyer 2011). The lack of the most basic resources and the fear of the police also undermines people's ability to participate consistently, and over the long term, in the struggle to secure better housing. However, even with all these constraints, these case studies show that although social mobilisation is fragmented and localised, community action through invited and invented spaces of participation and insurgent urbanism continues to play a major role in shaping the city and securing the 'right to the city' for all.

References

Bayat, A. (2010) *Life as politics: How ordinary people change the Middle East.* Stanford: Stanford University Press.

Huchzermeyer, M. (2011) *Cities with 'slums'. From informal settlement eradication to a right to the city in Africa.* Cape Town: University of Cape Town Press.

Pithouse, R. (2009) 'A progressive policy without progressive politics: Lessons from the failure to implement "Breaking New Ground"'. *Town & Regional Planning,* 54: 1–14.

Posel, D. and Marx, C. (2013) 'Circular migration: A view from destination households in two urban informal settlements in South Africa'. *The Journal of Development Studies,* 49(6): 819–31.

Settlement story 6.3 The contested phases of the N2 Gateway project in Joe Slovo informal settlement, Cape Town[5]

DAVID JORDHUS-LIER

Joe Slovo forms an outer band surrounding Langa township, the oldest black township in Cape Town with a history dating back to the 1920s. Joe Slovo informal settlement was established in the periphery of the Langa township in 1990–1 by backyard dwellers in Langa and migrants looking for jobs. Of informal settlements with a certain size, Joe Slovo is the one located closest to the city centre and, therefore, in relative terms, is a very attractive place to move to for poor job seekers.

In 2004, just when the African National Congress (ANC) government had unveiled their new housing policy *Breaking New Ground*, and when South African cities had begun preparations for hosting the FIFA 2010 World Cup, the N2

Gateway project aimed to address the huge housing backlog and the sprawl of informal housing along the highway. The N2 Gateway project was initially a joint effort between three tiers of government, and both local and national ANC politicians were protagonists of the project (Smit 2008). While several settlements along the N2 highway were identified for formal upgrading through the N2 Gateway project, the first phases took place in Joe Slovo from 2005.

By 2013, the Joe Slovo section of the project had seen two out of three phases completed. However, all stages of the development have been met with community contestation and protest. After a large shack fire in January 2005, initial plans of relocations to nearby locations were left in favour of mass-scale emergency relocations to the Delft out on the Cape Flats. Informal settlement residents in Joe Slovo and backyard dwellers in the neighbouring area have been challenging each other over the limited housing opportunities the N2 Gateway project offered. The identification of target groups has been done by a combination of individual applications and collective, area-based solutions, leading to widespread confusion and resentment. The battles have been many and the issues have been complex, and also included concerns over the quality of housing (particularly in the rental units of Phase I) and demands for casual job opportunities during the construction process. Finally, the lack of community participation has been a constant source of frustration throughout the planning and implementation stages.

Collective action among residents in Joe Slovo informal settlement has involved a plethora of community organisations, the most important being the Joe Slovo Task Team. Other groups, such as the Joe Slovo Residents' Association, the Joe Slovo Area Committee, the local branch of South African National Civics Organisation (SANCO), and the ANC Youth League, have also played important roles during particular phases of mobilisation. Observing how local civil society has mobilised in response to the N2 Gateway project, two characteristics emerge. First, the residents of Joe Slovo have chosen to pursue different strategies at different points in time, and as a result community resistance to the project has gone through several distinct phases. Second, in all of these phases local leaders and their organisations have strategically engaged with networks beyond the community of Joe Slovo and the Langa township.

Confrontational phase

When Joe Slovo residents first learned of the N2 Gateway project plans, it led to demands for detailed information about the development plans and housing models. The fire in January 2005 triggered a new set of responses from the community. Fire victims were told that they could not re-erect their shacks on the fire site as it had been designated as a development site for the N2 Gateway. This clearly entailed relocation, in one form or another, and the need arose for an organisation that would formulate residents' concerns about where people would be relocated and who was going to be relocated.

Popular resistance to relocation was the immediate trigger for the establishment of the Task Team. Task Team representatives claim to have had more than twenty meetings with authorities during this phase. After a period of consultation, the organised community structures decided it had not led to an accommodation of the residents' concerns, and they decided to change to more militant methods of action – as 'action speaks louder than words', according to one of the leaders. The blockade of the N2 Gateway marks a climax in the timeline of community mobilisation. On 10 September, 2007, community members blocked the main highway into town for several hours during the night and early hours of the day. During this phase, the Joe Slovo Task Team was supported by other social movements. Some of these, like the Western Cape Anti-Eviction Campaign, have been highly mobilised networks making their mark on housing politics in Cape Town throughout the last ten years.

The blockade divided opinion, and led to some critical media coverage and a heated public exchange of words between the Minister of Housing and the Joe Slovo residents and their sympathisers (Legassick 2008, Makinana and Phaliso 2007). The form of action was symbolic: just as the N2 Gateway project had targeted the settlements surrounding the highway due to their visibility in this main portal into the city centre, so did the Joe Slovo residents use this 'strategic location' to make their protest seen and heard. The blockade was followed by a series of demonstrations in 2007, which perhaps can be seen as ending the most confrontational phase in the Joe Slovo case. While expressions of collective protest might be short-lived, they also sometimes evolve into durable organisations, which go through learning processes, networking and develop their working methods in sophisticated ways (Ballard, Habib and Valodia 2006). As we will see, such opportunities were presented to the Joe Slovo Task Team, both when the case entered the court system and when the project invited community representatives to be part of decision-making structures.

Legal phase

At the same time they were generating a high level of popular mobilisation, the organised community was also getting acquainted with the legal system. This paved the way for a protracted legal phase that served to give parts of the community limited victories, but also de-mobilised and disciplined the informal settlement dwellers. For example, in the wake of the protests, eight Joe Slovo residents were charged with public violence (Legassick 2008). More importantly, however, Thubelisha and national/provincial government sought to get an eviction order from the Cape High Court for the area targeted for housing developments. The Court ruled in favour of the applicants, and ordered an eviction on 10 March, 2008. The Task Team established relationships to various NGOs and lawyers during this period in order to access legal expertise. These provided the community with documentation, argumentation and representation during the legal processes dating back to September 2007 (e.g., Constitutional Court Affidavit 2008, COHRE 2009). The legal process shaped the form of mobilisation – over time community protests gave way to solving technical matters. Some activists claimed that the community at this point failed to main-tain mobilisation and entered a lull.

The Constitutional Court (ConCourt 2009) handed down five judgments on 10 June, 2009, which had an impact on community mobilisation in more than one way. First, in spite of internal differences between judges, it upheld the eviction order from the High Court. Second, it prescribed in detail the circumstances under which eviction should take place. This included 'meaningful engagement' with the community (de Satge *et al.* 2009). This was interpreted as a victory for the Joe Slovo residents, but it also required that the community prioritised engagement over protest in their relationship to the state and the developers. Third, it stated that 70 per cent of the houses should be reserved for former Joe Slovo residents, with the remaining 30 per cent being allocated to people residing in Langa backyards.[6] This would mean that Phase 3 would have to prioritise low-income families in a different way than the rental housing of Phase 1 and the bank-mortgaged housing of Phase 2 had done. However, the 70:30 ratio created tensions between Joe Slovo settlement dwellers and groups living outside the area – particularly backyarders who tend to have a longer history in Cape Town and are sometimes referred to as 'borners'. Fourth, the order specified the timeframe, transport arrangements and standards of temporary accommodation, which the state and the developer had to offer to those relocated. In sum, these requirements were seemingly too specific and too demanding for Thubelisha and the state departments. Consequently, little had been accomplished by 2011 both in terms of relocation and meaningful engagement. In fact, so little had been done from the authorities' side that the Constitutional Court discharged their own eviction order on 31 March, 2011 on the grounds that the failure to comply with the 2009 judgment had created 'exceptional circumstances' sufficient to discharge (ConCourt 2011). This was celebrated as a huge victory by the Joe Slovo settlement dwellers. Despite the prolonged legal phase and the delays this entailed, the planning of the large-scale Phase 3 of fully subsidised housing slowly reached its construction stage, which again would change the dynamics of the community.

Phase of engagement

The mobilisation of communities in the Joe Slovo informal settlement also generated another form of politics beyond the highly visible street protests and resistance through legal processes. An approach favouring engagement and knowledge-generation as a means of mobilisation was becoming more visible. Efforts to create arenas for engagement with local authorities and knowledge sharing date back to (at least) 2004, when Joe Slovo residents together with the Community Organisation Resources Centre (CORC) approached the authorities to conduct surveys and joint planning with residents. This never materialised because a private contractor was chosen as the preferred agent. In the wake of the fire and the protests in 2005–07 the relationship between CORC and its affiliates and the Joe Slovo community became somewhat cautious. According to one representative of Slum Dwellers International, hostility and scepticism were directed towards NGOs during the confrontational phase, and they were seen as a threat to the autonomy of the community.

However, following smaller fires in the shack settlements in 2008 and 2009 there was a renewed engagement between the Joe Slovo Task Team, the CORC affiliates and the City of Cape Town officials. The leadership in the Joe Slovo Task Team became less involved with confrontational social movements and took part in establishing the Informal Settlements Network (ISN). The ISN is part and parcel of the South Africa Slum Dwellers International (SDI) Alliance. In April 2009, the Joe Slovo residents got involved in surveying the settlement (enumeration), a tool for generating independent and community-driven information. What was crucial about the enumeration exercise is that it was conducted by community members 'in sharp contra-distinction to other information-gathering efforts in the settlement, where external actors, linked and sponsored by the state, were suspected of hidden agendas' (enumerator cited in Baptist and Bolnick 2012: 63). Parallel to the enumeration, the community with support from CORC and the Federation for the Urban and Rural Poor started to re-block an area of the settlement, and engaged the City of Cape Town in constructing an ablution block. It seemed that crises, in the form of fires and floods, provided the impetus for the Joe Slovo community to turn to a more direct engagement with the local state and NGOs. Interestingly, SDI representatives described the fires as 'opportunities' and 'catalysts' for community-driven development (Baptist and Bolnick 2012). More critical voices, however, argue that SDI's role shifted from a critic to a collaborator, and that the latter role included 'facilitating the unpopular relocations *through* an "enumeration process"' (Huchzermeyer 2011: 145, my emphasis). Seen from this perspective, the enumeration process was 'intended to share information about pending developments or unavoidable relocations, empower ordinary residents and facilitate the organisation of communities' (Huchzermeyer 2011: 146).

Leadership in the Joe Slovo community also got actively involved in the scaling-up of informal settlement politics – the chairperson of the Task Team became vice-president of the ISN and has been on exchange trips to other settlements within and beyond Cape Town. While many in the settlement, prominent leaders in particular, embraced the SDI method, pockets of resistance to this form of engagement have also emerged. Nevertheless, engagement-oriented strategies have become the dominant mode of community response to the project since the eviction case was discharged from the court system. As the construction of Phase 3 began, the politics in the settlement of Joe Slovo changed into contestation over casual construction jobs, housing entitlements, and the right to be consulted in the housing allocation process – in particular through the facilitation role of the Joe Slovo Task Team. The local community was also involved in project's Phase 3 through several Community Liaison Officers who functioned as the link between the developers and the community, and who recruited local casual workers to construction tasks. But as it became clear that the development would not include everybody, many residents felt excluded or marginalised. Some of these turned to the Joe Slovo Residents' Association (or to the newly formed Joe Slovo Area Committee) to voice their complaints. At times during 2012, the rivalry between these organisations became hostile.

The dynamic character of resistance and engagement that the residents of Joe Slovo have pursued through several distinguishable phases was enabled by several factors: the lack of community involvement in the early phase led to the initial protests; the progressive nature of the South African constitution opened a bigger role for progressive NGOs; and the fact that a significant share of the community became beneficiaries in the final phase, thus fragmenting the community into winners and losers, meant that the Task Team was allowed a dominant role in the latter phase of engagement.

References

Ballard, R., Habib, A. and Valodia, I. (2006) *Voices of protest: Social movements in post-apartheid South Africa*. Scottsville, SA: University of KwaZulu-Natal Press.

Baptist, C. and Bolnick, J. (2012) 'Participatory enumerations, in situ upgrading and mega events: The 2009 survey in Joe Slovo, Cape Town'. *Environment & Urbanization*, 24(1): 59–66.

COHRE (2009) *N2 Gateway Project: Housing rights violations as 'Development' in South Africa*. Geneva: Centre on Housing Rights and Evictions.

ConCourt (2009) Judgment 10 June, 2009. Case CCT 22/08. Johannesburg: The Constitutional Court of South Africa.

ConCourt (2011) Judgment 31 March, 2011. Case CCT 22/08. Johannesburg: The Constitutional Court of South Africa.

Constitutional Court Affidavit (2008) Applicant's written argument. CC Case No CCT 22/08. Johannesburg: Constitutional Court of South Africa.

de Satge, R., Kahanovitz, S., Kubukeli, L., *et al.* (2009) 'Learning from Joe Slovo'. *NCHR workshop on advancing Socio Economic Rights: Session 7 – Group 1*. Gordon's Baai, Western Cape: NCHR. Available at: www.phuhlisani.com (accessed on 10 May, 2011).

Huchzermeyer, M. (2011) *Cities with 'Slums': From informal settlement eradication to a right to the city in Africa*. Claremont, SA: University of Cape Town Press.

Jordhus-Lier, D.C. (2015) 'Community resistance to megaprojects: The case of the N2 Gateway project in Joe Slovo informal settlement, Cape Town'. *Habitat International*, 45(3): 169–76.

Legassick, M. (2008) *Western Cape housing crisis: Writings on Joe Slovo and Delft*. Cape Town: A Western Cape Anti-Eviction Campaign and Socialist Alternative publication.

Lemanski, C.(2009) 'Augmented informality: South Africa's backyard dwellings as a by-product of formal housing policies'. *Habitat International*, 33(4): 472–84.

Makinana, A. and Phaliso, S. (2007) 'Sisulu slams Joe Slovo residents. Settlements say they won't be moved'. *Cape Argus*, 6 August, 2007.

Smit, W. (2008) 'Le grand project N2 Gateway'. In A. Dubresson and S. Jaglin (eds) *Le Cap après l'Apartheid*. Paris: Karthala, pp. 23–44.

**Settlement story 6.4 Collective contestation of the
Vía Parque Rímac mega-project from the low-income
settlements along the river Rímac in Lima[7]**

LISA STRAUCH AND MICHAELA HORDIJK

Introduction

The low-income settlements of the 'Margen Izquierda' and 'Margen Derecha del
Río Rímac' (MIRR and MDRR: left and right bank of the river Rímac) represent
fascinating case studies for studying community responses to large-scale urban
development projects. The settlements are located along the river Rímac next
to the city centre and belong to some of Lima's oldest *barriadas* (low-income
settlements) with a long history of collective action and social mobilisation.
This case study examines the residents' current resistance against a mega-project
intervening in their neighbourhoods, while taking into account their socio-
historical background. This allows us to reveal changes in the social mobilisation
mechanisms among Lima's urban poor, as well as shifts in power dynamics in the
city.

Lima's low-income settlements have historically provided their residents with
an important space in the city. From within the *barriadas*, residents organised
collectively to upgrade their neighbourhoods and to request or demand pro-poor
responses from the state. Already since the 1950s Lima's *barriadas* had expanded
rapidly, and therewith they developed into an important pressure group in the
city. As the government recognised that the urban poor's demands for housing
could not be neglected, their collective practices have been allowed, sometimes
supported and, eventually, almost always legalised. Peru is known for its early
acceptance of 'self-help housing' as a strategy to provide shelter to the poor, as
evidenced by the progressive 'law for the *barriadas*' adopted in 1961 (see Box 3.1).
Furthermore, collective organisation in the settlements was strongly encouraged
by stipulating that the government would only discuss land issues with elected
neighbourhood councils, not with individuals. Thus, the neighbourhoods along
the Rímac have well-established neighbourhood councils with their elected
leaders. Some neighbourhoods have been emblematic in their collective action
and social mobilisation (see Box 7.1).

Today, many of the initial squatter settlements have undergone remarkable
changes towards upgrading. Social dynamics in the settlements are also changing
as the need for collective mobilisation considerably decreases with the improvement of a neighbourhood's infrastructure. However, organisational structures
usually do not disappear. Rather, neighbourhood organisations lay dormant and
can be re-activated once the community faces new collective challenges – such
as displacement through large-scale development projects – as is the case with
the settlements of the MIRR and MDRR and the Vía Parque Rímac project.

Contested Relocation

The Vía Parque Rímac expressway is a mixed-use mega-project that is currently under construction along the river Rímac in the centre of Lima. It combines conventional road infrastructure with urban redevelopment, including public green spaces in the city centre. The project will displace various low-income settlements located along the river – a fact that has sparked extensive community resistance. As argued in Settlement story 4.5, one of the main factors that led communities to contest the issue of relocation was the secretive planning nature of the project and the exclusionary management of information. Indeed, affected communities had never been informed nor consulted about the project that entailed their displacement and were caught by surprise when it was publicly announced in the media.

However, once residents became aware of the threat the mega-project posed to them, resistance could be quickly organised through existing organisational structures. Neighbourhood councils got re-activated and got engaged in informing and mobilising the population through assemblies, protest festivals, and the dissemination of flyers and community newspapers. Dwellings to be demolished were draped with slogans voicing resistance 'This house is private property – the presence of any companies contracted by OAS is prohibited' (OAS is the private developer responsible for the project). Spontaneous resistance activities included preventing project personnel from entering the settlements or evicting them when they wanted to conduct surveys or soil studies.

More organised collectively expressed reactions to the project have gone through several distinct strategic phases, depending on the project's stage of implementation.

Confrontational phase: demanding engagement

In spring 2010 communities staged two massive street marches, one to the headquarters of the company and another to the congress. Given the authority's lack of engagement with the communities, these constituted the invented spaces in which resisters tried to make their voices heard. Besides the two big protest marches communities organised various roadblocks and smaller street protests within the neighbourhoods. The main objectives of these mobilisations were to: demand transparency and access to information; prevent the pending eviction and defend the right to housing; and fight the municipal ordinance passed in 2007, which declared the settlements along the riverbank as high risk areas and legitimised the displacement of residents with a low compensation (Interview, resident MIRR, 23 November, 2012).

The two marches constituted an effective form of bringing resistance into the public eye and putting pressure on political authorities. Indeed, the conflict became heavily politicised during the 2010 municipal elections and when the new mayor Susana Villarán took office, she negotiated several changes in the project with the contractor (see Settlement story 4.5).

Furthermore, communities managed to link up with political actors that supported their claims. In March 2010 members of the Peruvian Nationalist Party visited the settlements and publicly denounced the discriminatory treatment of the residents by the current municipal management and the company. Furthermore, they established a clear link between the 2007 ordinance and the execution of the mega-project. Subsequently, congress representatives supported the population in pleading for the unconstitutionality of this ordinance at the Constitutional Court, arguing that it violated the residents' right to property.

In June 2011 the resistance movement scored a small victory when the Constitutional Court emitted its judgment. Although it did not overturn the ordinance, it obliged the municipality to implement an adequate relocation plan for the residents occupying the risky banks of the river Rímac. It further mandated that a relocation scheme needed to be set up with the participation of the residents. However, even after the judgment, no meaningful dialogue was estab-lished between residents and project authorities. The low level of information provided to the communities and the complete lack of communication continued to be a consistent source of frustration and was still the top concern of all interviewees during fieldwork conducted in the settlements in 2012–13 (Strauch 2013).

Resistance as a tool for negotiating compensation and resettlement

Due to the social contestation of the project, the land-clearing process could not be implemented and the project was put on hold until the mandate of the local government under Luis Castañeda Lossio (2003–10) ended in December 2010. After the new mayor, Susana Villarán, took office in 2011, the protest movement achieved some successes. The project was re-designed, the monetary compensation improved and the number of families affected by displacement reduced. Therefore, the new mayor partially responded to the demands of the resistance movement. Although the amount for compensation and the form of resettlement continued to be hotly contested, the improvements, such as the higher compensation offered, altered the basis for decision-making about resistance. Rather than resisting relocation, some residents came to acknowledge the possibility of accepting relocation under adequate conditions and committed themselves to fighting for an improved compensation scheme.

Thus, residents did not challenge the project in itself but thought to nego-tiate a just compensation. They were careful not to portray themselves as opponents to the development of the city, but demanded a fair distribution of the benefits of this process, as one neighbourhood leader argued:

> we believe that the project is a necessity, all the streets are very congested. But if they want to remove us from here, the centre of Lima, to send us to who knows where, what we want is at least a fair compensation.
>
> (Authors' interview, 20 October, 2012)

Many residents indeed feared the devastating consequences of relocation. Given the fact that in the settlements one dwelling often houses various generations, the 60 square metre apartment offered by the company as alternative housing was insufficient. Furthermore, it meant that residents would be cut off from homebound income sources such as shops and workshops located within their dwelling or from the possibility of renting out parts of the house to tenants. On the other hand, people who refused to accept the apartment would be forced to move to the outskirts of the city, as land prices in the centre would prevent them from being able to purchase land in the central districts. Similarly, this entails a threat of impoverishment, as people are disconnected from their current place-related income sources and the urban opportunities that characterises the central location of the settlements. Moreover, all residents perceived relocation as uprooting. The settlements' collective history gave them a strong incentive to demand the recognition of the social-cultural sacrifices they were forced to make, as one interviewee lamented:

> Here in this neighbourhood we have been able to transform a sanitary landfill into a home. And we've done that with our own efforts, the government has given us absolutely nothing, not a penny. We want that they respect us for this. We are Peruvians and from our country they want to evict us. All we want is that they recognise our efforts.
>
> (Authors' interview, 6 December, 2012)

Following in the footsteps of past collective strategies, neighbourhood councils assumed the role of defending the residents' interests. Strategies and objectives of the negotiation process, however, diverged among the settlements, indicating the diversity of interests that formed the basis for different collective activities. One neighbourhood association hired an independent appraiser to conduct a price evaluation of some houses and invited the company to do the same. Significantly, the evaluations turned out to be quite different. The company established that the value of the land was USD 65 per square metre, whereas the independent appraiser set the price at USD 300 per square metre. Furthermore, as apart from the apartments neither the company nor the municipality planned a resettlement scheme for the affected communities, the neighbourhood council took up the initiative to look for a suitable place for relocation and proposed certain conditions under which they would agree to relocation: the provision of a serviced plot with the first storey already built, even accepting relocation to the periphery.

Another neighbourhood organisation centred its strategy on the rejection of relocation and tried to negotiate a new roadway design. Given that this specific community did not occupy the bank of the river, the neighbourhood council claimed that there was ample space to move the street closer to the river and therewith render displacement unnecessary.

The residents tried to negotiate directly with the company as well as with the municipality. However, negotiation strategies did not bring about results and the company proved unresponsive to the collective demands. Furthermore, authorities from the municipality and the company emphasised that compensation of the affected residents would be elaborated through the '*trato directo*' (direct treatment) mechanism – establishing that project authorities will deal with each resident case by case, defining the problem as an individual, not a collective, one; certainly a strategic decision to weaken collective organisation.

Factors hindering collective claim making: the diversity of the displaced

The settlements along the river Rímac, like many low-income settlements in Lima, draw on a long history of collective action in the upgrading of their neighbourhoods. Confronted with the threat the mega-project posed to the settlements, resistance could be quickly organised by re-activating existing organisational structure in the communities.

Yet, more than sixty years after their original foundation, these settlements today are highly diverse, both in physical and social terms. Inevitably, this means the mega-project will affect people in different ways. For families who live in precarious conditions on the steep banks of the river Rímac, relocation is a sheer necessity to prevent risk. For the many owners of multi-storey houses, relocation will be a change for the worse. This degree of internal diversity played an important role in the development of and participation in resistance. The resistance movement represented the interests of those that perceived they were exposed to the highest losses. A key theme in their discourse included the articulation of the right to housing and the defence of property. As a neighbourhood leader argued:

> We did the protest marches on the basis of the right to housing. We know that under the constitution we all have rights, we have already resided in the area for years, we have titles, we have all the services, we are recognised, we pay taxes. The authority cannot just remove us because they feel like it, as if we were invaders, as if the land was property of the state and not private property.
>
> (Authors' interview, 23 November, 2012)

Residents strategically aimed to position themselves as rightful inhabitants of their settlements, either through having a legal property title or through the length of their specific stay. De facto, the most deprived in the settlements were therewith excluded from the fight for justice. The heterogeneity of housing conditions in the settlements hence presented a challenge for finding common objectives and concrete translations for the resistance movement, as a resident from the steep riverbank argued:

> The problem here is that the urban conditions are very different from each other. There are houses that are better located. Therefore they have another vision of the compensation. And they have better legal weapons to fight,

too. But the problem for us is that we are close to the river. For us staying is not a possibility.

(Authors' interview, 23 November, 2012)

Furthermore, there is not only a broad spectrum of different dwelling conditions, but within many communities only a part is affected by displacement. The company considers those not affected by displacement the 'neighbours of the project' and invests in the upgrading of the settlements, educational programmes and charity events (Interview, 26 September, 2012, LAMSAC). Residents that stay hence benefit from the company's 'benevolent' interventions. These project features hence weakened unified resistance and proved a well-functioning strategy to lessen opposition within the settlements – a characteristic identified as inherent to many 'new' mega-projects (Lehrer and Laidley 2009).

Conclusion

Drawing on their history of collective mobilisation, residents and neighbourhood leaders from the banks of the river Rímac were dedicated to drawing attention to the inequities and injustices inflicted upon them through the Vía Parque Rímac mega-project. Resistance could be quickly organised through re-activating existing neighbourhood councils that used a variety of strategies to defend the interests of the residents. However, in the now-much-more heterogeneous settlements, interests diverge, which impedes sustained collective action. Furthermore, the case of this mega-project exemplified how authorities increasingly aim at dealing with poor citizens on an individual basis. This stands in sharp contrast to past practices and the collective culture in the settlements.

Mobilisation dynamics can no longer be understood in terms of the interaction between the local or national government and poor citizens, since power dynamics in the city are shifting. The elite is no longer only a national one, but has strong linkages to global capital and the interests of multinational corporations that are often even more powerful than local governments. In this scenario, the urban poor now find themselves under the pressure of global market forces that are unresponsive and not accountable to their collective demands.

Urban interventions led by the interests of multinational private capital – and backed by their power – that characterise contemporary urban planning in Lima, leave little space for the aspirations of the city's low-income residents.

References

Lehrer, U. and Laidley, J. (2009) 'Old mega-projects newly packaged? Waterfront redevelopment in Toronto'. *International Journal of Urban & Regional Research*, 32(4): 786–803.

Strauch, L. (2013) 'Seeking spatial justice in Lima – A case study of resistance mobilisation to an urban megaproject from Lima's *barriadas*'. Unpublished master's thesis, Amsterdam: University of Amsterdam. Available at http://dare.uva.nl/en/scriptie/454385 (accessed on 30 January, 2015).

Strauch, L., Takano, G. and Hordijk, M. (2015) 'Mixed-use spaces and mixed social responses: Popular resistance to a megaproject in Central Lima, Peru'. *Habitat International*, 45(3): 177–84.

Settlement story 6.5 A campaign for the right to shelter of the homeless in the context of the 2010 Commonwealth Games in Delhi[8]

VÉRONIQUE DUPONT

Slum clearance for the capital city's redevelopment and beautification, but without adequate rehabilitation, has often resulted in pushing unwanted settlements further into marginal physical and economic spaces, or throwing their dwellers into the streets without solving the issues of suitable shelter for the poor (Dupont 2008). This is exemplified by the case of people rendered homeless from Rajendra Nagar slum. The last eviction that affected this group of families triggered a campaign for the homeless that illustrates the mobilisation of the discourse of rights by civil society organisations (CSOs) and the crucial and protecting role played by the courts from the beginning of the campaign onwards.

Rajendra Nagar demolished slum and Pusa Road case: chronology of main events

The residents of Rajendra Nagar slum were rendered homeless following the demolition of their settlement in 2000 for the construction of a metro line, and their exclusion from the resettlement scheme. They were unable to pay the required fees for the resettlement plots they were entitled to and they relied on unscrupulous agents to whom they gave their original proofs of identity and residence. They lacked unity, organisation and mobilisation, were manipulated and were victims of fraudulent practices by a nexus of property dealers, corrupt municipal officers and often violent police.

During winter, the same group of about 125 families used to shelter in tents temporarily put up by the Delhi government under a relief scheme. They were again evicted by a municipal squad who destroyed their tents on Pusa Road in December 2009 as part of the preparations for the 2010 Commonwealth Games. In this last eviction, an international event was a pretext for the beautification of the capital's landscape, as well as for its 'social beautification' (Broudehoux 2007: 390, Dupont 2011). The consequences were dramatic: two homeless people died from the cold.

This event triggered a protest movement and the *suo moto* intervention of the High Court of Delhi in January 2010, which ordered the Municipal Corporation to provide a shelter to the evicted families. Consequently, the families were resettled in the Motia Khan night shelter, where they were still staying in December 2014, supported by non-governmental organisations (NGOs) and charitable organisations.

A successful mobilisation and scaling-up campaign

The Pusa Road homeless case provides an example of a successful mobilisation and scaling-up campaign that reached much beyond the case of the demolition of one temporary night shelter, as it addressed: the larger issues of forced evictions of homeless people, the lack of adequate shelter for the homeless, and the right to life and to food for people dying in the street because of lack of shelter. Thus, aside from the resettlement of the 125 evicted homeless families, the campaign had additional outcomes. Many more night shelters for the homeless were opened in Delhi following the advocacy by housing rights organisations and the orders of the Delhi High Court. The issue of lack of shelter for the homeless in Indian cities was also brought to the Supreme Court under an ongoing Public Interest Litigation on the right to food, and broadened to all major cities in India, with the view that night shelters should be provided in the ratio of at least one per 100,000 population – as per the stipulations of the Master Plan for Delhi. The scope of shelters for the homeless was also broadened following the Courts' instructions: from providing night shelters in winter, to 24-hour shelters with adequate facilities, running throughout the year.

Furthermore, the recommendations of the working group on urban poverty at the National Advisory Council (a government think-tank under the Prime Minister's Office) for a national programme for shelters and other services for the urban homeless[9] were an indirect outcome of the campaign in March 2012. Their proceedings were not unrelated to the announcement by the President of India, in her address to Parliament on 12 March, 2012, of a new scheme, the National Programme for the Urban Homeless.

At the grassroots level, the mobilisation of the CSOs for the Pusa Road eviction case exceeded its initial focus. The success of this specific campaign boosted the larger movement for the homeless. A 'National City Makers Caravan' was organised to take up on a national level the various issues of urban homelessness. The caravan aimed to sensitise government authorities, the media, and the general public to those concerns. It collected data about the conditions of homeless people in various states, with respect to the provision of night shelters as directed by the Supreme Court. This caravan covered twenty-two states across India, from August 2010 to January 2011, spreading awareness of homeless people's rights and creating a network of concerned CSOs.[10] This initiative was led by a national NGO working with marginalised and vulnerable sections of the society, including homeless people; it was supported by two big organisations, members of international confederations (Caritas India and Oxfam India), and was conducted in collaboration with around forty various CSOs from across the country. Homeless people contributed significantly: around 1,500 of them from Delhi followed the caravan and were joined in each city by other groups. They conducted a signature campaign among themselves, took part in a series of rallies, and performed street plays about their day-to-day problems. At the same time, a very significant semantic change marked the campaign for the urban homeless: from 'homeless people' – a descriptive term – to 'homeless citizens', with an underlying stress on rights and entitlements, and finally to 'city makers' – a term that asserts their 'significant constructive role in a city's development', as 'the real builders of the city'.[11] The last term reflects 'a shift from entitlement citizenship to activism citizenship'[12] in the mobilisation for the homeless.

The organisation of rallies, informal public hearings and consultations[13] on homelessness-related issues further contributed to giving a voice to these marginalised people now claiming a proper place in the city, and in restoring their dignity, too often outraged by harsh living conditions. In such public meetings, homeless people, men as well as women, could speak to share their experience and articulate their demands on the same platform and on par with speakers from very different social classes, statuses and professional categories. The outcomes of this larger campaign can be definitely considered an achievement in terms of increased visibility and empowerment of the urban homeless. A last major success of the movement in this regard is the enrolment of homeless persons in voter lists, thanks to the unrelenting demands and support of NGOs. Although the distribution of voter cards, initiated in late 2012, is still limited, the right conferred – or rather reinstated – to the homeless is undoubtedly a crucial step in enhancing their agency as citizens.

The conjunction of several factors explains the success and scaling-up of this mobilisation campaign. Various CSOs, including NGOs (local organisations as well as national ones supported by international donors), human rights movements (such as the Housing and Land Rights Network), a grassroots organisation of homeless people, and individual activists who had been working in the field of homelessness for more than ten years, combined their respective strengths and fields of expertise within a coalition, *Shaheri Adhikar Manch: Begharon Ke Liye*[14] (SAM–BKL) – the Urban Rights Forum for the Homeless, formed in September 2008, now consisting of more than thirty organisations and activists. The previous years of work for and with the homeless, as well as the efforts in co-ordinating various initiatives, had prepared the ground for an efficient and quick mobilisation. The homeless people themselves took an active part in the movement: some – actual or former homeless – as activists in the community-based organisation, which is a core member of the coalition, and many others as participants in the public meetings and rallies organised by their grassroots organisation or other NGOs.

The efficacy of the coalition rests, in addition to its communication skills, on its vertical linkages from the grassroots level to the higher level of the bureaucracy and the judiciary. This coalition had already established good contacts with the media as a strategy to sensitise the public to the homeless' condition and to highlight the coalition's initiatives. Thus, the media were promptly alerted, especially through press conference and press releases, and they subsequently publicised the case and raised the issues.

Additionally, some coalition members had good contacts with the judiciary, which was thus alerted and promptly took action to protect the homeless. The Delhi High Court's and the Supreme Court's interventions were decisive and allowed the campaign to scale up. Mobilisation by CSOs would not have translated so quickly into actions by the concerned government departments without the support of the judiciary. Both courts continued to monitor their orders regarding the provision of adequate shelters to homeless people.

The members of the coalition played an active role in providing support and information (including reports with action plans and recommendations for Delhi's homeless) to the High Court of Delhi for its *suo moto* case, which continues to date. They used the space provided by the regular hearings of the Court to highlight a range of issues related to the condition of the homeless. Not restricted to the Pusa Road shelter demolition case, they included other cases of evictions, poor maintenance and lack of proper facilities at night shelters, and police brutalities.[15] Thus, the CSOs have maintained the pressure on the concerned government departments through the Courts, preferring this 'pleading' space to express themselves and promote the cause of the homeless.

In contrast, the 'invited' spaces for participation provided by the government proved to be less effective or controversial. Thus, the Joint Apex Advisory Committee for the Homeless constituted in 2002, and projected at that time as a model of government–NGO partnership, became inactive for several years; it was revived at the end of 2011 owing to the Court's advice, but lacks efficiency. As for the Homeless Resource Centres created by the government of Delhi under its Mission Convergence (a flagship programme launched in 2008 to reach the poor through a single window system and promoting public–community partnership), they were affected by diverging views among NGOs.

In short, the success of this campaign in attaining tangible achievements for the homeless ensues from the combination of long-term structural work at the grassroots level and the timely reaction and mobilisation of various connected actors in different spheres (civil society, media, justice) and at different institutional levels (High Court of Delhi, Supreme Court, National Advisory Council). These achievements are significant in the context of Delhi, generally fingered for its weak social mobilisation, especially with regard to slum-related issues (Bautès, Dupont and Landy 2013, Kumar 2008).

Main challenges: sustainability of the campaign outcomes

Yet, the sustainability of the campaign outcomes faces several challenges. First, the living conditions of the families resettled in municipal shelters demonstrate that creating dependency on voluntary organisations does not provide a sustainable solution. This cannot be a substitute to a proper rehabilitation policy going beyond the sole issue of shelter, namely including measures not only to address housing needs but also to address the issue of access to social services, and, most importantly, livelihood opportunities.

Second, the commitment of certain government agencies, especially those implementing the night shelter scheme, is questionable, as revealed by recurrent problems reported during the court's hearings. Moreover, no comprehensive policy addressing the real causes of homelessness was developed. This reveals the major challenge associated with the judiciary pronouncing orders that protect the rights of the homeless in an inadequate policy frame, with weak government agencies that then transfer the responsibility to CSOs.

Last, the coalition of CSOs working with the homeless shows some weaknesses. There is a certain competition between some NGOs, and the only community-based organisation is not on an equal footing. For example, the use of English in the Courts and, at times, in meetings between CSO representatives and high-ranking government officers, is a concern for deepening participation of the grassroots. Moreover, significant divergences of views have emerged regarding the modalities of action vis-à-vis the state: while some promote co-operation and participation in invited spaces, others put forward the benefits of confrontational interactions with the state.

To sum up, despite the active engagement of some CSOs and the continuing intervention of the courts, the achievements regarding the cause of the homeless are still fragile, unconsolidated and subject to setback.

Concluding remarks

The story of the Rajendra Nagar demolished slum and Pusa Road eviction case highlight the CSOs' different spaces of participation on homelessness-related issues. According to the distinction proposed by Miraftab (2004) between 'invited' and 'invented' spaces of citizenship,[16] spaces provided by the government (such as the Joint Apex Advisory Committee for the Homeless and the public-community partnership initiated under Mission Convergence) are 'invited' spaces, whereas press conferences, public hearings and rallies organised by the CSOs qualify as 'invented' spaces for collective protests and claims. In the mobilisation campaign examined here, a third and very significant type of space seems to have emerged – one I call a 'pleading space', namely the courtrooms where the CSOs advocate their cause in a confrontational manner vis-à-vis state institutions but within the codified structure of the judicial system.

The scrutiny of this specific campaign points to more general trends. The courts' decisive role exemplifies the increasing intervention of the judiciary in urban governance in India, though, unlike in this case, not necessarily in the interests of the urban poor (Dupont and Ramanathan 2008, Ghertner 2008; see also Box 5.3). Furthermore, the provision by the government of 'invited' spaces for participation to the civil society illustrates 'a trend characteristic of contemporary urban governance in India' (Tawa Lama-Rewal 2011: 18). At the same time, diverging positions among CSOs and activists regarding the merits of participation versus those of confrontation with the state reflect recurrent debates that have taken place on a broader scale in civil society in India (Jenkins 2010), like in other countries, as discussed in Chapter 7.

References

Bautès, N., Dupont, V. and Landy, F. (2013) 'Acting from the slums: Questioning social movement and resistance'. In F. Landy and M.-C. Saglio-Yatzimirsky (eds) *Megacity slums. Social exclusion, urban space and policies in Brazil and India*. London: Imperial College Press, pp. 363–407.

Broudehoux, A.-M. (2007) 'Spectacular Beijing: The conspicuous construction of an Olympic metropolis'. *Journal of Urban Affairs*, 29(4): 383–99.

Dupont, V. (2008) 'Slum demolition in Delhi since the 1990s. An appraisal'. *Economic & Political Weekly*, 43(28): 79–87.

Dupont, V. (2011) 'The dream of Delhi as a global city'. *International Journal of Urban & Regional Research*, 35(3): 533–54.

Dupont, V. (2013) 'Which place for the homeless in Delhi? Scrutiny of a mobilization campaign in the 2010 Commonwealth Games context'. *Samaj (South Asia Multidisciplinary Academic Journal)* [on line] 8. Available at http://samaj.revues.org/3662 (accessed on 28 January, 2015).

Dupont, V. and Ramanathan, U. (2008) 'The courts and the squatter settlements in Delhi. Or the intervention of the judiciary in urban "governance"'. In I. Baud and J. de Wit (eds) *New forms of urban governance in India: Shifts, models, networks, and contestations*. Delhi: Sage, pp. 312–43.

Ghertner, D.A. (2008) 'Analysis of new legal discourses behind Delhi's slum demolitions'. *Economic & Political Weekly*, 43(20): 57–66.

Jenkins, R. (2010) 'NGOs and India politics'. In N. Gopal Jayal and P. Bhanu Mehta (eds) *The Oxford companion to politics in India*. Oxford: Oxford University Press, pp. 409–26.

Kumar, Ravi (2008) 'Globalization and changing patterns of social mobilization in urban India'. *Social Movement Studies*, 7(1): 77–96.

Miraftab, F. (2004) 'Invited and invented spaces of participation: Neoliberal citizenship and feminists' expanded notion of politics'. *Wagadu*, 1: 1–7.

Tawa Lama-Rewal, St. (2011) 'Urban governance and health care provision in Delhi'. *Environment & Urbanization*, 23(2): 1–19.

Settlement story 6.6 Evictions in the Chennai IT corridor and new threats: low resistance in squatter settlements along the Buckingham Canal

VÉRONIQUE DUPONT AND R. DHANALAKSHMI

Arignar Anna Nagar, a squatter settlement in an area under rapid transformations

The Information Technology (IT) corridor area in Chennai provides compelling cases for issues pertaining to substandard settlements, as the development of this corridor has been associated with land speculation, the extension of the Mass Rapid Transport System, and 'beautification' operations, especially along the Buckingham Canal that flows parallel to the IT corridor – in short, transformations that usually entail evictions. The larger resettlement complexes built in Chennai since the 2000s for evicted slum families are also located in the IT corridor zone, namely Kannagi Nagar and Semmenchery.

Arignar Anna Nagar (AAN) is one of the Canal Bank Road squatter settlements, known also as Canal Puram. It is located in the former Neelankarai *Panchayat*,[17] and was included in the Chennai Municipal Corporation Area in November 2011 following the extension of the corporation limits. The first settlers arrived between thirty and thirty-five years ago, and today between 1,500 and 2,000 households are living in this locality, which stretches along 1.5 km on both sides of the Buckingham Canal. Settlers there are mostly Tamils, some Chennai natives but more often migrants from other districts of Tamil Nadu previously residing in other areas of the city. The most recent settlers include migrants from North India, bachelors working in the nearby industrial area, who are tenants. People belong mainly to backward classes or scheduled castes (the former untouchable castes) and are mostly Hindus, with nevertheless a notable Christian community and Muslims.

The settlement is considered an 'objectionable slum' due to its location on the banks of the Canal, on land that is the property of the Public Works Department. Consequently, the inhabitants have no tenure security. Earlier settlers could occupy the land free of cost, but successive settlers had to 'buy' it from the politicians and local real estate dealers or landlords who controlled the area; they received a document called 'B-memo notice' for this transaction. They also paid property taxes to the former *Panchayat*. Whereas some dwellers believe that such documents will help them prove their ownership to the land, or even consider the 'B-memo notice' to be a land title, this notice is in fact a 'statement showing the details of unauthorised encroachments on Government lands, the use of which is regulated by [the] village *Panchayat*'.[18]

The area is prone to flooding, and the settlement was characterised by an acute deficit in basic urban services, including potable water, as well as physical and social infrastructure. The lack of a drainage and sewage system, and until very recently of garbage collection, contributed in making the locality highly unsanitary. The canal has become an open drain filled with polluted water and dumped garbage – a breeding place for mosquitoes. In addition to individual toilet outlets, industrial effluents and untreated (or not properly treated) sewage water are also released into this canal. The last field visits in 2013 revealed notable improvements, especially in water supply, street lighting, garbage collection and upgrading of roads, due to the extension of the Municipal Corporation area. This shows that being in the city (as per its administrative delimitation) or outside matters in terms of access to urban amenities for informal dwellers.

The remarkable feature of the social organisation in AAN is the lack of a local leader, as well as of community-based organisations and resident welfare associations. Moreover, no church association nor NGO works in the settlement. Furthermore, volunteers and cadres from the two main political parties, both populist, are not active in this settlement, although the inhabitants are part of their vote bank. The Democratic Youth Federation of India (DYFI), affiliated with the Communist Party of India (Marxist) – CPI(M) – is the only organisation with active local members tackling some issues in the settlement. Small self-help women's groups present in the locality are involved in micro-credit activities, but not in collective action at a larger scale.

Collective responses to critical issues in the settlement

The residents of this settlement continuously struggle to get more amenities, especially through repeated representations to the local authorities (village

Panchayat and now the municipal councillors). The DYFI local members played an active role in addressing some of the settlement problems, although their impact proved to be mainly limited to one street. Nevertheless, they collected financial contribution from the residents in order to build a pedestrian bridge over the canal, demonstrating that people can organise themselves when necessary and achieve results. The DYFI members are supported in their endeavour to improve the living conditions in their settlement by the CPI(M). The patronage of this political party is also a way for the DYFI members to scale up their demands: they participate in party activities and try to address their problems to the government during party meetings.

The most critical issue in the Canal Bank Road squatter settlements, as in all 'objectionable slums', is the risk of eviction. Several settlers were initially not aware of the illegality of their tenure. Some were under the impression that the 'B-memo notice' that they got when they purchased the land from private realtors and the property taxes that they paid to the village *Panchayat* were proof of ownership. Such illegal transactions and subsequent benefits for the *Panchayat* suggest rather a connivance between land grabbers and local politicians. Other settlers were informed of the risk of eviction when buying their plot, but did not take it seriously as many others were also buying land at that time and, in any case, they could not afford to buy a plot in an authorised residential colony. Some residents who settled in the locality in the early years said that they were warned against occupying the land, and were instructed to vacate the places by some officials. They used to leave for a while, but then returned to the same places. This was a regular occurrence at the time. Since there was no strict action taken by the public authorities to evict the settlers, the settlement extended gradually and most of the houses were consolidated.

The situation had radically changed by the 2000s, when plans to restore the waterways of Chennai were in the pipeline. By that time the width of the Buckingham Canal had shrunk considerably. To allow the desilting of the canal as part of the flood alleviation programme, the Ministry for Public Works declared in July 2002 that about 5,000 houses had to be removed along the Buckingham Canal (Ahmed 2002). Subsequently, from the last week of July to the first week of August, about 2,300 families were evicted from the canal banks, in the IT corridor zone, including almost 500 from AAN.[19] The remaining families were to be evicted within the following months. For an operation of that scale, officials of the Public Works Department, the Slum Clearance Board, the Revenue Department and the police were mobilised. Evicted families were relocated in Kannagi Nagar resettlement colony, although the flats were not habitable: they were soiled, with clogged toilets and without electricity and water supply.

The eviction was described in the press as 'a swift, low-resistance operation' (Ahmed 2002), which was confirmed by our interviews in AAN. Evicted residents explained that they co-operated with the government officers who came to survey them, took their photos and distributed tokens for allotment, for fear of losing their entitlement to a flat and becoming homeless if they opposed. The large deployment of police forces was another deterrent factor. In fact, families to be displaced were informed of the exact date of eviction around one week before, and some realised only on the eve of the eviction when they got their allotment tokens.

The lack of resistance in the settlements at the time of eviction did not exclude prior collective action to protest against it. Although residents were informed at the last moment of the exact date of eviction, for the last five years there were oral warnings through the *Panchayat* officers that the settlements in the area would be demolished for the 'beautification' of the canal. After each new threat, residents reacted by meeting government officials or submitting petitions to the Chief Minister. For instance, a signature campaign conducted through the All India Democratic Women Association (affiliated with the CPI(M)) collected 5,000 signatures from the Canal Bank Road settlements dwellers. Before the 2002 eviction, a road blockage was organised in a big road junction, as well as a later rally to the Secretariat (seat of the State Government) to make representations to the Chief Minister (the demonstrators were not allowed to enter the premises). Residents from all the settlements along the Canal participated in this rally (around 750–1,000 people).[20] The main demands included: no eviction, provision of all civic amenities, and ownership rights with proper land titles. However, this protest had no effect, and ironically the actual demolition in AAN took place on the day when its inhabitants were demonstrating in the city. The demonstration was organised by the CPI(M), but all other political parties participated. The CPI(M) also helped the evicted families to get their allotment tokens (in case they missed the distribution, or for any other reason) and during their resettlement process in Kannagi Nagar.

Following this major demolition drive no one could ignore the risk of future evictions. Plans for the IT corridor area and recent developments bear new threats of demolition for the squatter settlements along the Buckingham Canal. These include plans to beautify the canal as part of the IT corridor project, and to revive it as a navigation channel for efficient and cost-effective transportation. The construction of a wall all along both sides of the canal also started in 2011, officially for flood control, with a possible hidden agenda to protect the banks from new encroachments. Last, in March 2012, the removal (though not yet implemented) of all squatter settlements located along waterways, including the Buckingham Canal, was announced. Faced with the pending threat of eviction, most residents in AAN seem to accept the fact that, being on government land, their future relocation is inevitable, although they remain very critical of the living conditions in the big resettlement complexes.[21] There is indeed a discrepancy between the dwellers' resignation and pragmatic vision (as explained below), and the more radical stance of the CPI(M) activists.

Factors limiting social mobilisation and protest

This case study allowed us to evidence a combination of factors limiting social mobilisation. Some are specific to the Canal Bank Road squatter settlements and their geographical marginalisation on the fringe of the city. As a result of this situation they remained out of the reach of the major social movements for workers and slum dwellers in the city, which have a greater impact in the old industrial northern areas of Chennai. Furthermore, the location of these settlements in the same zone as Kannagi Nagar resettlement colony makes relocation there comparatively less disruptive to them, and thus more acceptable than to people from inner-city slums.[22] An additional obstacle in AAN stems from the weak social organisational structure in this settlement. On the whole, the residents are not organised to represent their demands and defend their interests, and their level of political awareness seems low.

Other observed factors have a broader significance in understanding the low resistance to eviction in squatter settlements. One is the lack of accurate information sufficiently in advance regarding the date of eviction. According to some residents, this is a deliberate government strategy to avoid the organisation of protests.

Another hindering factor is the divide between house owners and tenants, whose presence is very significant in the Canal Bank Road settlements. The former suffer heavy losses with the demolition of their house and the wiping out of all the investments made to improve their habitat and local environment (in addition to the initial cost of the plot). On the other hand, the latter are winners in a resettlement programme as they have no loss of fixed asset and gain a flat under a highly subsidised hire-and-purchase scheme.[23] This is a unique opportunity for them to improve their residential status. Tenants are not excluded in the government resettlement programmes for slum dwellers, providing they can submit proof of identity and residence. This usually generates struggles on the ground between house owners and tenants, with owners trying to grab more allotments by barring the tenants from claiming their entitlements, or fierce negotiations between the two parties where the tenants eventually need to pay compensation to their landlords to be able to claim their allotment. Barring some exceptions, it remains difficult to expect co-operation between owners and tenants and hence to organise mobilisation among people divided into two groups with such diverging interests.

Economic precariousness proves to be another structural factor that limits the possibility of sustainable mobilisation campaigns in these squatter settlements, as also observed in Delhi (Kumar 2008, own fieldwork). In other words, poor people cannot afford to spend time and thus lose money in long-lasting collective actions.

In addition, one should also consider the coping strategies and rationale of the affected households, in the highly constrained context of removal of objectionable slums. If the eviction is seen as inevitable, efforts are better focused on getting some compensation in the form of a resettlement flat: an asset and a prospective profitable good that they can rent out or resell for monetary returns (irregular transactions of flats in resettlement colonies being a frequent practice).

Finally, the weakening of social mobilisation observed in the Canal Bank Road squatter settlements also reflects the 'gradual weakening and eventual collapse of slum-based, struggle-oriented collective action against evictions' since the 1990s (Coehlo and Raman 2010: 23, Coehlo and Venkat 2009).

References

Ahmed, F. (2002) 'Evicted slum dwellers shifted to Okkiyam Thoraipakkam'. Chennai: *The Hindu*, 30 July, 2002.

Arabindoo, P. (2011) 'The spatial (il)logic of slum resettlement sites in Chennai'. Paper presented to the conference *The city in urban poverty*, 10–11 November, 2011. London: University College London.

Coehlo, K. and Raman, N. (2010) 'Salvaging and scapegoating: Slum evictions on Chennai's waterways'. *Economic & Political Weekly*, 45(21): 19–23.

Coehlo, K. and Venkat, T. (2009) 'The politics of civil society: Neighbourhood associationism in Chennai'. *Economic & Political Weekly*, 44(26 & 27): 358–67.

Coehlo, K., Venkat, T. and Chandrika, R. (2012) 'The spatial reproduction of urban poverty. Labour and livelihoods in a slum resettlement colony'. *Economic & Political Weekly*, 47(47 & 48): 53–63.

HLRN (2014) *Forced to the fringes. Disasters of resettlement in India. Report two: Kananagi Nagar, Chennai.* New Delhi: Housing and Land Rights Network.

Kumar, R. (2008) 'Globalization and changing patterns of social mobilization in urban India'. *Social Movement Studies*, 7(1): 77–96.

PUCL (2010) *Report of PUCL fact finding team on forced eviction and rehabilitation of slum dwellers in Chennai. Fact finding report.* Chennai: People's Union for Civil Liberties.

Notes

1 Where other sources are not referred to, this text is based on Braathen *et al.* (2013).
2 On the broader issue of violence and criminality in the *favelas* of Rio de Janeiro, see Machado da Silva (2008).
3 Durban is the popular name for the eThekwini Municipality, which is the administrative entity that manages the urban and rural areas that collectively form Durban.
4 *Toyi-toying* is an African dance that is used in South Africa during protest demonstrations.
5 This text draws on and contains extracts from the following published article: Jordhus-Lier, D.C. (2015) 'Community resistance to megaprojects: The case of the N2 Gateway project in Joe Slovo informal settlement, Cape Town'. *Habitat International*, 45(3): 169–76.
6 For a discussion of 'backyarders' in Cape Town, see Lemanski (2009).
7 This text draws on and contains extracts from the following published article: Strauch, L., Takano, G. and Hordijk, M. (2015) 'Mixed-use spaces and mixed social responses: Popular resistance to a megaproject in Central Lima, Peru'. *Habitat International*, 45(3): 177–84.
8 This text draws on and contains extracts from the following published article: Dupont, V. (2013) 'Which place for the homeless in Delhi? Scrutiny of a mobilization campaign in the 2010 Commonwealth Games context'. *Samaj (South Asia Multidisciplinary Academic Journal)* [online] 8. Available at http://samaj.revues.org/3662 (accessed on 28 January, 2015).
9 'National Programme for Shelters and Other Services for the Urban Homeless'. Recommendations of National Advisory Council & Explanatory Note. National Advisory Council (Government of India, Prime Minister's office), Working Group on Urban Poverty (Convener: Shri Harsh Mander), Communication to the Government on 14 March, 2012.
10 See 'Caravan for homeless', *Civil Society News*, February 2011, and the report on the IGSSS website, the NGO that organised this campaign. Available from www.igsss.org/newsevents/national-city-makers-caravan (accessed on 23 August, 2014).

11 See the *IGSSS Newsletter* (Nov–Dec 2010, Vol. 11, Issue 6, p. 2), published by the NGO that promoted the designation 'City Makers'. Available from www.igsss.org/wp-content/uploads/2013/07/6.IGSSS-Newsletter-nov-dec.pdf (accessed on 23 August, 2014).

12 This idea and phrasing is borrowed from Vyjayanti Rao (talk on 'Cities and citizenships – new political subjectivities', Paris: CEIAS, 12 June, 2012).

13 For instance, 'Making Delhi a caring city: Review and way forward', National Consultation organised by IGSSS in Delhi, 13 March, 2012. Available at www.igsss.org/newsevents/making-delhi-a-caring-city-review-way-forward (accessed on 23 August, 2014).

14 Recently changed to *'Begharon Ke Sath'*, this new semantic shift from *'for* the homeless' to *'with* the homeless' is again significant as it underlines homeless people's agency.

15 See the interim orders of the High Court of Delhi on this case. Available at http://delhihighcourt.nic.in/dhc_case_status_oj_list.asp?pno=528490 (accessed on 23 August, 2014).

16 See Chapter 7 in this volume for a discussion on these concepts.

17 The *Panchayat* is the basic administrative unit in rural areas.

18 Source: The Tamil Nadu Panchayat (Restriction and Control to Regulate the use of Porambokes in Ryotwari Tracts) Rules, 2000. [*Poramboke* land means village or government land set apart as common land for the whole community, and on which private construction is not authorised.]

19 The exact number of evicted families from AAN is not known; 500 is a rough estimate taking into account the information provided by different respondents.

20 Source: Interview with the General Secretary of CITU (Centre of Indian Trade Unions, affiliated with the CPI(M)) for the industrial area in this zone, 16 February, 2012.

21 The living conditions in Chennai's big resettlement colonies were also denounced by human rights organisations (PUCL 2010, HLRN 2014) and scholars (Arabindoo 2011, Coehlo, Venkat and Chandrika 2012).

22 If Semmenchery and Perumbakkam resettlement colonies are much farther southward in the IT corridor, the comparative distance of displacement (and subsequent impact) remains much more important for slum dwellers living and working in the inner parts of the city than for the residents of AAN.

23 The monthly instalments were initially INR 150 for 20 years, recently revised to INR 250.

7 Modalities of social mobilisation in substandard settlements

Véronique Dupont, David Jordhus-Lier,
Einar Braathen and Catherine Sutherland

Research questions and approach

This chapter addresses the ways residents in substandard settlements mobilise and organise in their struggle for decent housing and in resisting evictions and relocations. The innovative thrust of our research was to focus on the role of civil society organisations and their networks, and analyse how they operate horizontally and vertically in tackling issues related to housing for the poor.

Rather than focusing on social movement at the metropolitan level, we wanted to examine specific mobilisations rooted in selected settlements or city areas affected by larger urban transformations, particularly those resulting from the implementation of large-scale projects or the preparations for mega-events. In each case study the initial trigger for mobilisation was first identified. However, the history and contemporary dynamics of urban social movements shape the development and outcomes of any place-based and time-framed campaign and hence need to be recognised. To do so, we must consider each case carefully. On the one hand, they can be read quite narrowly as reactive social mobilisations to interventions. On the other hand, they must simultaneously be understood as part of progressive mobilisations, which have achieved changes in the legal framework and in the lived experiences of human settlements. For instance, the Citizen Campaign for the Right to Housing in Peru, in the first decade of this century, influenced the enactment of a law that incorporated the demands of populations of informal settlements in Lima (see Box 7.1).

To analyse mobilisations, we adopted an explicitly bottom-up and actor-centred approach, starting from the settlement level. We inquired into the specific issues people mobilise for or against, and tried to identify key actors driving social mobilisation. Moreover, our research has been guided by a recognition that people can act politically in many different ways, and we have therefore sought to map the different modalities of mobilisation in each case. Finally, we wanted to see if local social struggles have managed to articulate with other civil society networks or scales of governance – put simply, whether the mobilisation of informal settlement dwellers is being 'scaled up' (McIlwaine 1998). By looking at the connections between sub-local contestation in each settlement and wider urban social and political networks, we did not limit each settlement as an isolated case study. Rather, we included alliances and governance arrangements at the city scale. Before drawing evidence from the settlement stories to highlight different modalities of social mobilisation in various urban contexts, we present the analytical and conceptual framework that we have utilised to frame this research, with reference to contemporary theoretical debates on social mobilisation in political science, sociology, anthropology and urban geography.

Box 7.1 The main phases of social mobilisation for land and housing in Lima since the 1970s

Carlos Escalante Estrada

Social mobilisation for access to land and housing in Lima has changed since the 1970s. These changes are related to the nature of the mobilisation, its main features, and especially its capacity to influence the urban development processes of a city that has also experienced great transformations (see Box 3.1). Three phases can be identified during this period.

From the centralisation to the fragmentation of the dwellers' movement

Social mobilisation in the 1970s claimed for the right to have a place to live in the city (land titling of informal land occupations) and for minimum living conditions (water and sewerage services). This movement was led by neighbourhood leaders, who were very often supported by strong ideological bases and even political structures. These mobilisations were part of a process that centralised organisations and enabled the creation of the National Confederation of Shantytowns and Popular Urbanisations of Peru (*Confederación Nacional de Pueblos Jóvenes y Urbanizaciones Populares del Perú:* CONAPJUV) and the Departmental Federation of Shantytowns and Popular Urbanisations (*Federación Departamental de Pueblos Jóvenes y Urbanizaciones Populares*: FEDEPJUV), among others.

After the fall of the military government in 1977 and the return of representative democracy in the 1980s, two processes that affected neighbourhood movements developed together. First, the call for the election of government representatives, especially municipal authorities, turned several neighbourhood leaders into mayors, councillors, etc. Second, the intensification of the Shining Path's subversive violence aimed to co-opt and control neighbourhood organisations as part of its strategy to lay siege to the national government. To achieve this objective, the Shining Path relied on proselytising and on intimidation mechanisms, such as the assassination of opposing social leaders. Political violence is undoubtedly a crucial factor in the retreat and fragmentation of the Peruvian dwellers' movement.

The paradigm shift generates new conditions

The change of the country's economic model in the 1990s implied market opening, privatisation and the systematic and maximalist application of a neoliberal economic policy that cut labour rights and devaluated the national currency against the US Dollar (the economic shock of August 1990). Those measures increased poverty and informality but at the same time enabled the development of a social compensation policy that included the creation of the National Fund of Compensation and Social Development (FONCODES) and the National Programme of Food Support (PRONNA). In relation to housing and urban land, the policy was managed by several government spheres such as the Bank of Materials (*Banco de Materiales*) and the Commission for the Formalisation of Informal Property (*Comisión de Formalización de la Propiedad Informal*: COFOPRI).[1]

Economic crisis, assistantship, the dominance of individualist approaches intensively promoted by the media, corporate groups, and government sectors, led to a framework where pragmatism overwhelmed social and neighbourhood leadership. In addition, other dimensions, such as income and health, were incorporated in the social agenda and gained momentum over old claims for land and basic services. In general, representative schemes got rid of pyramidal models and relied on more fragmented organisation types that responded to a larger set of claims and more diluted economic processes.

A process of national consultation and democratic transition initiated after the fall of Alberto Fujimori's corrupt and dictatorial regime (1990–2000) took place due to massive popular mobilisation. Spaces such as the Consultation Board for Poverty Fighting (*Mesa de Concertación de lucha contra la Pobreza*), Participatory Budgeting, and local and regional Participation Councils, were articulated as part of the new political scenario. They also boosted a citizen movement different from the existing neighbourhood organisation movement.

On the one hand, the land formalisation policy conducted by the COFOPRI could not solve informal tenure problems and, on the other, it favoured informal occupation since it opened the possibility to eventually reach legal tenure. This was aggravated by the deactivation of Municipal Housing Programmes that eliminated any kind of planned access to land.[2] Thus, new land occupations kept occurring in the periphery of Lima and Peru's main cities.

The rise of new expressions

At the beginning of the 2000s, several neighbourhood organisations and NGOs that provided land tenure assistance to dwellers, decided to promote a Citizen Campaign for the Right to Housing in Peru (Escalante 2005). It aimed to denounce the habitable conditions of more than a million urban poor households, to develop advocacy activities, and to claim housing as a human right. This campaign developed a proposal for including an article on Right to Housing in the draft for a reform of the National Constitution,[3] and two law proposals for promoting land access and developing adequate financing mechanisms for low-income populations. Both proposals were part of a Supporting System for Social Housing and Habitat Production for the urban poor. The campaign led to a number of mobilisations to the National Congress, debate forums, and to several neighbourhood assemblies for presenting and discussing norm proposals and even establishing links with bodies from the United Nations (UN-Habitat and the UN Special Rapporteur on adequate housing, who came on a Mission to Peru in 2003). As a result of this process, the National Congress issued a new law on land and housing that partially considered the campaign's demands. In addition, main leaders of the mobilised populations agreed to form a Federation of Neighbourhood Organisations from Lima and Callao (*Federación de Organizaciones Vecinales de Lima y Callao*: FOVELIC) that was disabled after a few years.

It is important to mention that more recent human settlements are much smaller, more scattered and less visible in the urban spread than those from the 1970s. Furthermore, these newer land occupations are no longer the result of initiatives from homeless populations, but are generally organised by informal real estate agents commonly referred to as 'land traffickers'. New urban dwellers rely on the direct negotiation of small public works for their urgent necessities, such as stairways or roads, with authorities or even candidates. This situation has also permitted the rise of more centralised organisations, such as the General Coordinator of United Shantytowns from Lima and Callao (*Coordinadora Nacional de Pueblos Unidos del Perú*: CONAPUP), and some others that aim to mediate the clientelistic relationship between the state and the population (Cruz *et al*. 2011).

Nevertheless, a number of transformations took place in the domain of urban policies and development. A housing policy for lower-income sectors that went beyond the mere recognition of occupations and the marginal support to self-construction was approved for the first time ever. In addition, municipalities progressively acquired greater financial means and promoted the development of large-scale projects based on private initiatives for modernising the city. These new urban policy components generated new conditions for popular mobilisation. A first housing-related mobilisation, that united the potential beneficiaries of the *Techo Propio* ('My Own Roof') subsidised programme under this policy, emerged in September 2009, but could not survive due to organisational problems.

Ollanta Humala won the presidential election in 2011 with a social transformation programme. Neighbourhood leaders that supported his electoral campaign decided to constitute the Roofless People Movement (*Movimiento de Pobladores Sin Techo*: MST), formed by tenants who demanded housing programmes suitable for low-income populations. It is currently the most active neighbourhood organisation at the metropolitan level, convoking several mobilisations and advocating for the approval of a metropolitan policy that includes the promotion of low-income housing programmes. It has also presented similar initiatives to the National Congress.

However, this process has not yet established relationships with other actors that promoted mobilisations around specific agendas. Among these actors are organisations from the 'Huascar' informal settlement, who asked for the suspension of their expropriation process; organisations from the Left Bank of the Rímac River (MIRR); and organisations from many new human settlements dispersed on the outskirts of the city. It is still a challenge to establish a stronger link between more proactive movements that, to a certain extent, fight for the transformation of the current social model, and those whose vindictive claims are more focused.

References

Cruz, V., Escalante, C.E., *et al.* (2011) *La vivienda y el hábitat en el Perú 2009 y el 2010.* Lima: Grupo por el Derecho a la Vivienda.

Escalante, C. (2005) 'Producción Social del Hábitat en el Perú'. *Análisis y Propuestas.* Lima: Comité de Campaña por el Derecho a la Vivienda para Todas y Todos, pp. 59–60, 77–88.

Theoretical debates, analytical and conceptual framework

This section focuses on theoretical issues and concepts that we found the most relevant to analyse and interpret the findings of our case studies. Thus, concepts such as social movements and civil society, coping strategies and collective action, and spaces of citizenship are defined and discussed.

Social movements and civil society organisations

The notion of civil society organisations (CSOs) and its relationship with the concept of social movements needs to be defined and explored. According to Wilkinson (1971: 27) 'a social movement is a deliberate collective endeavor to promote change'. Social movements take on many forms, from those that are well established to those that are more temporary, such as protest movements, which emerge and disappear as issues and events arise and as they integrate into broader organisations or society. They include self-defined social movements, riots and strikes, crowds and mobs and they may be supported by CSOs. They must be considered in relation to the political parties, institutions, international agencies and social agents within whom they interact. Goodwin and Jasper's (2009: 4) definition of a social movement reveals its broad nature. They state that 'a social movement is a collective, organized, sustained, and non-institutional challenge to authorities, power-holders, or cultural beliefs and practices'. Della

Porta and Diani (1999: 16) suggest that social movements are '(1) informal networks, based (2) on shared beliefs and solidarity, which mobilize about (3) conflictual issues, through (4) the frequent use of various forms of protest'. Thus, it is not only processes of collective action that characterise social movements, but in addition the ideas of protests, resistance and opposition, aim at change. CSOs, although a potential component of social movements, refer to arrangements that may, or may not, endorse the same type of agenda and mode of action.

Given that the notion of civil society indeed is ubiquitous and marked by conceptual ambiguity (Jenkins 2010), our use of civil society organisations and networks calls for some operationalisations to be made. Among the various CSOs, a major distinction is often made between, on the one hand, non-governmental organisations (NGOs) and, on the other, community-based organisations (CBOs). Whereas the latter are membership-based, the former are not (Sen 1999). In the Indian context, for instance, Jenkins' (2010) literature review of the divide between NGOs and social movements, identifies the following differences:

- social movements are depicted as working at the grassroots level, seeking people empowerment, being radical, political, choosing the path of confrontation, and challenging state orthodoxy and political frame;
- NGOs are considered to be office-based, creating new forms of dependency for the poor, reformist, 'depoliticising', preferring the path of negotiation, and preserving the existing system and political frame (Jenkins 2010, see also Kumar 2008).

There is also a difference of scale, magnitude and complexity (de Souza 2013). However, relationships and hybrid organisational forms are also emerging, blurring the boundaries and bridging the differences in the binary of 'social movement versus NGOs' (Jenkins 2010). The distinctive characteristics presented above do not always fully coincide with reality. In fact, scholars such as Pithouse (2004: 181) have criticised the binary as 'utterly unhelpful' in that it glosses over, on the one hand, how mass-based organisations can be directly controlled by NGOs or funders and, on the other hand, how many NGOs are the sites of popular contestation.

While many of our case studies are dominated by strategic interactions between mass-based organisations and the expertise and activism of NGOs, the line is often difficult to draw and changes over time. In Lima, for instance, certain NGOs and CBOs tended to endorse the most political stance, whereas some social movements on the contrary were limited to a pragmatic and depoliticised approach (however, not in the case under study). In Brazil, new social movements emerged during the struggle for democracy in the 1970s and 1980s. In the 1990s many of them became professionalised organisations with bureaucratic capacities resembling NGOs. However, many have been helpful in supporting the development of new protests and movements that have emerged since 2010 (see Box 7.2). Thus, when we use an historical perspective, the binary of 'social movement versus NGOs' is somewhat lacking in analytical clarity.

Box 7.2 Brazil's World Cup protests, 2013–14[4]

Einar Braathen

In June 2013 the Confederations Cup, the test-run for the football World Cup 2014, was played out. The mass demonstrations that spread across Brazil against precarious and over-priced urban collective transport, corruption and grossly expensive World Cup projects took the mass media in Brazil and worldwide by surprise. Ten million people showed up in the streets in almost 500 cities, the largest demonstrations in Brazil's history (Maricato 2013).

The 'Vinegar Uprising' in June 2013

The events were ironically nicknamed the 'Vinegar Uprising' by social movements and protesters. The first demonstrations in São Paulo were organised by the movement for free public transport, *Movimento Passe Livre*, on 6 and 13 June. What started out as peaceful demonstrations turned into violent clashes between protesters and the police, who used weapons such as tear gas, rubber bullets and batons to control the demonstrations. Vinegar can be used to alleviate the effects of tear gas, and is therefore something that many protesters carried. On 13 June, some 60 protesters were arrested for possessing this 'weapon', which has been widely ironized by protesters. Vinegar therefore soon became a symbol for the movement. A Facebook campaign to 'legalise vinegar' was launched, and the 'March for Legalising Vinegar' gathered tens of thousands of participants. While there was a humoristic spin on these initiatives, it underlined the absurdity of the situation where the police, who were supposed to protect and serve the population, engaged in a full-on confrontation with peaceful protesters. The police did not distinguish them from the handful of people who had taken advantage of the general confusion to commit acts of vandalism (Braathen, Sørbøe and da Silva 2013).

World Cup versus people's needs

Among the banners carried by protesters in the mass mobilisations across Brazil, a frequent slogan demanded 'FIFA standards' on education, health and security. The Confederations Cup spurred debate over the massive public spending on stadiums and infrastructure for the mega-event when the quality of public services was of alarmingly poor quality.

The World Cup 2014 cost more than the past three World Cups combined. While the Ministry of Sports' official figure was USD 11.6 billion of public money spent, recent estimates put the World Cup's total cost closer to USD 15–20 billion (Zimbalist 2014). The mega-sports events were to showcase a modern and developed Brazil. In the case of Rio de Janeiro, the World Cup in combination with the 2016 Olympics was part of a marketing strategy to become a 'global city' (Mascarenhas 2014).

Over the last decade Brazil has had a steady economic growth and social uplift. 10 per cent of the population, nearly 20 million people, has moved out of extreme poverty (Singer 2012). However, Brazil suffers from insufficient and inefficient public services, due to corruption and the lack of political will to prioritise their proper delivery. Brazil spends only 3 per cent of its Gross Domestic Product (GDP) on education, and two-thirds of Brazilian fifteen-year-olds are incapable of more than basic mathematics and half cannot draw inferences from what they read. Brazil spends only 3.77 per cent of GDP on health, much of it in the private health services for the well-off classes (IPEA 2011, *Carta Capital* 2012). The country ranks lower than comparable economies in Latin America on infant mortality, life expectancy and a range of other indicators (UNDP 2014).

Instead of increasing health and education spending, billions of public funds have gone towards white elephant projects related to the World Cup. In total Rio de Janeiro spent BRL 3.4 billion (around USD 1.4 billion), 65 per cent more than estimated. The beloved Maracanã stadium in Rio underwent its second renovation in seven years in order to meet the FIFA standards. The upgrade for the 2014 event amounted to BRL 1.050 billion (Comitê Popular 2014: 131). The accusations were that the construction consortium has tapped into the public coffers to the maximum.

The street demonstrations were, however, not against the mega-sport events themselves. The excessive economic costs, the illegal evictions because of the public works, and other side-effects of the events were in focus. The Confederations Cup served as an arena for international and national media attention, and its corrupt management became an evident symbol of what has been perceived as the large political evils at the national level.

The youth versus the power

What was fascinating about the June 2013 demonstrations was how quickly they spread from being a handful of leftist youth activists marching for cheaper public transportation to becoming an all-encompassing movement with the support of 81 per cent of the population (*O Globo* 2014). The majority of the people taking to the streets in June were young people from the lower-middle and working classes, with some education but many living in the precarious peripheries of the cities. They did not have much political formation or prior experience with demonstrations. They were at large mobilised through social media platforms such as Facebook, Twitter and YouTube. Social media had not only been used to mobilise people but also as a political tool. Videos portraying police violence uploaded online gave credibility to the demonstrations. While the conservative media in the beginning characterised the protesters as a gang of vandals and troublemakers, justifying the police repression in order to protect public property, they were forced to change their discourse as the demonstrations spread. From one day to the next, the major Brazilian news corporation – O Globo – turned around and supported the demonstrations. In other words, the protests became a huge wake-up call for the traditional power centres.

President Dilma's turn-around

While President Dilma Rousseff was notoriously quiet during the first week of the demonstrations, she radically changed her approach on Monday 24 June. After having met a delegation of activists from *Movimento Passe Livre*, she delivered a televised speech to the nation. She praised the demonstrators who used their democratic rights and raised their voices. She claimed they contributed to a much-needed 'oxygenation of the political system' by resisting the 'money power in politics'.

She denounced the excessive use of force by the police, promised to deepen citizen participation in policy-making and announced several initiatives. The key ones were: first, a popular referendum on political reform; second, earmarking oil revenues for education; and, third, a national transport plan elaborated in a participatory way with full civil society involvement from the city to federal levels, to be supported by massive investments to improve 'urban mobility'.

The urban transport reform

Millions of low-income people live in the peripheries of Rio de Janeiro and commute to more central parts of the metropolitan region to get access to jobs, schools, shopping centres, sports and cultural venues. To commute they depend on public transport, on which they spend more money and more time every year – the latter due to congestion and poor services. A more affordable and expedient public transport system is a key to improve the quality of living in the mega-cities. Henceforth, people applauded President Rousseff's promise to allocate an additional BRL 50 billion (USD 25 billion) to investments in urban transport systems. São Paulo, Rio de Janeiro and other cities were quick to reverse the price increases on public transport, which had initially triggered the demonstrations. The announced decrease in the price of user fares was to be compensated by the city government in the form of increased subsidies to the companies operating the public transportation. However, these companies and their shady connections to politicians who had given them concessions were one of the targets of the protesters.

Therefore, the *Movimento Passe Livre* criticised these measures, and the movement called for public inquiries into the linkages between transport concessionaries and politicians. In Rio de Janeiro, popular pressure led to the decision to establish a Parliamentary Inquiry Commission to investigate the concession contracts between the municipality and the bus companies. However, counter to 'good governance practice', the municipal council in Rio did not allow those who pushed for the inquiry to lead the commission. The pro-Inquiry-Commission councillors therefore pulled out of the commission, which never produced any open hearings or reports.

The *Movimento Passe Livre* initially demanded that urban transport became a free-for-all public service, as part of the right to the city, which is already embodied in the federal City Statute from 2001. In some cities, urban authorities partly addressed the demand, by making transportation free only for students and unemployed, while 'freezing' the general fare.

The national transport plan that President Dilma Rousseff proposed was to be elaborated with the full involvement of the civil society, as prescribed by the 1988 Constitution. In the 1990s, many cities run by the Workers' Party (PT) excelled in participatory democracy. After Lula became the president of Brazil in 2003, almost every national policy sector formulated its priorities and guidelines through conferences starting at the municipality level, then carried on at state levels and finalised at the federal level. This participatory type of governance was discontinued by President Rousseff. Typically, the president did not follow up her promises for the transport sector.

2014

By 2014, the president, her government and the local governors were not any more concerned with 'the voice of the street' raised in June 2013. Instead they paid most of their attention to two interrelated issues: first, carrying out the football World Cup safely and without the embarrassing mass demonstrations as seen in 2013; second, ensuring their re-election thus helping their 'heirs' to win the federal and state elections in October 2014.

There were several attempts to continue the movement of 2013. However, the initiatives to protest against the World Cup itself were met by a massive police force equipped with even more weapons and new legal powers (Amnesty International Brazil 2014). At the end of the day, most Brazilians were probably far more interested in football and how their national team would get on in the Cup than in continuing to show their anger at the politicians.

References

Amnesty International Brazil (2014) 'Brasil, chega de Bola fora. Protestos durante a Copa 2014: balanço preliminar'. July 2014. Available at http://issuu.com/anistiabrasil/docs/balanc__o_parcial_-_copa_-_final (accessed on 12 January, 2015).

Braathen, E., Mascarenhas, G. and Sørbøe, C.M. (2015) 'A "City of exception"? Rio de Janeiro and the disputed social legacy of the 2014 and 2016 sport mega-events'. In G. Poynter and V. Viehoff (eds) *Mega-event cities: Urban legacies of global sports events*. Surrey and Burlington: Ashgate.

Braathen,E., Sørbøe, C.M. and da Silva, A.L. (2013) 'Brazil's Vinegar Uprising and its effects'. NIBR's International Blog, 3 July, 2013. Available at http://blog.nibrinter national.no/#post61 (accessed on 12 January, 2015).

Carta Capital (2012) 'De pires na mão'. 25 January, 2012.

Comitê Popular (2014) *Megaeventos e Violações dos Direitos Humanos no Rio de Janeiro*. Rio de Janeiro: Comitê Popular da Copa e Olimpíadas, June 2014. Available at https://comitepopulario.files.wordpress.com/2014/06/dossiecomiterio2014_web. pdf (accessed on 12 January, 2015).

IPEA (2011) 'Governo gastador ou transferidor? Um macro diagnóstico das despesas federais'. Comunicado n° 122. Brasília: Instituto de Pesquisa Econômica Aplicada.

Maricato, E. (2013) 'É a questão urbana, estúpido!' In *Cidades Rebeldes: Passe Livre e as Manifestações que Tomaram as Ruas do Brasil*. São Paulo: Boitempo Editorial, pp. 32–46.

Mascarenhas, G. (2014) 'O Brasil urbano na era dos megaeventos: uma nova geografia para 2014'. In V. Melo, F. Peres and M. Drummond (eds) *Esporte, cultura, nação, estado: Brasil e Portugal*. 1. ed. Rio de Janeiro: 7 Letras, 1, pp. 188–200.

O Globo (2014) 'Cresce rejeição de brasileiros às manifestações, diz Datafolha'. 24 February, 2014. Available at http://oglobo.globo.com/brasil/cresce-rejeicao-de-brasileiros-as-manifestacoes-diz-datafolha-11694381#ixzz3PHBTf8tK (accessed on 12 January, 2015).

Singer, A.V. (2012) *Os sentidos do Lulismo. Reforma Gradual e o Pacto Conservador*. São Paulo: Companhia Das Letras.

UNDP (2014) *Human development report 2014. Sustaining human progress: Reducing vulnerabilities and building resilience*. New York: United Nations Development Programme.

Zimbalist, A. (2014) 'Get ready for a massive World Cup hangover, Brazil'. *Time Magazine*, 27 June, 2014. Available at http://time.com/2930699/world-cup-brazil-spending (accessed on 15 July, 2014).

Still, we would argue that these concepts are relevant and part of a still on-going debate, as illustrated by the recent forum on 'NGOs, Social Movements and the City' in the journal *City* (2013a and 2013b), that discusses the convergences and divergences between these two categories. Several issues are addressed, which are reflected in our case studies, such as: to whom these actors are accountable and how they claim legitimacy; how they give voice and representation to people – 'who speaks for whom?'; the circumstances under which they can be manipulated and co-opted by nodes of power; and what their different institutional logics are (Lipietz 2013a and 2013b, Pithouse 2013, de Souza 2013, Cabannes 2013). Even more importantly, categories such as NGOs and social movements are often used actively by the actors involved in our case studies, for self-identification and legitimation purposes.

Given the large and rather ideological and normative debate on what constitutes a social movement, we chose to adopt a broad definition of the social movement in our research based on Wilkinson (1971) and Goodwin and Jasper's (2009) conceptualisation (see above), without a priori excluding any non-state organisation. We argue that research on social mobilisation should be more grounded on empirical analysis, focusing on one of its core characteristics, namely that of collective action (as developed in the next section). In our analytical framework, we have therefore included all types of organised non-state actors without developing a pre-conceived hierarchy related to their role in mobilisation. We further paid special attention to the configuration of actors forming the CSO network and the relationships between the different actors in each case study. We nevertheless recognise that the notion of the CSO network does not necessarily imply strong networking between the various actors, who instead may compete for a hegemonic position or oppose each other. The relations and interactions between actors are important to explore as a means of explaining the success and scaling-up of a mobilisation campaign.

From coping strategies to collective action

To analyse the forms of popular agency and mobilisation, we explored the varied responses from the poor, ranging from those highlighted by the subaltern approach that stresses the urban poor's coping strategies, to those emphasised by the insurgency approach that puts citizens' claims to the fore. The contrast between what Bayat (2010) depicts as 'the quiet encroachment of the ordinary' and insurgent urbanism leads us to ask whether they reflect distinct moments in time, through a process of mobilisation. In what follows, we address this question in more detail.

Although informal settlements are spaces of deep inequality and deprivation, we argue that in informal settlements in most of the selected cities the mundane and survivalist everyday arrangements characterise these settlements rather than social mobilisation or protests. Life in informal settlements is therefore dominated by coping forms of resilience and familial strategies rather than collective action at the settlement level. Such situations may be best understood as 'the quiet encroachment of the ordinary', or 'the [social] non-movement of the urban dispossessed', analysed by Bayat (2010: 15) in the context of Middle Eastern cities,[5] and that 'encapsulates the discreet and prolonged ways in which the poor struggle to survive and to better their lives by quietly impinging on the propertied and powerful, and on society at large' (Bayat 2010: 15). However, external interventions or changes in the settlement can trigger social action, resulting in mobilisation and protests as a response to these interventions.

In all circumstances, we must appreciate the agency of the urban poor. Thus, to study 'subaltern urbanism'[6] (Roy 2011), we followed an actor-centred approach, namely 'an approach that consists of restoring to the actors involved their share of initiative in working out their own lives' (Godard 1990: 9 – our translation). This is the approach adopted in India by the subalternist school of thought, that recognises 'the exercise of agency by subaltern subjects' (Baviskar 2003: 97), even in the context of slum evictions (Dupont and Vaquier, 2013). Similarly, Berry-Chikhaoui and Deboulet (2002) emphasise the abilities and skills of ordinary city dwellers, in order to understand the making of the city.[7] Such an approach implies considering the urban poor and vulnerable groups as *not* mere passive recipients – or victims – of public policies and external interventions.

As a contrast to Bayat's 'non-movement of the urban dispossessed' we can consider the notion of insurgent urbanism. Developed in the Brazilian (Holston 1995, 2008) and South African (Miraftab and Wills 2005, Miraftab 2009) contexts, it refers to 'radical planning practices that challenge the inequitable specifics of neoliberal governance operating through inclusion', or, to be more specific, to a type of formal inclusion that does not correspond to substantive inclusion (Miraftab 2009: 40–41). The general background of insurgent urbanisation is further defined as a situation where:

> the majority of marginalized people take in their own hands the challenges of housing, neighborhood and urban development, establishing shelter and earning livelihoods outside formal decision structures and 'professionalized planning'
>
> (Miraftab 2009: 42)

The fact that Holston and Miraftab developed their conceptualisations based on national contexts radically different from India indicates that different regimes of governance, as discussed in Chapter 3, play a key role in shaping how poor people express their political agency. Still, the notion of insurgency resonates well with the experiences of Indian cities too. However, the practices of insurgent planning, defined as the 'purposeful actions that aim to disrupt domineering relationships of oppressors to the oppressed' (Miraftab 2009: 44), necessitate a degree of political consciousness, along with united mobilisation. This may be difficult to achieve in many fragmented slum communities (or rather non-communities as we could argue). Nevertheless, the insurgency approach has inspired some Brazilian academics who worked with the People's Plan of the community of Vila Autódromo in Rio de Janeiro (Settlement Story 4.4). They refer to this experience as an 'effort of urban self-planning in a conflict situation', an effort they define as 'conflictual planning' (*planejamento conflitual*)[8] (Vainer *et al.* 2013: 4 – our translation).

Similarly, 'occupancy urbanism' was propounded by Benjamin (2008) in the context of Indian cities. The concept articulates the assertion of territorial claims by poor groups, the practice of vote-bank politics or clientelism, and the interactions with the lower level of state bureaucracy. This could be a pertinent framework to explain the possible transition from 'the quiet encroachment of the ordinary' to insurgent urbanism. When citizens from settlements that are considered illegal engage with both the political and administrative apparatus, it is primarily to secure their 'quiet encroachment' of land in the city. But we can also read into such tactics a conscious strategy to subvert the dominant planning rules.

Indeed the notions of 'the quiet encroachment of the ordinary' and insurgent urbanism raise the following questions: Do these contrasting approaches reflect different modes of actions embedded in different socio-political contexts as well as different national and local contexts? Or, do such different practices rather correspond to distinct moments over time, through a *process* of mobilisation? For instance, Cindi Katz distinguished three main forms of community responses that highlight a progression throughout evolving phases of resistance: (i) 'forms of resilience that enable people to survive without really changing the circumstances that make such survival so hard', (ii) 'forms of reworking that alter the organisation but not the polarisation of power relations', and, finally, (iii) 'resistance that involves oppositional consciousness and achieves emancipatory change' (Katz, quoted by Sparke 2008: 424).

In short, do the informal settlers' practices and community responses observed in the six cities under investigation allow us to evidence a continuum of mobilisation, across different spaces and over time? Depending on the contingency of the local situation, we do find different ways to articulate the claims of the urban poor to land and shelter. And we do observe *processes* of mobilisation that need to be understood with a long-term perspective. This will be presented in detail and discussed in the last part of this chapter.

In order to understand the dynamics of mobilisation, or lack thereof, it is important to reflect on the rationales behind collective action.[9] In *The logic of collective action*, Olson (1977) adopts a utilitarian perspective to explain group behaviour, based on individuals' rationality understood as weighing costs and benefits at the individual level (not at the group level). He argues that collective action occurs when the 'total worth' exceeds the level of 'total cost' of the actors involved, and that the group will not mobilise until and unless the individuals are provided with 'selective incentives'. In our empirical material, there is certainly plenty of evidence seemingly supporting this utilitarian approach, for instance in how civil society was divided into beneficiaries and non-beneficiaries from the housing project in Joe Slovo, Cape Town.

Still, there are also continuities and forms of solidarity that do not seem to lend their support to Olson's rational choice approach. Since Olson published his theory, several scholars have proposed alternative explanations where emphasis is placed on the role of group solidarity and responsibility (Tilly, Tilly and Tilly 1975, Zald and McCarthy 1979). In their resource mobilisation theory, McCarthy and Zald place formal organisations at the core of social movements and examine the role of external and internal actors in their dynamics (McCarthy and Zald 1977). Bebbington (2006: 4) further discusses the effect of the actors' heterogeneity in social movement, stating that:

> while the actors involved in these movements do not need to share exactly the same visions either of the reasons for protest or for the alternatives being sought, there does need to be a significant overlap among these visions in order to sustain the movement and give it its coherence.

Ostrom (2000) further argues that 'contextual variables' are vital to have a thorough understanding of the path to co-operation and collective action. Among the many contextual variables identified as 'conducive or detrimental to endogenous collective action' (Ostrom 2000: 148), we can underline those that resonate with situations encountered during our field studies in informal settlements:

> [T]he size of the group involved; the heterogeneity of the group; [. . .] common understanding of the group; the size of the total collective benefice; [. . .] the size of the temptation to free ride; the loss to cooperators when others do not cooperate; having a choice of participating or not; the presence of leadership; past experience and level of social capital; the autonomy to make binding rules; and a wide diversity of rules that are used to change the structure of the situation.
>
> (Ostrom 2000: 148)

Our empirical studies across cities and countries highlight the various dimensions of mobilisation, as well as the significant role of contextual factors, organisations and group solidarity for collective action. This does touch upon a longstanding debate in sociology, namely the centrality of 'contextual factors' in explaining social movements. What the approaches outlined in this section have in common, however, is that they carry a strong actor-centred focus on *how* collective action comes to be. This contrasts with the tradition known as theories of new social movements, championed by sociologists such as Alain Touraine (1985) and Alberto Melucci (1989), emphasising *why* social movements emerge in post-industrial societies. While we acknowledge that a study of the politics of informal settlements in the global South at its heart is shaped by a political economy that creates the unequal cities we have studied, we find that the focus on collective agency in the literature presented here is the most useful framework for analysis.

The literature on social mobilisation also strongly emphasises the political and cultural dimensions of social movements, especially their identity content, while the role of emotions in protest is also given due recognition (Goodwin and Jasper 2009). The way in which actors employ frames of collective action greatly influence how they manage to mobilise different constituencies and identities (Benford and Snow 2000). How frames are assembled to assign an *us* (e.g., informal settlement dwellers or residents of a particular settlement) and a *them* (e.g., the state), depends on structural opportunities and existing identities in each case.

Spaces for participation and confrontation

Another important dimension of social mobilisation is how various popular actors engage with formal authorities in order to realise their demands. To better understand the tactics and strategies deployed in the context of specific settlements, we examined how different spaces of participation and contestation were used at different stages of mobilisation. In the above-mentioned resource mobilisation theory, these are often conceptualised as 'political opportunity structures', and refer to the different degrees of state repression shaping collective mobilisation (e.g., McAdam, McCarthy and Zald 1996). We rely on a distinct, yet related, literature on political participation to develop our own analytical framework. Here, the notion that different social actors have access to different 'spaces of participation' was first articulated by Cornwall (2002). It was later refined by Miraftab (2004), who distinguishes between 'invited' and 'invented' spaces of participation and citizenship. According to her:

> 'invited' spaces are defined as the ones occupied by those grassroots and their allied non-governmental organizations that are legitimized by donors and government interventions. 'Invented' spaces are those, also occupied by the grassroots and claimed by their collective action, but directly confronting the authorities and the status quo.
>
> (Miraftab 2004: 1)

As Miraftab suggests, while both NGOs and social movements might enter into 'invited spaces' of engagement, 'invented spaces' are characterised by being firmly controlled by mass-based social movements. These 'invented' spaces of citizenship, also termed 'spaces of insurgent citizenship' (Holston 1995, Miraftab and Wills 2005),[10] have to be analysed as distinct from the 'invited' spaces of participation, although these are not necessarily mutually exclusive. Thus,

> fluidity characterizes insurgent practices: through the entanglement of inclusion and resistance they move across the invited and the invented spaces of citizenship.
>
> (Miraftab 2009: 35)

Rather than seeing it as a sharp binary, we see the invented/invited coupling as encapsulating various modalities and phases of mobilisation (see Sutherland 2011).

This link between participation and mobilisation remains a matter of empirical investigation, such as to what extent invited spaces are controlled by state or corporate authorities. After all, as discussed in Chapter 4, the capacity to decide *who* participates, and *who* defines the agenda, and *who* sets the rules, also represents a dimension of power (see Braathen, Attwood and May 2012). When processes of managerial governance exclude certain subjects from real and meaningful participation while including others, this is a way to curb contestation.

Various modalities of mobilisation

The settlement stories from six cities in four countries depict different tactics and strategies, as well as various phases in the mobilisation process. We have identified the following broad modalities of mobilisation. First, we observe various forms of everyday resilience (cf. Katz 2004) across all cases, most of which would probably be categorised as 'quiet encroachment' by Bayat (2010). Second, in most of the cases we have also observed social protest, where tactics turn towards confrontational mobilisation and where claims of insurgent citizenship are made through what Miraftab (2009) labels 'invented spaces'. Third, a common modality in several mobilisations we have studied is what we have labelled 'judicialisation'. The way in which CBOs are claiming, and are being caught up in, the spaces of the judicial system neither seem to fit the 'invented' nor the 'invited' categories. Moreover, these legal phases appear to completely dominate political dynamics in the process. Fourth, many civil society organisations do at strategic points in time chose to engage in 'invited spaces' of local state actors through tactics that we have labelled engagement and partnership. Fifth, another important moment of mobilisation is also examined, the divisive effects of interventions on collective action and the resulting demobilisation. Sixth and last, we also observe in our case material situations characterised by the absence of mobilisation over time, despite external intervention affecting the settlement.

All our cases show how different modalities of social mobilisation are used at different times in particular local spaces. We will now turn our attention to each of these main modalities and discuss them in detail.

1 Everyday forms of resilience

In all the different urban contexts studied, resilience is manifested in the everyday practices of informal settlers and the homeless as they struggle to assert and secure their place in the city. Thus, the genesis of all informal settlements exemplifies the way in which their residents have been striving to access basic urban services and to improve their living environment, ranging from the continuous efforts of individual families, to small group initiatives and larger collective actions. The story of the squatter settlements along the Buckingham Canal in Chennai illustrates this point (Settlement Story 6.6). In Delhi, the return of evicted slum dwellers to their previous sites as long as the land remained vacant (Dupont 2008), or the homeless squatting on the pavement and changing their sleeping places to escape being chased away by the police (Settlement Story 6.5), also demonstrate forms of resilience and acts of resistance. Moreover, everyday practices may turn into inventive tactics, in response to specific circumstances and events. For instance, in the Ocean Drive-In settlement in Durban, the simple fact of putting blankets on their doors, thus hiding house numbers, was an act of resistance by some residents against the community mapping process initiated without involving them adequately (see Settlement Stories 4.3 and 6.2). These examples further reveal the informal settlers' 'agency in times of constraints' (Bayat 2010: ix).

2 Protest or confrontational mobilisation

When external interventions threaten to significantly disrupt life in a settlement or result in evictions, when projects affecting informal settlers are fraught with opacity that engenders anxiety, and when residents experience acute injustice in the resettlement or the housing process, many informal settlers do not remain passive victims. The recognition that formal entitlements (as those inscribed in national constitutions) do not guarantee substantive rights to the city further encourages practices of 'active citizenship' (Miraftab and Wills 2005).

We thus found many examples of collective protests across the cities, aimed first at making the informal settlers' claims heard and giving visibility to the movement. Several forms of protest are employed across the six cities, including street demonstrations, sit-ins, and road blockades. Other insurgent practices of citizenship reflect the subalterns' creative agency and are more embedded in their local context and culture, such as *toyi-toying*, a dance with chants used in social protests in South Africa, or street plays used in India to highlight the plight of the slum dwellers and the homeless.

However, for resistance and protest to be translated into effective and sustainable mobilisation, some crucial factors are required. Efficient organisational structures in the settlement or community, such as grassroots organisations, neighbourhood associations and elected neighbourhood councils, residents' or area committees and task teams, emerged as a prerequisite in our study. In some cases, support from organisations or strategic actors outside the settlement is equally important. To that end, we find that CBOs established linkages beyond the settlement to, for instance, NGOs or human right activists (as in the campaign for the homeless' rights in Delhi), or political actors that support the residents' claims (such as city councillors from the political opposition in Rio de Janeiro). In this respect, our settlement stories provide striking instances of vertical linkages to actors from the higher echelons of power. In the Vila Autódromo case in Rio de Janeiro, the community managed in the 1990s to get support from the state governor against the city mayor (see Settlement Story 4.4). In V.P. Singh Camp, a squatter settlement in Delhi, the residents successfully resisted an attempt of demolition by the Delhi Development Authority in 1989–90 by gaining the support of the then Prime Minister of India, V.P. Singh, who stalled the demolition, hence the present name of this settlement (Saharan 2012).[11] In other instances, the role of horizontal linkages needs to be stressed. Thus, in Durban, organisations within a settlement often gain support from similar organisations within neighbouring informal settlements, who join forces and show solidarity with each other as settlement specific protests arise, reflecting a horizontal network of support.

What matters for a successful protest movement is the capacity to build alliances or coalitions including different types of actors, from different sectors, intervening at different levels. Mobilisation of networks beyond the community and backing from outside the settlement are essential to scale up the campaign to the city level or even beyond. This point is well illustrated by the campaign for the right to shelter of the homeless initiated in Delhi, in Rio by the city-wide mobilisation in the context of mega-sport events entailing urban renewal operations, and in Durban through the shack dwellers' movement, *Abahlali baseMjondolo*. In the process of mobilisation, support from political parties is also frequently sought. On the one hand, politicisation of the mobilisation helps to scale up the campaign, as observed in Rio and Durban. Yet, on the other hand when politicisation is circumscribed by local politics, it may turn into co-optation of CSOs into political client–patron relationships. This will eventually curb mobilisation, as observed in Durban in the case of Ocean Drive-in. For instance, when political allies lose local elections, a community may end up even more politically marginalised and frustrated.

3 The judicialisation of struggle

While this is not necessarily the case across the global South, in India, South Africa, Brazil and Peru, national constitutions and/or laws provide informal settlers with legal instruments they can employ to defend their rights when confronted with external interventions affecting their settlement. Under the Constitution of India (1949), the right to shelter is indirectly recognised and guaranteed as a subset flowing from the fundamental right to life (Article 21). The courts, approached by activists defending slum and pavement dwellers, especially through the Public Interest Litigation procedure, have often passed stay orders that prevented forced eviction (Ahuja 1997). Likewise, Section 26 of the Constitution of South Africa (1996) states that everyone has the right to have access to adequate housing. The South African state is thus obliged to take reasonable legislative and other measures, within its available resources, to achieve the progressive realisation of this right. In Brazil, the City Statute Law (passed in 2001) includes the right to the city, recognising all city dwellers as right holders. With the enactment of the Law for Marginal Settlements (the 'Barriadas Law') in 1961, Peru was the first country to regularise informal settlements based on self-help principles (see Box 3.1).

As an increasing share of public policy is being settled through the court system in liberal democracies, a process coined as 'judicialisation' by Ríos-Figueroa and Taylor (2006), is arguably applicable to the issue of pro-poor housing in India, South Africa, Brazil and Peru. We use the term judicialisation more specifically to refer to how local political dynamics around informal settlement upgrading and relocation tended to change character as they entered the judicial system. Judicialisation can happen as popular actors try to use progressive laws and constitutional reforms to back their cause, or by other actors such as states or developers to secure eviction orders to realise their development plans.

Taking the struggle to legal spaces requires co-operation with allies who know how to navigate the judicial system, a quest that often takes CBOs outside the community in search of support. This is a feature observed across all our cases. Morro da Providência activists in Rio de Janeiro managed to persuade the public defenders to file a case against the municipality. In Lima, communities affected by the Via Parque Rímac project got support from a left-wing mayor candidate, as well as congressmen of the Peruvian Nationalist Party, to fight their cause in court. In the Joe Slovo informal settlement of Cape Town, a community Task Team sought help from NGOs and lawyers to access legal expertise. In Durban the social movement *Abahlali baseMjondolo* uses its knowledge of the legal system to defend the rights of informal settlers in the city, directly challenging the African National Congress government through the Constitution. In Delhi, the Urban

Rights Forum for the Homeless included members with special contacts in the High Court of Delhi and the Supreme Court.

Are legal strategies used as a last resort when all the other modalities of mobilisation have failed? Not necessarily, but it always changes the dynamics of mobilisation. In several cases, it led to decisive outcomes. It may also direct the protestors towards more engagement with the state and the developer who are implementing the resettlement or rehabilitation project (see the cases of Joe Slovo in Cape Town, or Kathputli Colony in Delhi). This may, however, result in diverting the claims and collective protests on the ground. Because court orders are binding, they delegitimise to some extent protests and other acts that are not in accordance with the judgments.

A legal route has no guarantees, of course, as court decisions may not support the informal settlers' petition, and other actors use the judiciary system against the informal settlers or their activists (as observed in Joe Slovo). In Rio, residents of Morro da Providência and their supporters had to face a counter-judicial offensive by the city authorities. In the case of divided communities, adverse complainants may even be from within, as observed in Kathputli Colony where the implementation of a slum redevelopment project created new lines of division among residents with diverging interests (see Settlement Story 4.1). Furthermore, in Indian cities, many slum demolitions were the result of petitions filed in the court by civil society organisations or activists, as illustrated by the large-scale demolition drive along the banks of the Yamuna river in Delhi (see Box 5.3).

4 Engagement and partnership

Evidence from our research reveals that engagement and partnership with the local state should be considered as a means of mobilisation. However, it is important to question whether the participation of CSOs in 'invited spaces' influences the success of a mobilisation campaign, or whether it is a manipulative way of the state to curb and manage protests. At a time where requirements of community participation have gained acceptance in international development discourse as a guarantee of good governance (Christens and Speer 2006), and where government-initiated 'invited spaces' of participation reflect a broader trend in contemporary urban governance, it is worth paying attention to this question. Given the various forms of engagement and partnership, and the variety of actors involved, there is no straightforward answer.

When actors choose to participate in 'invited spaces' provided by the government, this is often met with diverging views within a CSO network, as evidenced by the coalition working on homelessness issues in Delhi. From the perspective of actors who favour public–community partnerships, many of whom might base their strategies on previous experiences with participation in government schemes, a process of mobilisation will often reach a stage where co-operation with the government must be sought in order to alert the latter to the problems on the ground. Engagement is a way to ensure that the government develops a better understanding of the grassroots' perspective. Others fear that close association with the government will deprive CSOs of their autonomy and position to oppose government policy and decisions, even when these fail to serve the interests of the people they are supposed to represent and speak for (see Pithouse 2013, de Souza 2013). In other words, there is a risk that the distance between CSOs and the state will disappear as a result of the former's strategies of engagement. This lack of autonomy resulting from collaboration with formal authorities is what we refer to as co-option. Co-option of voluntary organisations in implementing government schemes could be a way of silencing dissenting voices and preventing challenging mobilisation (Mohan and Stokke 2000). Activists critical of the benefits of participation in invited spaces, tend to rather advocate actions through 'spaces of insurgent citizenship'. These different arguments reflect ubiquitous debates. In Cape Town, for instance, Slum Dwellers International was criticised for playing the role of a 'collaborator' at the expense of its expected role as a critic.

Nevertheless, empirical evidence from the case studies indicates that while entering these 'invited spaces' tends to lead to several painful compromises, it does often offer tangible concessions to the local community – or more often to *parts* of the local community. The eagerness on the part of formal authorities to remove obstacles to their development plans, or to display participatory practices for the sake of democratic legitimacy, does offer local informal settlement dwellers some leverage. But in most of the settlement stories above, these forms of engagement and partnership are most effective when they are combined with, or backed by, other more confrontational methods.

5 Division and demobilisation

There are many factors likely to cause division of a movement and consequent demobilisation. Divisions usually arise as the result of divergence of interests within the affected communities. It can also originate in differences between organisations who support community members, as well as other intervening elements.

Division of collective action in the face of displacement threats often reflects the heterogeneity of socio-economic conditions in the settlement. The settlements we have studied display a diversity of housing conditions and occupancy statuses, as highlighted by settlement stories in Lima and Delhi (Kathputli Colony). Those families staying in the most precarious conditions can improve their situation through resettlement or rehabilitation, whereas the better off are more likely to be impacted negatively by resettlement, and thus are more eager to resist displacement. In other words, residents who have made greater investments in incremental upgrading of their houses have more to lose from relocation.

The 'tenants–house owners' divide is another case in point, with various outcomes. The initial relocation scheme for the Via Parque Rímac project in Lima provided differential compensation between the two categories. In Chennai, the resettlement scheme for squatter families evicted from the banks of the Buckingham Canal turned some tenants into winners, as they acquired a flat, and most house owners into losers, as a one-room flat in a remote area was a meagre compensation for their demolished house. In Ocean Drive-In in Durban, both owners and tenants were relocated to Hammonds Farm, although this is often not the case in relocation processes in South African cities. In most instances tenants or lodgers are displaced, and this has led to intense social protest as witnessed in the Cato Crest settlement in Durban in 2013. Last, in Kathputli Colony in Delhi, tenants were even excluded from the identification and eligibility surveys for the rehabilitation project.

Division of collective action may also stem from different perspectives among the residents: between those focusing on the short term and who want to prioritise achievable goals, and those with a longer-term vision, who are not satisfied with small gains, and want to pursue a more transformative politics that will maximise benefits in the future.

When eviction targets only certain sections of the settlement (as in Rio's *favelas* or in the squatter settlements along the Rímac river in Lima), when resettlement projects are implemented in a phased manner leaving parts of the residents behind (as in Durban Ocean Drive-In settlement), when eligibility criteria (as in India) or waiting lists (as in South Africa) for a rehabilitation or upgrading project are applied, turning only parts of the families into 'beneficiaries', these processes inevitably entail the fragmentation of communities – and subsequently that of the protest movement. Braathen suggests that scattered removal is a psychological weapon adopted to weaken resistance in Rio's *favelas* (see Settlement Story 6.1).

To summarise, the way slum resettlement or upgrading projects tend to be implemented, combined with the heterogeneous nature of many informal settlements, creates fragmented communities where divisions between (relative) winners and losers dominate politics – an effect called 'social diffraction' by Navez-Bouchanine and Chaboche (2013: 331). Subsequently, this hinders effective mobilisation. In the long run, desperation and weariness may, by themselves, also contribute to a demobilisation phase.

To compound matters, the diverging positions of supporting organisations within and beyond the settlement, in particular their dividing lines regarding the modalities of collective action (as developed above), or more generally rivalries between organisations, necessarily weaken mobilisation. Power struggles and political competition at the city level, more acute during election campaigns, also have an adverse effect on the sustainability of protest movements in informal settlements, especially when the latter are seen as vote banks (as in India). Rivalry between different political parties, given the strong influence of party politics in South Africa, has fragmented mobilisation in the country. In specific contexts, violence and fear of the police proved to be an additional factor curbing informal dwellers' movements – the violence of the Shining Path in the 1980s in Peru or the violence linked to drug traffickers in Rio's *favelas*. The frequent use of force by the South African police to control social protests both during and post-apartheid also supports this observation.

6 Weak mobilisation

We make a distinction between *demobilisation*, where an initial state of high mobilisation is quelled by various circumstances, and *weak mobilisation*, where the state of mobilisation remains low throughout the external intervention. In our study, we came across cases of settlements where mobilisation remained at a very low level, or was absent despite threats of eviction, such as in Chennai squatter settlements along the Buckingham Canal (see Settlement Story 6.6). This helped us identify potential obstacles to mobilisation. Both socio-economic and knowledge-related factors might act as disincentives to organise. At the outset, the lack of basic information may hinder mobilisation when the residents are not even aware of the interventions that will affect them, or when uncertainties are too many, as discussed in Chapter 5. Also, the lack of social and economic resources proved to be a hindrance in the most disadvantaged communities, as pointed out by Kumar (2008) in relation to social mobilisation in Indian cities.

Some other core issues for mobilisation emerge from the comparison of settlements stories across cities, especially from stories showing strong mobilisation and significant achievements on the one hand, and those highlighting weak collective action or poor outcomes on the other. As expected, solidarity, a crucial ingredient for collective action, is difficult to sustain in heterogeneous and divided communities. Collective action is further affected by the type of leadership within the settlement, which similarly often remains split along political, regional, social and religious lines. On the other hand, the lack of organisational structure in project-targeted communities is certainly detrimental to their mobilisation (as found in the squatter settlements studied in Chennai).

The role of NGOs may be ambivalent, especially when they operate in divided communities, and when competition and rivalries between organisations further hinder solidarity and unity at the settlement level. The support of NGOs with good connections with the state or judiciary apparatus is also not sufficient. Other factors, such as the involvement of the grassroots through community-based organisations and, above all, co-operation and co-ordination among the CSOs, are equally essential. Last, the role of resourceful external actors may be crucial on the one hand, but also limiting on the other hand or in other cases, as patronage may undermine people's self-reliance and proactive endeavours or autonomy of action.

The factors identified above, through the case studies, that may curb mobilisation should not be considered as absolute, insurmountable obstacles. First of all, mobilisation does not follow a linear and straightforward trajectory. Mobilisation should instead be seen as a process that unfolds, often over the course of many years, and is embedded in specific socio-spatial and historical contexts. Hence, phases of intense and successful mobilisation with tangible outcomes might be followed or preceded by phases of weak collective action or mundane, everyday practices. Also, the above-mentioned division of communities, and the related rivalries among organisations, has in some cases been overcome – at least temporarily – by strategic alliances. Conversely, just because social mobilisation is unified does not automatically make the movement strong and successful.

Intertwined modalities

The modalities of mobilisation discussed above are not comprehensive at a general level. However, they reflect the main approaches adopted by informal settlers in the six cities under investigation.[12] We should hasten to reiterate that the categories above do not represent strategic alternatives that community-based organisations are free to pick between. Rather, they are often telling of difficult circumstances that circumscribe action and force community representatives to make less-than-ideal compromises. Moreover, the various strategies identified are not exclusive of each other, as we have to recognise mobilisation as a multifaceted and evolving process. Thus, our findings show how some modalities are related to specific historical and urban contexts, but also how various tactics and strategies may be combined over time – or at the same time – in the same settlement or by the same community.

For instance, social mobilisation in the *favelas* of Rio de Janeiro highlight how protests, street demonstrations and judicial battles were strategically articulated, sometimes followed by engagement and dialogue (as in the case of Morro da Providência, see Settlement Story 6.1), and how phases of mobilisation and demobilisation alternated. In Delhi, the 2010 campaign for the right to shelter of the homeless, which exemplifies the recourse to the judicial system, was combined with forms of protests in 'invented spaces' of citizenship, as well as participation in government schemes for the homeless (see Settlement Story 6.5). In Lima, in the case of the Via Parque Rímac mega-project affecting a string of settlements located on the banks of the Rímac river, the negotiations with residents who were to be relocated were preceded by confrontational mobilisation, as well as a battle in court (see Settlement Story 6.4). While the judicialisation of politics might be temporary, it is not insignificant. When a struggle exits the legal system and returns to a politics of engagement or confrontation, it is often subject to a new balance of power created by a court order.

In Cape Town, reactions to the N2 Gateway project by the residents of Joe Slovo informal settlement have been many (see Settlement Story 6.3). While most of them were never collectively expressed, the organised forms of community response alone play out across a spectrum where forms of engagement (with authorities and implementing agencies) and levels of mobilisation (of local popular constituencies) have varied. Different strategies were pursued at different points in time, resulting in several distinct phases of community resistance to the project. The residents of Ocean Drive-In informal settlement in Durban have also adopted a wide range of strategies to improve their poor living environment and address issues related to their relocation to a formal housing project (see Settlement Story 6.2). However, these remained at the local scale, without linking up with the broader social movement supporting informal settlement dwellers in the city.

Conclusion

The settlement stories in the previous chapter and the theoretical discussion in this chapter serve a common purpose, by showing us that the social mobilisation of residents in substandard urban settlements tend to share similar modalities and go through certain phases of mobilisation across six cities on three continents. We also identified some common factors limiting or weakening collective action, in particular how upgrading and resettlement programmes are instrumental in shaping new lines of division among residents.

By way of conclusion, we will attempt to articulate in more explicit ways how these findings address some of the theoretical debates introduced above. First, we asked whether the notions of 'quiet encroachment' and insurgency identified in the literature can be seen as distinct modalities or whether they might in fact be different expressions of poor people's agency in ways that are mutually reinforcing. Our comparative empirical material offer hints as to how these two are linked in cities in the global South. The local political dynamics in our settlement stories do seem to indicate that the everyday resilience built up through coping on the margins of the city are indeed instrumental in allowing for insurgent citizenship to emerge. For instance, the acts of insurgency witnessed in this study tend to be based on existing associational networks, such as re-activated neighbourhood councils and resident associations. In this regard, the 'quiet encroachment' and 'insurgent practices' are indeed connected. This evolutionary process has occurred in situations where the communities were 'besieged' or under extreme external pressure. Moreover, most often some element of external instigation supported by a leadership already committed to insurgent practices was essential in connecting these modalities of action.

Second, it is worth asking whether the 'invited spaces' that actors have made use of in our case studies constitute real arenas for influence for residents of substandard settlements and their organisations. We argue that the extent to which 'invited spaces' *do* offer opportunities hinges in part on what takes places in 'invented spaces' of participation. When people have protested on the streets and in community halls in our six cities, this has indeed placed pressure on local government. Sometimes, such actions force authorities to make concessions to informal settlement dwellers and allow participation in places and at times when there was no invitation. In many other cases, however, protests are firmly quelled by governing practices, at times through state repression and at other times through active co-optation of movement leaders. In general, the discourses and experiences of informal settlement dwellers do not easily find their way into policies and practices. Nevertheless, when social mobilisation follows a path to the judiciary, this can result in significant shifts and, on several occasions in the cases studied in this book, to (partial) recognition of informal settlement dwellers' interests and rights.

Third, mobilisations of substandard settlement dwellers in Rio de Janeiro, Lima, Durban, Cape Town, Chennai and Delhi all testify to the importance of alliances. Mobilisation campaigns with strong internal coherence and constructive connections to external organisations are more influential. But, as mentioned above, this is not always a choice, but rather the result of politically and socially favourable contexts. Particularly in settlements that are newly established, social networks are weak and community representatives depend on connecting with expertise outside the settlement, not least when mobilisation is judicialised. This being said, representatives of substandard settlements also remain vulnerable to marginalisation within these alliances. Still, our overall observation is that such links are necessary for marginalised communities to influence the conditions of upgrading and relocation.

The fourth concluding point is that divisions fragmenting solidarity in many of the communities we have researched are often directly related to external interventions of upgrading and relocation. When development plans create potential winners and losers, communities who otherwise had achieved a certain level of mobilisation and had overcome difference easily fall prey to internal divisions and resulting demobilisation. We realise there is a danger in over-emphasising this point, and in the process implying that substandard settlements are united and homogeneous prior to these interventions. Still, in settlement after settlement presented in this volume, local politics seem inescapably caught up in conflicts of interests relating to threats of relocation and opportunities for upgrading.

On a final methodological note, we would argue that studies of the politics of informal settlements are best based on long-term perspectives. Our settlement stories are all marked by constantly evolving configurations of actors, which makes it difficult to draw definite conclusions regarding their success, their ability to scale up or to forge alliances. As Bickerstaff and Agyeman (2009: 783) suggest, social movements are not 'static, reified entities but are continuously being constituted, contested, reproduced, transformed or replaced during the course of social movement activity'. They are constituted by the action of ordinary people, their relations to broader political systems, and their interactions with wider urban communities (Larmer 2010). These modalities of social mobilisation further provide insights into the agency of the poor, as well as the way they frame and attempt to secure their 'place in the city'.

Notes

1 Created by the Legislative Decree No. 803, 15 March, 1996.
2 They were implemented by the *Izquierda Unida* administration and dissolved by the following *Partido Aprista Peruano* administration.
3 It was eliminated from the 1993 Constitution approved during the Fujimori Administration.
4 For a more extensive analysis, see Braathen, Mascarenhas and Sørbøe (2015).
5 Although Bayat's analysis pertains to the situation before the Arab Spring that started in December 2010, it remains very relevant to understand the evolution of a social 'non-movement' into civil uprising and political protests.
6 'Subaltern urbanism' is a 'formation of ideas' that writes 'against apocalyptic and dystopian narrative of the slum' and 'provides accounts of the slum as a terrain of habitation, livelihood, self-organization and politics' (Roy 2011: 224).
7 These authors further refer to Michel de Certeau's (1980) everyday practices of ordinary people, their 'arts of doing', which include tactics to re-appropriate urban space and its use, hence subverting what the institutions seek to force on them.
8 'Conflictual planning is based on the capacity of the conflictual processes to constitute collective subjects capable to occupy, in an autonomous way, the public stage' (Vainer *et al.* 2013: 18).

9 This paragraph and the next one draw on Goodwin and Jasper (2009) and Saharan (2012).
 10 Cornwall and Coehlo (2007: 1) referred to 'conquered' spaces.
 11 This occurred in the context of unprecedented initiatives launched by V.P. Singh at the city level towards the recognition of slum dwellers through their enumeration and by issuing them identity cards and ration cards (Sriraman 2013).
 12 To enlarge this comparative research with an emblematic case of community resistance in the Asia's largest slum, see Weinstein's (2014) in-depth monograph of 'Dharavi and the right to stay put in globalizing Mumbai'. For a broader international perspective of the inhabitants' reactions to urban restructuring in regions not covered in this book, in particular southern Europe, North Africa and the Middle-East, see for example the comparative studies co-ordinated by Berry-Chikhaoui, Deboulet and Roulleau-Berger (2007), Navez-Bouchanine (2012).

References

Ahuja, S. (1997) *People, law and justice. Casebook on public interest litigation*. New Delhi: Orient Longman.
Baviskar, A. (2003) 'Between violence and desire: Space, power, and identity in the making of metropolitan Delhi'. *International Social Science Journal*, 55(175): 89–98.
Bayat, A. (2010) *Life as politics. How ordinary people changed the Middle East*. ISIM Series on life in contemporary Muslim societies. Amsterdam: University of Amsterdam Press and ISIM, Stanford (CA): Stanford University Press.
Bebbington, A. (2006) 'Social movements and politicization of chronic poverty'. Working Paper 63. Institute of Development Policy and Management, Manchester: University of Manchester.
Benford, R.D. and Snow, D.A. (2000) 'Framing processes and social movements: An overview and assessment'. *Annual Review of Sociology*: 611–39.
Benjamin, S. (2008) 'Occupancy urbanism: Radicalizing politics and economics beyond policy and programs'. *International Journal of Urban & Regional Research*, 32(3): 719–29.
Berry-Chikhaoui, I. and Deboulet, A. (2002) 'Les compétences des citadins: enjeux et illustrations à propose du monde arabe'. *L'Homme et la société*, 1(143–4): 65–85.
Berry-Chikhaoui, I., Deboulet, A. and Roulleau-Berger, L. (eds) (2007) *Villes internationales. Entre tensions et réactions des habitants*. Paris: La Découverte.
Bickerstaff, K. and Agyeman, J. (2009) 'Assembling justice spaces: The scalar politics of environmental justice in North-East England'. *Antipode*, 41(4): 781–806.
Braathen, E., Attwood, H. and May, J. (2012) 'The role of politics in telecentres: Cases from South Africa'. *International Journal of E-Politics*, 3(3): 1–20.
Cabannes, Y. (2013) 'Urban movements and NGOS: So near, so far'. *City*, 17(4): 560–6.
Christens, B. and Speer, P.W. (2006) 'Tyranny/Transformation: Power and paradox in participatory development'. *Forum Qualitative Social Research*, 7(2): Art. 22.
City (2013a) 'Forum discussion on "NGOs, social movements and the city: Part one"'. *City*, 17(2): 251–61.
City (2013b) 'Forum discussion on "NGOs, social movements: Convergences and divergences: Part two"'. *City*, 17(4): 558–66.
Cornwall, A. (2002) 'Making spaces, changing places: Situating participation in development'. IDS Working Paper 170. Brighton: Institute of Development Studies.
Cornwall, A. and Coehlo, V.S. (2007) 'Spaces for change? The politics of participation in new democratic arenas'. In A. Cornwall and V.S. Coehlo (eds) *Spaces for change? The politics of citizen participation in new democratic arenas*. London: Zed Books, pp. 1–29.

De Certeau, M. (1980) *L'invention du quotidien. Vol. 1, Arts de faire*. Paris: Union Générale d'Editions, Coll. « 10–18 » [1984, *The Practice of Everyday Life*. Oakland: University of California Press].

De Souza M.L. (2013) 'NGOs and social movements. Convergences and divergences'. *City*, 17(2): 258–61.

Della Porta, D. and Diani, M. (1999) *Social movements: An introduction*. Oxford: Blackwell Publishers.

Dupont, V. (2008) 'Slum demolition in Delhi since the 1990s: An appraisal'. *Economic and Political Weekly*, 43(28): 79–87.

Dupont, V. and Vaquier, D. (2013) 'Slum demolition, impact on the affected families and coping strategies'. In F. Landy and M.-C. Saglio-Yatzimirsky (eds) *Megacity slums. Social exclusion, urban space and policies in Brazil and India*. London: Imperial College Press, pp. 307–61.

Godard, F. (1990) 'Sur le concept de stratégie'. In C. Bonvalet and A.-M. Fribourg (eds) *Stratégies résidentielles*. Paris: INED, Plan Construction et Architecture, MELTM, pp. 9–22.

Goodwin, J. and Jasper, J. (2009) 'Editors' introduction'. In J. Goodwin and J. Jasper (eds) *The social movements reader. Case and concepts* (second edn). Oxford: Wiley-Blackwell, pp. 3–7.

Holston, J. (1995) 'Spaces of insurgent citizenship'. *Planning Theory*, 13: 35–52.

Holston, J. (2008) *Insurgent citizenship: Disjunctions of democracy and modernity in Brazil*. Princeton: Princeton University Press.

Jenkins, R. (2010) 'NGOs and India politics'. In N. Gopal Jayal and P. Bhanu Mehta (eds) *The Oxford companion to politics in India*. Oxford: Oxford University Press, pp. 409–26.

Katz, C. (2004) *Growing up global: Economic restructuring and children's everyday lives*. Minneapolis: University of Minnesota Press.

Kumar, R. (2008) 'Globalization and changing patterns of social mobilization in urban India'. *Social Movement Studies*, 7(1): 77–96.

Larmer, M. (2010) 'Social movement struggles in Africa'. *Review of African Political Economy*, 37(125): 251–62.

Lipietz, B. (2013a) 'NGOs, social movements and the city. Introduction'. *City*, 17(2): 251–2.

Lipietz, B. (2013b) 'NGOs, social movements: Convergences and divergences: Part two. Introduction'. *City*, 17(4): 558–9.

McAdam, D., McCarthy, J.D. and Zald, M.N. (1996) *Comparative perspectives on social movements: Political opportunities, mobilizing structures, and cultural framings*. Cambridge: Cambridge University Press.

McCarthy, J.D. and Zald, M.N. (1977) 'Resource mobilization and social movements: A partial theory'. *American Journal of Sociology*, 82(6): 1212–41.

McIlwaine, C. (1998) 'Civil society and development geography'. *Progress in Human Geography*, 22: 415–24.

Melucci, A. (1989) *Nomads of the present: Social movements and individual needs in contemporary society*. New York: Vintage Books.

Miraftab, F. (2004) 'Invited and invented spaces of participation: Neoliberal citizenship and feminists' expanded notion of politics'. *Wagadu*, 1: 1–7.

Miraftab, F. (2009) 'Insurgent planning: Situating radical planning in the global South'. *Planning Theory*, 8(1): 32–50.

Miraftab, F. and Wills, S. (2005) 'Insurgency and spaces of active citizenship. The story of Western Cape anti-eviction campaign in South Africa'. *Journal of Planning Education & Research*, 25(2): 200–17.

Mohan, G. and Stokke, K. (2000) 'Participatory development and empowerment: The dangers of localism'. *Third World Quarterly*, 21(2): 247–68.

Navez-Bouchanine, F. (ed.) (2012) *Effets sociaux des politiques urbaines. L'entre-deux des politiques institutionnelles et des dynamiques sociales*. Paris: Karthala.

Navez-Bouchanine, F. and Chaboche, M. (2013) 'Gagnants et perdants des politiques urbaines. Apports et limites de la maîtrise d'ouvrage sociale dans les projets de résorption des bidonvilles. L'exemple du Maroc'. In A. Deboulet and M. Jolé (eds) *Les mondes urbains. Le parcours engagé de Françoise Navez-Bouchanine*. Paris: Karthala, pp. 327–42.

Olson, M. (1977) *The logic of collective action – Public goods and the theory of groups* (sixth edn). Harvard (MA): Harvard University Press.

Ostrom, E. (2000) 'Collective action and the evolution of social norms'. *The Journal of Economic Perspectives*, 14: 137–58.

Pithouse, R. (2004) 'Solidarity, co-option and assimilation: The necessity, promises and pitfalls of global linkages for South African movements'. *Development Update* (Special issue: Mobilising for change – The rise of new social movements in South Africa), 5(2): 169–99.

Pithouse, R. (2013) 'NGOs and urban movements'. *City*, 17(2): 253–7.

Ríos-Figueroa, J. and Taylor, M.M. (2006) 'Institutional determinants of the judicialisation of policy in Brazil and Mexico'. *Journal of Latin American Studies*, 38(4): 739–66.

Roy A. (2011) 'Slumdog cities. Rethinking subaltern urbanism'. *International Journal of Urban & Regional Research*, 35(2): 223–38.

Saharan, T. (2012) 'Dynamics of urban social movements in informal settlement – Case study of V.P. Singh Camp in Delhi, India'. Paper presented to the N-AEREUS XIII Conference, Paris, 22–24 November, 2012.

Sen, S. (1999) 'Some aspects of state-NGO relationships in India in the post-Independence era'. *Development & Change*, 30(2): 327–55.

Sparke, M. (2008) 'Political geography– political geographies of globalization III: Resistance'. *Progress in Human Geography*, 32(3): 423–40.

Sriraman, T. (2013) 'Enumeration as pedagogic process: Gendered encounters with identity documents in Delhi's urban poor spaces'. *South Asia Multidisciplinary Academic Journal* [Online], 8. Available at http://samaj.revues.org/3655 (accessed 27 January, 2015).

Sutherland, C. (2011) 'Shifting away from binaries: The entanglement of insurgent urbanisms, formal participation and state action'. Chance2Sustain, Opinion Paper No. 1, Bonn: EADI. Available at www.chance2sustain.eu/29.0.html (accessed on 27 January, 2015).

Tilly, C., Tilly, L. and Tilly, R. (1975) *The rebellious century, 1830–1930*. Cambridge (MA): Harvard University Press.

Touraine, A. (1985) 'An introduction to the study of social movements'. *Social Research*, 52(4): 749–87.

Vainer, C., Bienenstein, R., Megumi, G., Oliveira, F.L. and Lobino, C. (2013) 'O Plano Popular da Vila Autódromo. Uma experiência de planejamento conflitual'. In XV *Encontro Nacional da ANPUR –Desenvolvimento Planejamento e Governança*. Recife.

Weinstein, L. (2014) *The durable slum. Dharavi and the right to stay put in globalizing Mumbai*. Minneapolis (MS): University of Minnesota Press.

Wilkinson, P. (1971) *Social movement*. London: Macmillan.

Zald, M.N. and McCarthy, J.D. (eds) (1979) *The dynamics of social movements*. Cambridge (MA): Winthrop Publishing.

8 Conclusion

Catherine Sutherland, David Jordhus-Lier,
Einar Braathen and Véronique Dupont

This book focuses on the large number of people living on the 'margins' of fast-growing cities in the global South, who create their place in the city through their own innovative action and their engagement, or dis-engagement, with the state. These poor urban citizens both construct and defend their spaces of residence and livelihoods, and in so doing produce new forms of urbanism and citizenship. However, they are also extremely vulnerable. Although many of the case studies presented as 'settlement stories' in this book are centrally located in their respective metropolitan areas, their position in the city is far from central. People living in these settlements experience substandard living conditions, and often find themselves on the margins of the agendas of city governments and private-sector interests, and hence of urban life. With urban authorities pursuing so-called 'global city ambitions' and mediating the interests of domestic and international capital, the drive to produce 'world class cities free from slums' and realise the value of the land on which marginalised urban communities reside is often stronger than the will to respond to their social needs and to protect their rights as urban citizens. The empirical research for this project has focused on substandard settlements that are directly impacted by large-scale developments. As this research has shown, these communities find themselves caught up in intense political contestation. Their right to the city is jeopardised by the combination of their informal status and their location on attractive urban land.

Large-scale developments form part of the entrepreneurial urbanism being adopted by many countries in the global South. Large-scale developments and informal settlements share two important characteristics: first, they both tend to bypass formal planning procedures and second, neither of these phenomena is temporary in nature (cf. Roy 2005). Contrary to earlier expectations of urban planners and decision-makers, they are 'here to stay'. The juxtaposition between these high-income 'exceptional projects' and the action of the urban poor in securing their place in the city, reveals the challenge of developing more sustainable and just cities, in the face of dominant pro-growth or neoliberal national agendas.

Initially in our research we focused on two main questions: how policies address substandard settlements; and how civil society organisations mobilise and engage with these policies, including their implementation. However, during the research a third question emerged around the politics and power of knowledge in these processes. These three questions have been used to explore the politics of slums, focusing on the different tactics and strategies of social mobilisation around substandard housing in six cities across four countries in the global South. *Social mobilisation* has been explored in relation to *policy-making*, with a focus on how substandard settlements are addressed in policy or trigger policy responses. This has in turn led us to examine *the politics of knowledge production*, as it shapes practices and interventions, in our case settlements. The comparative research conducted has enabled us to develop an understanding of these processes and to identify broad trends in all three research themes. To that end, it has been essential to implement a comparative approach in designing our methodology and in carrying out our urban analysis.

We recognise that our results are not comprehensive, nor can they be used to make generalisations across all countries in the developing world. All six cities are dynamic and have different local and national contexts, and therefore our results are nuanced and complex. There are global trends that are influencing these cities, including the neoliberal or pro-growth agenda, democratisation processes and reforms, as well as the more socially progressive global discourse that now recognises slums and the role they play in housing the poor. However, in all six cities it is the national and local context that seems to matter the most. As Holston (2007) argues, specific contestations assume a particular expression because their historical construction continues to shape their present form or production.

We found that particular state interventions and the manner in which they have been conducted, rather than the policies themselves, have been the immediate triggers of social mobilisation across our case studies. For many of the residents interviewed in this research, legal and policy frameworks are seen as harbouring a progressive potential, but suspicions that other agendas rather than official policy are driving interventions cause mistrust in state–society relations.

One interpretation is that this is a result of 'weak governance' on the part of the state, or that poor communities are 'uncivil' and 'disobedient'. Alternatively, one could combine these explanations and argue that there is simply a lack of trust between members of local communities and civil society organisations, on the one hand, and state and corporate actors, on the other. While it is true that mistrust permeates all these case studies, we believe that our analysis offers a more sophisticated argument as to what underlies this lack of trust in six different cities of the global South, bringing in dimensions of politics, power and knowledge to better understand how to (re-)build trust. In the next section we summarise some of the cross-cutting issues that have emerged from our analysis, as we argue that issues of public policy-making in urban housing, the use of knowledge in urban governance and social mobilisation by marginalised groups are entangled.

From policies to politics – and back again?

One of the main questions framing this research was how substandard settlements are addressed through urban *policies*. The research process revealed how difficult it is to answer this question, as policies shift over time and are complex, as a result of the multiple layers of governance networks that produce and implement them. It was therefore not possible, for example, to develop a comprehensive list of policies for comparison across the four countries. We conclude, therefore, that policy-making is dynamic and fluid, with policy often being developed in response to social needs and pressure. Informal housing by its nature occurs outside of formal planning policy and practice, and yet it has prompted the development of a plethora of policy and practices to address its relationship with other elements of the city. The needs and rights of the urban poor have gradually become acknowledged in global and national policy discourse, in part thanks to the effective alliances of social movements and progressive NGOs. However, it remains clear that their success in shaping public policies has not been sufficient to protect the interests of marginalised urban communities. While we will devote most of this chapter to the *politics* of substandard settlements, we do acknowledge that progressive policies do matter, and can facilitate a real impact for people whose place in the city is at risk.

Given that appropriate policies are necessary but insufficient in protecting the interests of urban marginalised communities, our study became increasingly occupied with the *politics* surrounding the implementation of these policies. This corresponded to our second question, namely: how do civil society organisations (CSOs) mobilise and engage in the construction and implementation of these policies? Residents in substandard settlements mobilise through, and are mobilised by, civil society organisations in their struggle for decent housing. This is true for all our case studies, although their degree of militancy and their impact differs from settlement to settlement. CSOs are using both horizontal and vertical networks to resist evictions and relocations, meaning that they build links with other local actors as well as with higher echelons of power. Our settlement stories represent place-specific or local responses, while at the same time they reflect broader patterns of progressive mobilisations in the different cities' history. For instance, the social movement *Abahlali baseMjondolo*, that emerged from the social mobilisation of the Kennedy Road settlement in Durban, has since become a national social movement in South Africa, which directly challenges the state. In comparison, the empirical material presented in this volume reveals that slum dwellers and residents of *favelas* and *barriadas* have a limited capacity to challenge the state. This is not to say that these communities are bereft of agency. The settlement stories in Chapter 6 give numerous examples of how social mobilisation has impacted on policy-making and implementation. But we should not underestimate the power imbalances of cities in the global South: between marginalised communities and elites, or between poor urban residents and those who are governing them. This is an important point that permeates all our findings.

Hence, it is worth reiterating that politics and policies are both relational and co-constitutive: politics defines the perceptions of the state of 'something', which then requires or stimulates a response. This response may then be integrated into or reflected in new policy. New policies then in turn reshape political dynamics, set new agendas, open up new spaces for contestation and include new social actors – or reconfigure relations between current social actors. The mutual relationship between policies and politics is therefore critical to understand and explore if policies and politics are to be transformed so that they can play a role in achieving more equitable and sustainable cities.

Right to a place in the city

The most intensely contested politics in the research presented in this book revolves around the threat of relocation, underscoring how spatial disruption is a critical factor in shaping urban policies of informal and substandard settlements (see Figure 3.2 in Chapter 3). For many marginalised urban communities across the global South, the right to the city translates into a fight to defend their place – their location – in the urban landscape. Case studies such as Joe Slovo informal settlement in Cape Town and Vila Autódromo in Rio reveal the determined efforts by informal settlers to resist relocation, even when this offers the benefit of a 'formal' house. This does not mean that they do not struggle over other things, such as access to services or political influence, but it does illustrate how the fight against being removed often overshadows most other issues. This is in itself a strong argument in favour of the in-situ solutions proposed by various policies discussed in Chapter 3.

Moreover, and as a result of this, many of the attempts to generate community-based knowledge through mapping exercises is in part motivated by knowing one's place in the city, and making one's place in the city known. As emphasised by Harvey (2012: 4), the 'right to the city' is 'far more than a right of individual or group access to the resources the city embodies: it is the right to change and reinvent the city more after our hearts' desire'. Hence, for analytical purposes it is useful to distinguish between individual and community rights, on the one hand, and the right to collectively influence the development of the city as a whole by means of participatory budgeting and other democratic mechanisms on the other. While the first might include entitlements to tenure and other legal titles to land individuals have inhabited for a number of years, the second signals a move away from clientelistic and non-transparent politics towards class-based and transparent politics that can allow for the redistribution of resources. The only measure to avoid zero-sum game politics, making some disadvantaged subaltern groups 'winners' and others 'losers', is a politics where marginalised urban dwellers act in solidarity to enforce policies that benefit all of them. In cities where this has happened, such as in the famous example of Porto Alegre (Baiocchi 2005), this has forced urban authorities to take their role as responder much more seriously, and even to institutionalise this mandate in a way that we have not observed in our six cities.

Another major threat that jeopardises the right to the city for the residents of substandard settlements is their exclusion from policy and programmes, including the eligibility criteria of various upgrading programmes. The critical question that emerges from this finding is whether it is possible, or utopian, to design policies with only winners and no losers, given the socio-economic hetero-geneity of the concerned communities, the divergent agendas within communities and between affected communities and other stakeholders. In this instance city authorities have to act as 'mediators' between conflicting interests, finding a middle ground or creating winners and losers.

Policy–practice discrepancy and entrepreneurial governance

Our empirical research reveals that there have been some shifts in stated policy towards substandard settlements or slums from repressive approaches (i.e., a low degree of participation and high degrees of state intervention and spatial disruption as shown in Figures 3.1 and 3.2) to more integrated approaches (i.e., high degrees of state intervention and participation and a low degree of spatial disruption). These prescriptions are given labels such as 'in-situ upgrading', 'urbanisação' (in Brazil), 'in-situ rehabilitation' (in India and South Africa), 'integrated human settlements' or 'incremental development areas'. However, the implementation of the new policies, or policy in practice, leaves a lot to be desired in all the countries and cities observed. The 'old' policies of demolition, eviction and the lack of security of tenure continue to remain a threat – and in many cases are still being implemented.

There are several reasons for this policy–practice discrepancy. First, national state policies regarding 'slums' most often depend on city municipalities or regional states as implementing authorities, and these local governments tend to operate in strong partnership with the private sector when it comes to concrete interventions. Therefore, much is lost in translation when policy implementa-tion is moved from the public (policy) sphere to local government, private or community-controlled spheres. Second, the ongoing process of policy-making, with a lack of transparent consent from important stakeholders, results in numerous conflicts including judicial disputes at the stage of implementation. The 'practice' therefore becomes, in many cases, very different from what the managers of the intervention 'planned'. Third, most interventions in urban space are not guided by a single set of policies, for instance, slum-upgrading policies, but rather become the arena for contestation between housing policies and economic development policies or long-term planning devices, such spatial development plans.

The discrepancy between formulated policy and its implementation is a recurrent theme in comparative policy analysis. As Green and Hulme (2005: 876) aptly note, '[inequality and] poverty reduction does not simply require "good" policy: it requires creating the capacity of poorer people to influence, and hold accountable, those who make policies'. In other words, while state policies or 'politics from above' can promote certain types of urban development, social movement or 'politics from below' has to pressure the public authorities to implement policies, for instance through expropriating urban land for social housing purposes, or allocating resources for urban upgrading. This is particularly the case when policies demand some kind of radical redistribution of resources, and the political authorities therefore might lack the political will to implement these policies. Insurgent citizenship (Holston 2007) is therefore a prerequisite for making policies matter for marginalised communities. When this happens, city authorities are forced to assume the role of 'responder to the social demands of the demos of the city'. In this instance policies often follow practice as a result, reflecting the interaction between top-down and bottom-up processes.

This leads us to some general problems of policy-making. In the metropolitan societies in this study, there is a plurality of actors with conflicting interests. When state authorities establish forms of democratic or responsive governance, these interests tend to be incorporated into the governance process, generating contradictory policies. While a policy for social housing might reach a certain stage of implementation, a policy for economic growth may simultaneously offer support for real estate development. This can undermine and distort social housing projects, for instance, due to conflicting agendas over public land where informal settlements are located. We have not chosen to focus on the class foundations of these cities, and the way in which different elite actors organise pressure groups to achieve certain agendas, however we acknowledge the important role that such political processes play in the settlement stories above, particularly given the dominance of the pro-growth agenda.

Two quite different future scenarios can be projected from this current influence that representatives of marginalised urban communities and their NGO and academic allies have managed to exert over global, national and urban policy discourse. One possible trajectory is that this is the first step towards meaningful and real influence over how informal and substandard settlements are governed and serviced in the city. This is a cautiously optimistic reading of the situation. A more pessimistic understanding is to see this policy shift as an inroad into the realm of formal, policy-informed managerialism, that is gradually losing importance in an urban reality, overshadowed by the exceptionalism of large-scale projects and mega-events – in other words the urban entrepreneurialism that Harvey (1989) is concerned about.

Put differently, the struggle for coherent and pro-poor policy-making is a struggle for a democratic deepening and transformation of the state. The challenge of participation is to move beyond minimalist invited spaces and allow for substantial participation. This indeed represents one of the most fundamental governance challenges in cities in the global South. There is a deficit of participatory democracy in all the large cities we have observed. This deficit has several sources. First, Brazil, Peru and South Africa have a relatively long history of authoritarian rule and similarly short experience of majority-based democracy, while India could qualify as the 'world's largest democracy' only after the country gained its independence in 1947. Second, the processes of decentralisation that have occurred in most of these cities have been accompanied by an entrepreneurial governance discourse, where cities are supposed to act as drivers of an urban development agenda and as a mediator of the city visions of many other actors. Hence, this has reduced the scope of democratic urban governance, and what we have labelled as 'the city as a responder to social mobilisation'.

Perhaps as a reflection of these conflicting roles, it is quite striking how city governments in this study show a tendency to address growing urban informality and substandard housing through large-scale projects. While one should be careful not to label all these projects as signs of urban megalomania, after all the need for adequate housing is colossal and calls for heavy investment in social infrastructure, it can still be argued that these large-scale projects further limit the potential for participation. Large projects bring together a vast number of stakeholders, not only in terms of residents positively or negatively affected, but also as numerous state agencies and private contractors are brought into these interventions. Adding to this, large-scale solutions involve high political stakes and corporate investments that create tight time constraints and as a result circumscribe any real participation from citizens. The power asymmetries between powerful state and corporate actors and relatively weakly organised local communities are arguably more stark in these large-scale projects than in other approaches to upgrading. This being said, democratic deficits play out quite differently from case to case, and between the different urban governance contexts, in this study (see Figure 3.1 on degrees of participation and state intervention in Chapter 3).

Knowledge asymmetries and the alliances to overcome them

The asymmetry between the marginalised and the powerful becomes even more skewed when taking into consideration the knowledge dimension discussed in Chapters 4 and 5. Empirical evidence from the settlement cases shows just how complex and contested knowledge is in the interactions between local communities, their representatives and government authorities around upgrading and relocation projects. The most challenging issues in knowledge partnerships are the ways in which knowledge flows or is obstructed, the legitimacy of different forms of knowledge and the ownership and control of knowledge. The limited sharing of knowledge was a constraining factor and, indeed, a trigger for mobilisation in some of our cases.

While retention of information serves to entrench already existing power asymmetries, we have also found examples of how communities' own efforts to generate and systematise knowledge have led to empowerment in the face of powerful actors. In fact, knowledge has emerged as a critical factor in upgrading initiatives in substandard settlements. The local state needs strong evidence and knowledge about the target settlements and their population, and this can most appropriately be done through various forms of community mapping, as shown in cases in Rio de Janeiro and Durban, where residents are playing an active part in 'being known'. The critical task is to institutionalise participatory procedures, through the establishment and practice of participatory institutions. A main challenge is to do so without excessive bureaucratisation and the co-optation of substandard settlement leaders. There is a strong need for improved systems of knowledge production that include all actors and facilitate knowledge sharing with (and not simply about) residents of substandard settlements.

Given the exceptionalist and at times unpredictable nature of the large-scale projects in this research, residents were stressed by a lack of clarity, transparency and consistency on the part of the state. This makes it difficult for those living in these settlements, or those who represent them, to develop defendable knowledge that they can use to secure their right to the city. Knowledge is 'slippery' and often not made available by state agencies or private developers, impacting negatively on the capacity of marginalised communities to engage with or challenge the state effectively. The lack of transparency in housing allocations from Durban to Delhi, or related to the relocations along the Rímac river in Lima, are just a few examples of how housing projects hailed as progressive by their respective governments fail to live up to their own ideals. In these situations, development interventions continue to nurture fears of demolition and eviction. Secrecy around housing relocations is common, with affected communities often relying on hearsay and public media to gather necessary information. Depending on the concrete contexts, the knowledge factor contributed to the increase or decrease of conflicts, to social mobilisation or demobilisation.

The low degree of community participation in the upgrading and relocation projects depicted here thwarts the form of 'deliberation' proposed by Fischer (2000). For local knowledge to constructively interact with expert knowledge in decision-making processes, mandates and responsibilities must be renegotiated in a less top-down manner than they have been in many of our settlement stories. Neither the tacit knowledge of local communities nor the knowledge of external experts have been able to 'travel well' (cf. McFarlane 2006) in the settlement stories of Chapter 1. Hence, there is a need to develop new knowledge platforms for urban planning and settlement upgrading, to ensure a greater democratisation of 'appropriate knowledge' (cf. Fischer 2000), i.e., knowledge that makes sense to all involved.

The common denominator of the settlement stories that can be labelled as relative successes is how residents have taken part in knowledge alliances with external independent expertise. For instance, the cases of Vila Autódromo and Ocean Drive-In show that community-based enumerations or mapping exercises, where needs are identified, can play an important role in challenging the top-down approach of the state in relocation projects. Face-to-face communication in public meetings or assemblies is still important, even in an age of interactive technologies and social media. To build knowledge alliances, knowledge brokers play an important role in including community knowledge and informing affected communities about state interventions. Knowledge alliances also represent a success criterion in shaping the outcome of wider struggles. In fact, the shift we have seen in global policy discourse is also a result of knowledge alliances forged between the organisations and representatives of informal settlers, on the one hand, and NGOs, progressive lawyers, academics and others, on the other.

Research institutions can play a constructive role in bringing together the state and its citizens, by playing a supportive role in the production of community knowledge and in communicating expert forms of knowledge to various constituencies. Through their engagement with the state at national and local scales, both research institutions and NGOs have shaped policy and practice in all four countries. Consultants produce knowledge for policy but this is often technical scientific knowledge, or codified knowledge, that is produced through engagement with the state, rather than with and for communities. There are often competing rationalities in the knowledge and practices that are produced between technical experts and communities (Winkler 2013). Typically these are not negotiated or debated as participation and deliberation in decision-making relating to substandard settlement issues is weak in all four countries. Another challenge is that in many cases residents suffer from 'research fatigue', where they are continually called upon to provide information and produce knowledge but do not see the benefits of this knowledge production as their situation does not change. This was evident in the community-based mapping exercise undertaken in Europe informal settlement in Cape Town. Our research also reveals a number of pitfalls that local knowledge brokers might experience, including co-optation and community divisions.

All the case studies reveal that communities lack access to information and communication processes that are transparent, and to knowledge that they can trust. They would like to engage with the main actors involved in their particular project. They also need to develop the skills and have access to the infrastructure that enables them to navigate their way through the knowledge produced. Trust appears to be critical in the process of sharing knowledge and this can only be achieved through long-term engagement between different actors. Knowledge brokers play a major role in developing or undermining trust in knowledge-exchange processes. As the cases reveal, knowledge is often withheld, produced and communicated in a form that is codified (experts) or experiential (community members), which makes it inaccessible to other actors, often communicated at the wrong time, usually late in the planning process, and is manipulated in power struggles. This all serves to undermine the constructive sharing of knowledge. The politics of knowledge needs to be addressed, as knowledge exchange in itself is not the solution to empowering communities or making better decisions in upgrading or relocation projects.

Interactive and strategic mobilisation

Even though governance regimes and national regulatory contexts differ across our case studies, the agency of marginalised urban citizens seems to be one thing that binds all these cases together. Social mobilisation is a process that develops over many years and it is embedded in specific socio-spatial, economic and historical contexts. Because popular agency evolves over time in different contexts, and is employed in different ways by social actors, different modalities of social mobilisation are not mutually exclusive and they are often strategically articulated simultaneously. Struggles in all our researched cities range from subaltern approaches that reflect 'the quiet encroachment of the ordinary' (Bayat 2010) to the insurgency approach that places citizens' rights at the forefront of belligerent activism (Miraftab 2004), or a combination of these practices (Holston 2007).

In these approaches residents of substandard settlements are not passive victims of urban inequality, but rather actors claiming a right to the city. Periods of intense and powerful action can be followed by demobilisation. Moreover, the more spectacular forms of protest are always supplemented by, and arguably bolstered by, mundane and everyday practices. The forms of engagement and contestation identified in our cases made use of both 'invented' and 'invited' spaces of participation (cf. Miraftab 2004), indicating that a binary thinking around these concepts is too simplistic (Sutherland 2011). When studied over time, groups of residents and their representatives seem to both engage and dis-engage with formal authorities, depending on their experiences with 'invited spaces' of participation.

Moreover, progressive constitutions and alliances with progressive legal expertise might lead social mobilisation into a legal modality. Just as often, however, this judicialisation of struggle is triggered by developers or state authorities seeking permission to evict and relocate residents. Since judicial struggles take time and demand resources, they might induce groups of residents to become parts of larger social movements or organisations. If losing judicial battles, the movement might focus more on political struggles to change laws and administrative measures. Seen in isolation, this might not be any point of concern. However, in their commute between the courts and the city hall, many groups of residents might have lost hope and the movement may eventually become weakened.

The choice of appropriate strategies, their timely intervention and innovative combination appears to be critical to their success. Nevertheless, it is important to stress that even when communities are unified in social action this is not always sufficient for success. For example, some of the residents' associations we studied in Peru and Brazil needed to be connected with organisations and struggles in other places and at other scales in order to achieve legal success.

Concluding remarks

Our case settlements represent a truly diverse set of communities. A main insight that emerged from this research is that there is no singular concept that fully describes the nature of these settlements. To describe the materiality of deprivation and the poor living conditions that characterise the settlements studied in this volume, 'substandard' seemed like the most appropriate term. When describing their relationship to the state and their contested location on maps and in project plans, however, 'informality' more precisely captured their status. Finally, the stigma and socio-cultural marginalisation that many of these residents experienced in addition to lacking material means and formal recognition, brought us back to the discourse of 'slums'. Hence, all three words appeared in the various chapters of this book, including in the conclusion, but for good reason.

Housing the urban poor is not simply a question of finding the right policy. Addressing the challenge of urban substandard settlements requires that democratic authorities meet with their citizens in ways that bring informality into constructive engagement with formality, and where urban insurgency is allowed to shift formal policy and practice. The fact that the urban poor in India, South Africa, Brazil and Peru have to claim their right to the city through a variety of strategies that are often located outside of the state, indicates that the main challenge is the establishment of democratic processes through which such policies and practices can be jointly crafted and implemented. The overall impression given by the multitude of case studies presented here is that urban governments need to better regulate, plan for, manage and accommodate urban informality and urban insurgency. Citizens acting outside of formal political processes are likely to remain commonplace in these relatively young democracies. Upgrading substandard settlements on centrally located land, rather than eliminating them or relocating them on the city fringes, will arguably become a tenet of urban sustainability in the future. Furthermore, the increasing involvement of the private sector in social housing should not obliterate the responsibility of the state towards its poorer urban citizens. It is indeed the state's responsibility to protect those living in substandard conditions from unjust outcomes in the implementation of the projects affecting them.

We also recognise that the lack of information and consultation, and more generally the deficit of citizen participation in urban projects, is not limited to the experience of informal settlement dwellers in the global South. In metropolises from the global North, legal tenants in social housing targeted by urban renewal operations and eviction often face similar difficulties. This denial of urban citizenship has, for example, been documented in Marseille and the Paris region (Deboulet 2009). This brings us back to Jenny Robinson's (2006) proposal that all cities should be considered to be 'ordinary' cities and that we should deepen our comparisons between them, not based on their hierarchy or classification, but rather on the social relations being produced in all of them.

An interesting and somewhat unexpected finding that emerged from the research is the relationship between housing policy and environmental risk. This will become more important as climate change intensifies, as most risks in substandard settlements are associated with flooding and landslides. The urban poor resist relocations based on the threat of environmental risk as they trade this off against social and economic opportunities. Tension arises, as legislation and policy in most cities do not support informal settlers living on land exposed to high environmental risks. In these cases, city authorities will not support the upgrading of informal settlements on hazardous sites. Here the codified or scientific knowledge produced on environmental risk is challenged, as informal settlers contest its validity, not trusting its 'predications'. This reveals the conflict that emerges when an environmental risk is constructed differently by experts and communities. Currently, due to low levels of participation, there are no platforms available to negotiate and explore these different forms of expert and tacit knowledge and how they should shape decision-making.

The challenge of climate change therefore adds further complexity and pressure and increases the ongoing conflicts and tensions that city authorities experience as they attempt to balance different roles and responsibilities. These have grown in magnitude and scale as economic, social, and environmental challenges increasingly become the responsibility of the local state. So how do authorities who develop the narratives, discourses and practices of these fast-growing cities drive, mediate and respond to these challenges? Sustainable development is a useful framework as it promotes the integration of social, economic and environmental concerns within a system of participatory governance. However, even when this framework is adopted, it appears that the pro-growth agenda continues to dominate and participatory approaches are not well developed (Hansen and Wethal 2015, Scott *et al.* 2015). Upgrading substandard settlements lies at the heart of a better life for the urban poor, as housing is integrally linked to a wide range of urban opportunities and resources. However, as this book has shown, narratives around substandard settlements are constructed in a manner that marginalises rather than integrates these settlements and their residents into the future of these cities. They are construed as spaces to be eliminated, rather than spaces of hope and opportunity. Only when these settlements are described and understood in both policy and practice as spaces of 'habitation, livelihood, self-organization and politics', as Roy (2011: 223) suggests, will they become properly embedded in the future planning and development of cities in ways that are socially just and sustainable.

References

Baiocchi, G. (2005) *Militants and citizens: The politics of participation in Porto Alegre.* Stanford (CA): Stanford University Press.

Bayat, A. (2010) *Life as politics. How ordinary people changed the Middle East, ISIM Series on life in contemporary Muslim societies.* Amsterdam: University of Amsterdam Press and ISIM, Stanford (CA): Stanford University Press.

Deboulet, A. (2009) 'De l'épreuve à l'enjeu urbain: mobilisations collectives autour de la démolition et du délogement'. In M. Carrel, C. Neveu and J. Ion (eds) *Les intermittences de la démocratie. Formes d'action et visibilités citoyennes dans la ville.* Paris: L'Harmattan, pp. 101–20.

Fischer, F. (2000) *Citizens, experts and the environment: The politics of local knowledge.* Durham (NC): Duke University Press.

Green, M. and Hulme, D. (2005) 'From correlates and characteristics to causes: Thinking about poverty from a chronic poverty perspective'. *World Development, 33*(6): 867–79.

Hansen, A. and Wethal, U. (2015) 'Global sustainability and the rise of the South: Development patterns and emerging challenges'. In A. Hansen and U. Wethal (eds) *Emerging economies and challenges to sustainability. Theories, strategies, local realities.* London: Routledge, pp. 263–74.

Harvey, D. (1989) 'From managerialism to entrepreneurialism: The transformation in urban governance in late capitalism'. *Geografiska Annaler B, 71*(1): 3–17.

Harvey, D. (2012) *Rebel cities. From the right to the city to the urban revolution.* London and New York: Verso.

Holston, J. (2007) *Insurgent citizenship.* Princeton (NJ): Princeton University Press.

McFarlane, C. (2006) 'Knowledge, learning and development: A post-rationalist approach'. *Progress in Development Studies, 6*(4): 287–305.

Miraftab, F. (2004) 'Invited and invented spaces of participation: Neoliberal citizenship and feminists' expanded notion of politics'. *Wagadu, 1*(Spring): 1–7.

Robinson, J. (2006) *Ordinary cities: Between modernity and development*. London and New York: Routledge.

Roy, A. (2005) 'Urban informality: Toward an epistemology of planning'. *Journal of the American Planning Association*, 71(2): 147–58.

Roy, A. (2011) 'Slumdog cities. Rethinking subaltern urbanism'. *International Journal of Urban & Regional Research*, 35(2): 223–38.

Scott, D., Sutherland, C., Sim, V. and Robbins, G. (2015) 'Pro-growth challenges to sustainability in South Africa'. In A. Hansen and U. Wethal (eds) *Emerging economies and challenges to sustainability. Theories, strategies, local realities*. London: Routledge, pp. 204–17.

Sutherland, C. (2011) 'Shifting away from binaries: The entanglement of insurgent urbanism, formal participation and state action'. Chance2Sustain Opinion Paper 1, April 2011: 1–2.

Winkler, T. (2013) 'At the coalface: Community-university engagements and planning education'. *Journal of Planning Education & Research*, 33(2): 215–27.

Index